Catholics on the Edge

∽ TIM UNSWORTH ∽

CATHOLICS
ON THE
EDGE

CROSSROAD • NEW YORK

1995

The Crossroad Publishing Company
370 Lexington Avenue, New York, NY 10017

Printed in the United States of America

Library of Congress Cataloging-in-Publication-Data

Unsworth, Tim.
    Catholics on the edge / Tim Unsworth.
        p.   cm.
    ISBN 0-8245-1463-7
    1. Catholics—United States—Biography. 2. Catholic Church—
United States—History—20th century. 3. Church controversies—
Catholic Church. I. Title.
BX4670.U67 1995
282'.092'273—dc20   94-48890
[b]   CIP

To Jean

As it was in the beginning,
is now,
and ever shall be . . .

———◆◆◆———

To adore, or scorn an image, or protest,
May all be bad; doubt wisely; in strange way
To stand inquiring right, is not to stray;
To sleep or run wrong is. On a huge hill,
Cragged and steep, Truth stands, and he that will
Reach her, about must, and about must go.

John Donne, "Third Satire"

But a Pharisee in the Sanhedrin named Gamaliel, a teacher of the law, respected by all the people, stood up, ordered the men to be put outside for a short time, and said to them, "Fellow Israelites, be careful what you are about to do to these men. . . . For if this endeavor or this activity is of human origin, it will destroy itself. But if it comes from God, you will not be able to destroy them; you may even find yourselves fighting against God."

Acts 5:34, 38–39

Contents

Preface

D on't be misled. This is not a negative book. It is not a manual for gripers or whiners. The Catholics in this book would no more leave the Church than change the color of their eyes. They are bred-in-the-bone believers who, if excommunicated from the Church, would likely appeal the case. They are children of the Church, children of both the old and the new catechisms. Most of them memorized the 499 answers in the old Baltimore Catechism and have at least skimmed over the 2,865 answers in the new *Catechism of the Catholic Church*. Some, at least, once gave total acceptance to those responses. Now some answers give them pause. Now they wonder why the number of questions and answers has increased five times. They recognize the need to inform one's conscience but ask what has become of the primacy of the individual conscience. They question how a well-informed church can set aside overwhelming data about priestly vocations, the failure of celibacy, the broken ideals of marriage, and the virtual impossibility of considering a family without addressing the issue of birth control.

Catholics of a certain age—one stretching to pre-Vatican II years— once believed that any deviation was a heresy. They were fish-on-Friday, fast-before-Communion Catholics who were proud of the calluses on their knees. Now they have changed. An infinitely more complicated world has altered many of the moral and spiritual equations. Some Catholics on the edge respond that they have "simply grown up." They are no less idealistic or spiritual. They still view certain norms at least as ideals to be achieved. But they no longer view religion as a set of parameters.

In a talk presented at Loyola University of Chicago in 1992, Bishop Kenneth Untener of Saginaw, Michigan, said:

"Many, even Catholics, have the notion that religion is to set parameters. Religion establishes certain parameters, the moral framework within which you live your life. The task is to bring people 'into the sheepfold'—get them into the church—i.e., get them to live within certain parameters.

"The fact is, Jesus did the opposite. The purpose of religion, and of the Catholic Church is to bring freedom to people so they can dream dreams they never dared to dream before, have horizons that are deeper, richer, broader. Think of all the freedoms: freedom to forgive, freedom to be generous (to give things away rather than gather them). The caricature of religion is exactly the opposite. If those engaged in active ministry haven't communicated that, our ministries are wrong-headed."

Bishop Untener is clearly a bishop on the edge.

The Catholics introduced here were once as centered as anyone could be. But they attempted to dream dreams. Then, something happened to each of them that pushed them to the edge. They were pushed to their intellectual, spiritual, or emotional limits by an institution that is sometimes astigmatic, refracted, and punitive. They hang there by their fingertips, most of them hoping and praying that the Church they love will provide them with a moment of return to the center.

The late Jesuit theologian John Courtney Murray, who died in 1967, was a classic "Catholic on the edge." Indeed, he may have partially coined the term with his use of the phrase "the cutting edge." Murray was referring to original thinkers, like himself, whose ideas brought them to the cutting edge, only to find themselves rejected and later accepted. Yves Congar, O.P., a leading French theologian, was another cutting-edge thinker. He spent years in intellectual exile, forbidden to teach or write. Finally, in 1994 while in his ninetieth year, Congar was named a cardinal by John Paul II. Both Congar and Murray are examples of the experience of cutting-edge people. These great theologians were pushed to the edge, then rescued by the very church that forced them to the edge. Finally, they had the ironic experience of observing the institution take credit for their ideas!

"Why do we make it so hard on people to be Catholic?" Fr. John Cusick asks. "Why are we punishing them? I just can't get that through my head." Cusick is the director of the Young Adult Ministry for the archdiocese of Chicago. He views the situation with young adults versus the Church so darkly that he feels that the local church's evangelization efforts should be directed to young Catholic adults rather that non-Catholics, disenfranchised Catholics, or ex-Catholics. Cusick, who was interviewed by my friend Dick Westley for his publication *In the Meantime* and by me for an earlier book, believes that the Church has lost its ability to understand the "cultural mores" of its people. (See chapter 7 on Dick Westley; he uses the Latin term *sensus fidelium*, the common sense of the people, which is closely related to cultural mores.

Both terms imply that the Church's ideas simply do not tie in with the lived experience of the people.)

Cusick is a priest who doesn't bite, trying to help people make sense of a church that too often acts like moral police. He bristles at parishes that now have an endless list of rules for marriage—rules that insist that Catholics be members of the parish, sign up to be married at least a year in advance, and in general jump through a maze of legal hoops that even the official church does not require. (Canon law stipulates only that Catholics have a domicile in an area for thirty days prior to marriage. The couple need not be registered in the parish.)

In 1994, the *National Catholic Reporter* commissioned a Gallup Poll on attitudes of Catholics toward certain aspects of church teaching and practice. Basically, it revealed that U.S. Catholics are putting less and less stock in official church teaching. The poll revealed a dramatic rise in self-reliance among the people in the pews.

Some examples:

- 56 percent of Catholic women say a person can be a good Catholic without obeying the Church's teaching on abortion. In 1987, only 39 percent of Catholic women believed this.
- 62 percent of Catholics said that laity should have a role in the decision-making process of the institution, up from 48 percent seven years before.
- 56 percent said that lay administrators would be acceptable in parishes, up from 38 percent.
- 65 percent of women and 60 percent of men believed that the laity should have a role in deciding whether women should be ordained. This result came on the heels of John Paul II's pronouncement not only that women could not be priests, but also that the subject could not even be discussed.

The Gallup Poll was released about the same time that the Vatican declared that all Catholics living in invalid marriages were to be denied the Eucharist unless they regularized the marriage or agreed to live as brother and sister. In some dioceses, where careful estimates reveal that upwards of one-third of the marriages are invalid, this decree had the potential of pushing literally millions of Catholics to the edge. Should invalidly married Catholics take the edict seriously, they would exhaust virtually every canonical and pastoral resource within the institution.

"You can make a persuasive case against Catholicism if you want," Fr. Andrew Greeley wrote in the *New York Times Magazine* in July, 1994.

"The Church is resolutely authoritarian and often it seems to be proud of the fact that 'it is not a democracy.'" He adds that for the past thirty years the hierarchy and the clergy have done just about everything that could be done to drive the laity out of the church, but they have not succeeded. Greeley attributes the tenacity of the faith to the images. He makes a good case. Clearly, the Church since Vatican II has committed a cardinal sin: It has become more concerned about itself than about the truth.

Jesuit William J. O'Malley, writing in *America*, says that the objective nature of human beings must force us to accept that no one, not even the Church, can legitimately treat humans like cattle or adults like children. "What father would want his children to remain infants—much less sheep?" he asks rhetorically.

Some forty years ago, Italian monsignor Romano Guardini wrote that "the Church has always been the cross that Christ is crucified on." Franciscan priest Richard Rohr seems to embrace Guardini's sentiments as well as those who speak in this book. "I stay in the Church because all the new patterns are really old patterns," Rohr wrote in *Sojourners*. "I stay because everybody else can only address the symptoms. I stay because it continually clears new ground wider and deeper than mere ideology. I stay because Jesus alone creates a lifestyle that can't be bought off, an ethic that refuses power, position, and possessions, a vision that is subject to no judgment or vested interest less than God's plan for the whole. Nobody is possibly going to do better than that."

Now, enjoy these friends who continue to clear new ground.

Tim Unsworth
Thanksgiving, 1994

1

Carrie Kemp:
Helping Catholics to Come Home

------◆◆◆------

"**I** cried when I read that statement from the Vatican," Carrie Kemp said. "It must be easier for them to make such statements from afar. Statements like that seem to say: 'You're unworthy but I'm not.' They also reveal the Vatican's obsession with sex with all that talk about 'acts proper to married couples.' Don't they know that intimacy in marriage goes far beyond sex?"

So spoke Carrie Kemp, a fifty-six-year-old wife, mother, and grandmother, who devotes her working life largely to guiding and healing Catholics in second marriages. She was referring to the Vatican's decree of October, 1994, which declared that Catholics who are in irregular second marriages are forbidden to receive the Eucharist. Further, they are considered adulterers unless they agree to live together as brother and sister, avoiding those acts that are proper to married couples. The nine-page statement was signed by Cardinal Joseph Ratzinger, prefect of the Vatican's Congregation for the Doctrine of the Faith. It was viewed as a direct response to a 1993 proposal by three German bishops who wanted an exception clause added to this long-standing canon. The bishops had suggested that some Catholics, who in good conscience contend their first marriage is invalid but who cannot obtain an annulment, could receive the Eucharist.

"'Acts proper to married couples,'" Carrie said derisively. "There they go again. To hear them tell it, the only acts proper to married couples have to do with sex."

Matrimony was the last sacrament to be introduced. It was made a sacrament about the year 1012. In that year, the Church claimed to have total authority in all marriage cases. Early Christians viewed marriage as a civil contract and made no declarations about the validity of marriage and its relationship to sacrament. Gradually, around the fall of the Roman

Empire in 476, the Church increased its involvement in the legal aspects of marriage, but centuries passed before it was raised to its present status and the Church became involved in virtually every aspect. The involvement has been costly and complicated. Marriage tribunals now form the largest department in most chancery offices. Little discretion is left to the parishes. While no accurate figures are available regarding the number of Catholics who divorce annually, the number of annulment petitions has remained at a steady forty-five thousand to fifty thousand each year, a figure said to be only a small percentage of the Catholics who actually divorce each year.

The United States leads the world in annulment petitions. Some countries do not even have matrimonial tribunals. Even in Western Europe the number of annulments is small. Church legislation tends to draw its philosopical underpinnings from a Mediterranean model that deals with honor, respect, male power, and the passage of property. Concubines—secondary wives—are tolerated over divorce and remarriage.

When the Ratzinger document appeared, moderate American bishops attempted to soften its impact by pointing to the pastoral aspects of the letter. Conservative bishops, some of whom are equally well known for their ambition, lost no time in issuing statements of support for its more negative aspects. At the parish level, pastors winced in pain, knowing that perhaps 25 to 33 percent of the marriages in their parish are irregular.

"I just won't deal with the Eucharist and marriage issues in the same sessions anymore," Kemp continued. "Imagine! I have to deal with mothers who are preparing their children for Eucharist but cannot receive themselves because their marriages are invalid or illicit. That's blasphemy! Pedophiles can consecrate it, but I can't receive it. That's blasphemy!"

Carrie Kemp isn't an angry woman. In fact, although she has been through a virtual Gethsemane of therapy, clerical counseling, course work, reading, reflection, and prayer, she can still experience terror at the thought of confronting the Church. She is a gentle, almost fragile person. One gets the feeling that she is often shocked by the thoughts that fly out of her mouth. "I can't believe that I'm saying this," she said often during our several conversations. But the circumstances have emboldened her. She has a vital piece of steel inside her.

Carrie Kemp sparkles. She has a cheerleader's voice, but it is one with ears. Her sonar and radar are exceptionally fine-tuned. She can recognize pain even if it is buried deep within a career bishop's soul. She deals on a daily basis with people who have been spiritually abused, often by badly trained clergy who work for a system that is fueled by fear.

"Only a few get hurt, they say, only a few. Imagine that!" Carrie is referring to the response she sometimes gets from her clerical friends who supply knee-jerk answers in order to defend the dysfunctional system. "Imagine a system that justifies its existence because only a few get hurt!"

Carrie Kemp now devotes her life to insuring that people don't get hurt. She directs a service known as Kairos, which works primarily with people seeking annulments from bankrupt first marriages or who are preparing for a second marriage. In a sense, her entire life has been a preparation for this work. She has been through a painfully arid first marriage and a period of virtual economic and spiritual destitution caused when an unjust legal system permits the male spouse to escape with the bulk of the family's assets while leaving the wife with the children and a fraction of the assets. She has had to return to the work force while trying to raise four children and she has had to leap over the barriers of an annulment process that can be both enlightening and depressing. She has been tempted often "to slap my sandals together and walk away"—a typically Kempian paraphrasing of the Scriptures. Yet she remains in love with an institution that often cannot love her back. The experience has left her with a host of contradictory feelings. Thus, she holds many priests in high regard but has no desire to see the priesthood maintained. "They are asked to live in ways that are so unhealthy," she says with great sadness. "Especially those who hang around the chancery office. It's such an addictive corporation, such an unhealthy family."

She has set her experiences down in a book, *Catholics Coming Home* (with Don Pologruto, Harper, 1990). It's a handbook for churches who are reaching out to inactive Catholics—an estimated sixteen million of the nearly fifty-seven million Catholics in the United States.

Once her book was out, Carrie got too involved. "There was a lot of pain, a lot of loss with my freelancing. I just got too busy. Income wasn't a problem, numbers were. I lost a lot of one-to-one contacts when I left a parish structure and began freelancing from my home. But it has settled down."

Together with the statement on Catholics in invalid marriages, John Paul II issued a heart-chilling six-page statement that not only closed the door to any consideration of women priests but also forbade any discussion of the matter. Yet, it is clear that a conversation with Carrie Kemp is a conversation with a gifted priest in all but the greasy spot on the forehead.

Carrie is a native of St. Paul, the daughter of an immigrant Italian father, a blue-collar worker with Armour Meat Packing, and a rather rigid Danish Lutheran mother, a school teacher who was banished from her family when she married an ethnic Catholic. "There was a lot of pain regarding religion," Carrie recalled. "I felt closer to the Italian side of my family. There was noise, faith, joy, and pasta.

"But I was the second daughter and last child of a family that would be either black or white, right or wrong. My parents were determined that the dichotomy of their backgrounds and the accompanying hostility of my maternal grandparents could be overcome by a perfect marriage. I still wince as I recall the horrible moments of her condescending treatment of my father's family, the very people who took her in and loved her."

Her mother insisted that she and her sister attend public schools. "The public schools were better," Carrie recalled. "The Catholic schools simply couldn't pay the better teachers. My mother used to tutor the Catholic school kids and she found them to be woefully underprepared. Meanwhile, I studied my catechism with the sisters in the parish school and learned from them that salvation was not guaranteed to public school children and certainly not to their wayward parents who were sending us there.

"It was a very uncomfortable situation. I drew my strength from my grandmother, an immigrant Italian who was only forty when her husband died, leaving her with nine children. I was one of her forty-three grandchildren. I accompanied her back to Italy when I was sixteen. We stayed three months. My theology of the Communion of the Saints rests on my grandmother's soul."

At sixteen, Carrie had her first date. He was a good-looking Baptist who was as serious—and conflicted—about his religion as Carrie was about hers. They naively thought that they could solve the religion problem by simply not talking about it. Three years later, at only nineteen, she married the born-again Baptist who sincerely believed that his marriage to a Catholic was a ticket to hell.

The marriage lasted twenty-two years. There were four children, two girls, Angie and Cindy, while they lived in Winona, Minnesota, and two boys, Greg and Steve, after they moved to St. Paul. All were adopted.

"It hit me early on in the marriage that it wasn't working, but I saw myself as the mistaken one," she said. "As time went on, I began to develop my spirituality. It brought me confidence in myself.

"Then, our six-year-old boy got hit by a car. He was almost killed. I asked my husband to pray with me. He simply walked away. He honestly believed that to pray with a Catholic would jeopardize his salvation.

"Finally, after seventeen years, I got pregnant. After nearly five months, there was a violent miscarriage. My husband wasn't with me. Something more than the baby died at that point. Nothing was ever the same.

"I went back to work in a flunky office job. I was Mrs. Cleaver. The other wives would sometimes gather for coffee and complain about their husbands, but I never said a word. I left them all with the impression that our marriage was perfect."

Carrie's health began to deteriorate as a clinical depression set in. She became both physically and emotionally exhausted. Some relief came after she joined a charismatic group, but in time the group became too controlling. She withdrew.

Sometime during 1978 or 1979, she made a retreat. The experience opened an emotional dam inside her. Her pent-up emotions unraveled during a lengthy crying episode. The retreat leaders wisely just let her cry.

When she visited a therapist, the notion of divorce was mentioned for the first time. "I said 'No!'," she recalled. "Inside myself, I knew what I had to do, but I couldn't do it. I felt that I was going to lose my family and my church."

By Christmas, 1979, her daughter Angela was attending the College of St. Catherine in St. Paul. Carrie joined her on a five-week trip to Italy. The group needed a chaperon who spoke Italian and Carrie's was passable. Somehow, the trip opened her up. She viewed Michelangelo's creations and concluded that, for Michelangelo, the perspective was different. "Instead of carving and hammering to create something out of the blocks of marble," she said, "Michelangelo envisioned a creation in its perfection, something so beautiful and so complete that he had only to remove the necessary layers surrounding it in order to bring it into light. That's his gift to us—the freeing of what is already there. There is only one credential for those called to this art of sacred sculpture. We must have endured the hammer and the chisel."

As soon as she returned home, she asked out of the marriage.

It wasn't an easy parting. Telling the younger boys that she was moving out was very difficult. Her rigid Lutheran mother disowned her—a situation that lasted ten years. She became isolated from her lifelong parish community. Her pastor during this period was an nonrecovering alcoholic, totally dysfunctional in his role.

Typically, in divorces involving children, the mother gets the short end of the stick. Carrie moved from a nice home to an old farmhouse which she described as a "dump." Ironically, she has remained in the "dump," transforming in into a charming home.

"I couldn't even get a credit card," she recalled. "Sears turned me down flat. I applied later, using my dog's name. Sears immediately issued a credit card to Ted. I've never forgiven them!

"What really hurt was that there wasn't a word from the church. It was as if I had a big 'D' on my back. It was good old plastic suburbia at its best. In terms of men, I was completely neutered. I was working in an insurance office and Gary was there. We were friends but had no relationship. He was a divorced Methodist, not really practicing anything.

"I was forty. It was a real struggle. There was never enough money. My faith became very routine. I never really left the Church but, for a period of five years, I was just a Mass-on-Sunday Catholic.

"Then, I went to the Paulist church in Minneapolis. The priest gave a homily in which he actually talked about single mothers. It was the first time I had heard such a homily. You know, so many Catholics simply don't know that divorce doesn't exclude them from the Church. In time, Gary began to come to the talks with me. He had been married to a Catholic woman.

"Finally, both a priest and a therapist suggested that I go through the annulment process. It took the scales from my eyes. I saw all the dysfunctional stuff that I grew up with. And, perhaps for the first time, I felt that I was being ministered to.

"The whole process was a blessing. It's much more than filling out papers. It slows people down before they jump into something worse. It's now the reason Gary and I serve as field advocates and it's why we are involved in this second marriage preparation.

"You know, there's a movement now in some areas to change this process. Some want to exchange the testimony of spouses. That's not right. It's abusive. Much of this testimony is given in confidence. I'm afraid that if testimony is exchanged in this area, I'll have to get out of the loop."

Kemp is not a cheerleader for the entire annulment process. She views much of it as inconsistent, more of a legal process than a pastoral one. But she is convinced that a process is necessary for anyone contemplating a second marriage. "A broken marriage is an accumulation of deaths," she wrote in a Paulist publication. "It is the death of love, the death of hope, the death of promise. Grieving takes time and hard, honest work. If the marriage fails and we do not learn about ourselves in the failure, we become vulnerable to repeating our futile search in still another relationship."

Kemp now conducts six-session workshops in the archdiocese of St. Paul-Minneapolis and weekend workshops in the nearby diocese of New Ulm. She is the founder and director of Inactive Catholic Ministries. Today her work involves team development and training, facilitation of program series for parishes, preparation of grant requests and correspondence, consultation to diocesan and parish groups, and individual pastoral ministry.

"We cover all the issues in building intimate relationships, issues having to do with revealing oneself. We do spirituality, sexuality, intimacy. We stress the sacredness of the human condition. We don't use words such as 'right' or 'wrong,' 'good' or 'bad.' We don't use 'fault,' in groups or in private sessions. It's beautiful. You see conversion. I give people permission to be where they are and to find the meaning and mystery of the moment. I let them hear the voice of God in the reality of their lives and then to celebrate that in community, if that is fitting for them. Some of these tough farmers from New Ulm come in reluctantly and leave knowing that they are beloved of God. It's often their first concept of a God of love.

"If religion doesn't work for people in the broken parts of their lives, then it doesn't make any sense at all. I try to give people an opportunity to accept their vulnerabilities and to discover the kind of intimacy such acceptance permits in all their relationships: with self, with one another, and with God.

"But we also deal with the long-lasting effects of an abusive home and we deal with the fact that, in second marriages, divorces often happen because of the children.

"You know, shame is the original sin. It shuts us down. We don't want much light to come in. We're terrified of any admission of vulnerability.

"Divorced and remarried couples are the easiest to bring back to the Church. And there are so many out there! When I worked at the chancery, we used to get reports that, in a parish community of twelve hundred families, there were only three divorces. That's ridiculous! It means that only three couples came forward. Most just leave the Church because they believe that they can't be helped. So the Church believes its own statistics.

"Oh, yes, I did cry when the Vatican issued that statement about divorced and remarried Catholics. Honest relationships with the beloved of God, regardless of circumstances, foil our ability to judge anyone unworthy to approach the table. Rather than condemnation, the Church should be urgently soliciting the stories of baptized Catholics who have endured the ravages of divorce. I have been blessed by hundreds of these stories. Not once has it been suggested that the decision to divorce was an easy one or that the divorce experience lessened the value placed on marriage.

"The Church needs to shoulder some of the responsibility for these failed unions rather than pointing fingers at them. Instead, the Church has placed more emphasis on raising children than intimacy between partners. Instead, I see sacredness in couples called to live in second marriages.

"Again, I refuse to deal with the Eucharist and the marriage issues in the same sessions. I won't tell people to simply ignore the Church's teaching and approach the Eucharist but I won't tell them to stay away either.

"You know, this issue of second marriages is not unlike the gay-lesbian issue. We have to do forgiving work. It's not a 'mother' church, as they like to call it. It's really a 'father' church—strict, unforgiving. A true mother church opens up her arms. I don't have to hit someone over the head with canon law to get them back into the Church. I can just tell them that you have everything within you to be everything you want to be.

"People have been trying to work out relationships since Adam and Eve. For many people, divorce is a call from God. We can't have a group of nonrelational clergy telling us about divorce, remarriage, and the Eucharist."

That is how Carrie Kemp talks. She shifts gears, going from one perspective to another. At first, they seem unrelated, almost like the verbal wanderings of Molly Bloom in Joyce's *Ulysses*. But they tie together. One only has to listen.

Kemp is now in private practice, helping clients who are experiencing many of the problems she endured. There is no shortage of walking wounded coming for help. She is often booked months in advance. "After four years at St. Lawrence [the Paulist parish], I just got overwhelmed. I got into hospitality and sharing sessions. It got to be too much. Now, in private practice, I can have a separate, manageable apostolate."

Kemp's faith and apostolate was severely tested after she took a position at the chancery office, a cold and forbidding building, said to be purposely designed that way, located on Summit Avenue in St. Paul. Here, she worked in a variety of capacities leading to a position as an assistant to the director of finance and administration. From the very beginning, she suffered increasingly vicious sexual harassment from the building's janitor, a clearly troubled man with a long history of harassing female employees. When she complained, the janitor's supervisor informed the archbishop that, unless he was empowered to fire him, he could no longer supervise him. The archbishop responded by placing the janitor under the supervision of a priest who was moderator of the Curia. The priest encouraged employees to report any incidents of harassment. The complaints mounted; all were reported to the archbishop. His response was to shift the janitor's supervision to another priest.

One priest described the janitor's relationship with the archbishop as "very, very close." It was clear that the janitor often served as his driver, maintained his car—even his getaway cabin. He lived nearby, worked every day, and was always at the archbishop's beck and call.

In time, the janitor's harassment made Carrie fear for her safety. "Priests on the staff would witness his verbal assaults, including profanity," she recalled. "They would laugh about it afterward, telling me that he didn't do it to them." The janitor's tirades were often clearly overheard even by at least one of the archbishop's auxiliaries. But the bishop never acknowledged hearing the janitor. "I was immobilized," she said. "I realized that ethics, moral values, reasoning, and process had no effect in a dysfunctional family or system."

Gradually, Kemp realized that she had to take action. She began with her supervisor, who informed her that the archbishop had expressly forbidden him to reprimand the janitor. "Don't ask me to choose between you and the archbishop," he said. He assured her that the matter "would be taken care of." The janitor was spoken to, but nothing happened.

The great irony was that this harassment took place even as Archbishop John Roach, former president of the National Conference of Catholic Bishops, was calling for action at the archdiocesan level "to assure women of the dignity and equality which in justice is rightfully theirs, but which they do not always experience." It was another classic example of the Church's penchant for lofty rhetoric followed by inaction, especially on economic and social justice issues.

Carrie determined to take the case outside the chancery office to the Office of Human Rights for the State of Minnesota. While privately admitting that genuine harassment had taken place, her supervisors cautioned her that her job security was at stake and that the archbishop would support the janitor. She was cautioned: "Do something about your anger."

Kemp returned to her office where gradually the realization came that people whom she had trusted and respected would close ranks and shut her out.

The complaint went forward. Roach's attorneys investigated and found both clear evidence of sexual harassment and a failure of the archdiocese to act. They declared it "legally intolerable" and stated that "nothing has been put forward which would justify the failure to remedy the abusive situation this employee has created."

The janitor resigned. But he never left. Roach rescinded the resignation. "I was told that the archbishop had evaluated him," she said. "That is all that is necessary. You are to forget it."

Carrie had support from within. At least a dozen employees gave sworn testimony to her lawyers. The case was finally settled out of court for an undisclosed amount. The archdiocese also attempted to keep Carrie from discussing the case, but she refused.

She lost her job. The janitor remains in his. Roach remains archbishop but a coadjutor archbishop, Harry J. Flynn, was appointed in 1994. The appointment appears to be at Roach's request.

"The case left me asking just where my responsibility as a Catholic Christian begins and ends and where does my responsibility to myself, my family, my sisters in Christ begin and end. How do I deal with the deep sense of caring that I feel for John Roach as he lives with the demon within him, causing his complete disregard for me and my dignity, for all women and their dignity? How do you deal with priests and lay people whose ethics and discipleship center on the archbishop rather than Jesus? Why is this pattern so familiar in diocesan priests who end up in chancery offices? I have to ask myself: 'Can I, representing the Church, continue to offer such experience within the Church to these people, knowing how limited the hierarchial experience of female humanness is?'"

The case is closed and the wounds appear to be healing. Carrie Kemp touched some consciences. The archbishop and the janitor still have their jobs, but the religious and emotional pillars that once held the structure up were nearly destroyed by a tiny Samson who had the courage of her faith.

Carrie Kemp now pursues her apostolate of healing away from the misogynistic climate of the chancery office. "I tell people that their experience is valid, their loss is felt and their story is heard," she concluded. "I simply enjoy working with people in situations where the answers no longer fit their questions."

2

Bishops on the Edge

———————◆·◆———————

Bishops can get pushed to the edge, too. They can leave their episcopal installations glowing like a Renaissance painting and find, after a few months, that their purple beanies weigh heavily on their heads. Their pastoral sonar and radar are often short-circuited by circumstances they never envisioned.

There was a time when they ruled like the princes they claimed to be. They behaved like only children. They simply raised their ringed hands to cut off all further discussion of any issue. Now, however, all but the most ambitious or insensitive must pick their steps across rock-filled creeks and rushing waters.

"Congratulations," one gnarled cleric said to a seminary classmate who had just been appointed to a diocese, "you'll never get a bad meal and no one will ever tell you the truth."

If the meal that my wife Jean and I had with two bishops during a gathering in Washington, D.C. is any indication, the "no bad meal" axiom is certainly true. It was at an Italian restaurant not far from the hotel where the National Conference of Catholic Bishops (NCCB) meets each year. The little restaurant was filled with bishops, some treating old friends, some holding court at the center of a long table filled with lesser bishops.

Dinner with these two bishops was rewarding. It had a ripple effect that lasted for weeks. Some bishops may be tightly wound, but these two had rubber croziers. They made you feel good. They had the quiet confidence of two men who had long since arrived at an understanding of who they are. Tell them about another bishop who bristled when one of his clergy hoisted his drink and said: "Harry, don't go on like that. Don't you know that half your people have never heard of you." They will laugh with resigned recognition. Joke about bishops who seem to follow Alexander Pope's heroic couplet: "Be not the first by whom the new is tried,/ Nor yet the last to lay the old aside." They will tell you of bishops who would want the mindless couplet on their episcopal shields.

"Nothing must be done for the first time" could be another manifesto among the growing number of conservative bishops.

"The Church was the first to offer those frequent flyer miles," the taller bishop said with a feigned straight face. "After all, weren't we the ones that invented indulgences?"

The two bishops just wanted to relax, *sans* Roman collars and pectoral crosses. They are two really good men, blessed with more faith and humor than an Irish pub. They are solid, believing men, but not men who want to inflict the death penalty on anyone who isn't pro-life. Neither believes that just because they are bishops life has to be all heart surgery. Their spiritual DNA matches the Church's, but they don't have an astigmatic view of morality and they aren't trapped in the heresy of incidentals. They love their fellow bishops but fear that too many are becoming increasingly self-destructive, refracted, and punitive. For the most part, they see their colleagues as sincere men who work hard, even as they live in fear of the institution. They see no criminal intent in the appointments of their fellow bishops, just a lot of overweening ambition and compulsive little egos. They didn't say it, but I got the impression that they felt that too many of their colleagues have become baseball owners.

They said nothing that could be regarded as cruel or unusual, but it's best that they remain anonymous. Bishops generally line up crozier to crozier. Their gentle observations could be viewed as breaking rank.

I brought up one recent appointment. They winced when I informed them that a newly installed bishop had just announced that all Catholics living in his diocese who were in irregular marriages were adulterers. In an area where an estimated one-third of marriages are irregular, that's a lot of adultery. This new bishop was rumored to be installing rocket launchers around his desk. In this present climate, he'll go far. His edict was likely issued more to impress the Vatican than to bring sinners to their knees.

Perhaps these two men were accidental bishops, appointed before the punch list grew so long. One was appointed by Paul VI, the other by John Paul II. Surely, they would not be appointed today, nor do they have a career path within the present church. Their train has made its last stop. They know it and it has freed them up.

"Ambition," one said. "Ambition is still the password. The Vatican loves men with ambition. In Rome's mind, it means that they have a puppet on a string. An ambitious bishop will do anything Rome tells him."

"It starts with their background," the other said. "If they've written or said anything negative about *Humanae Vitae* [Paul VI's encyclical on birth control, 1968] or anything truly positive about women, they're already dead. They'll never make bishop."

I recalled a careerist priest I know who sensed incorrectly years ago that something positive needed to be said about women. He honestly thought that Rome was pointed that way, partly in an effort to overcome the negative effect of *Humanae Vitae*. So, he wrote some positive reflections about women, even suggesting that the question of their ordination be discussed. It's doubtful that he had any personal feelings in the matter; he is a lifelong careerist with fewer feeling mechanisms than a lobster. But his words found their way to his file and his career ended. They nodded knowingly. Career crashes are commonplace. Only about 10 percent of would-be candidates make the cut. Less than a tenth of one percent of priests are appointed to what is termed "the fullness of the priesthood."

"One mustn't write anything except accepted stuff," the taller bishop said. "The Blessed Mother, family values—that sort of thing."

He was enjoying himself. He had written a great deal, including diocesan pastorals that got good play outside his diocese. He had chosen his words carefully. On balance, his writings would be classed as moderate. But he believes in dialogue and that in itself short-circuited his career. Dialogue is superfluous when all has been divinely ordained.

The late President John F. Kennedy once addressed a group of religious sisters. Tongue-in-cheek, he told them that he viewed them as Democrats while the bishops were Republicans. It would be easy to establish whether or not nuns are Democrats, but the bishops guard their vote jealousy. One can't be certain what they're thinking; one has to examine what they're saying and doing. Based on that view, it's a good bet they vote Republican.

Bishops and many of their subordinates adhere to what Jesuit theologian David G. Schultenover calls the "Mediterranean Model." In his *A View from Rome: On the Eve of the Modernist Crisis* (Fordham University Press, 1993), Schultenover introduced the Mediterranean Model as the organizing model of the Church. Its principle support is "belongingness" and its primary social structure is the family (read Church). "A person's identity depends on belonging to and being accepted by the family," Schultenover writes. "But that belonging and acceptance depend on one's adherence to the traditional rules of organization and maintenance." The traditional codes are simple: honor and shame. In the Mediterranean culture, the male plays the dominant—or public—role; the female plays the private role. Indeed, a man's very identity hinges upon his upholding his honor.

Shame occurs whenever anyone disrupts or even criticizes this system. And, according to the Creighton University professor, "Shame falls primarily on whoever is responsible for maintaining order." Thus, subordinates are always a threat to superordinates because they might bring shame. Bishops then are always watching their backs, vigilant for any deviation from the norm. To lose control is to be shamed. Worse, to lose control to a woman is to be emasculated.

In this system, discussion is not in order. "The very concept of authority is based on the right and power to enforce socially accepted mores rather than on any power arising from personal, individual, self-authenticating charisms," Schultenover says. "Indeed, the concept of the 'personal' (in the sense of individual) has little place in Mediterranean society. Such a notion would be considered foreign, an outside influence, and therefore a serious threat to order."

Understanding this culture helps one to understand the convoluted and often wiggly hierarchal infrastructure. It helps explain why a bishop with utterly no pastoral experience is moved from Rome to head a major U.S. diocese. He had the essential qualification: he would maintain order and quickly declare anything new or different as trivial or faddish. His reward will likely be a red hat.

The Mediterranean model explains John Paul II's six-page apostolic letter ("On Reserving Priestly Ordination to Men Alone"). Women are perceived as the greatest threat in this model which is fueled by fear, distrust and suspicion. Theological distinctions have nothing to do with it and scriptural citations serve only as adornments.

Sadly, good will, trust, and love have little place in this model. Efforts at reforms are read as revolts. At diocesan levels, those who would call for change are routinely sent letters that contain the word "scandal." The letters threaten "dire consequences" if any external authority is challenged. Lately, it seems, episcopal candidates are being examined for internal as well as external assent.

In a large diocese, a bishop has the luxury of picking a chancellor who will exercise the vigilance and apply the lash. (Some readers will recall the novel and movie *True Confessions* in which the cardinal orders his chancellor to remove a pastor. "You'll be a bishop some day," the cardinal said, "and you'll have someone to do your dirty work.") Bishops' letters to subordinates often contain phrases that are linked to the system. Thus, the offender is charged with giving "grave scandal" that "reflected negatively upon the ordinary." It is rarely the offense that matters; it is the impact on the ordinary. He is shamed before his superiors; he should have finessed the matter. Clergy brought on the carpet routinely report that their bishop will plead: "Do you realize what you're doing to me?" There is never any space for individual conscience; those who stand against the collective conscience are seen as possessing malformed consciences. As Schultenover states, "The view that conscience represented access to God's will, independent of the teachings of the Church, was regarded as heretical."

The Catholic Church originated and developed within this culture. It still carries this model's strengths and weaknesses. The analogy of the Mediterranean model with the Church reminds one of the remark heavyweight champion Sonny Liston's manager made about the late pug: "You know, Sonny has a lot of good points. It's his bad points that aren't so good."

Earlier, Jean and I visited Washington's beautiful National Cathedral, an Episcopal shrine that could be called the nation's church. We spotted two bishops taking in its spectacular architecture and wonderful chapels. Both had their clerical collars covered lest they give "scandal" even in these ecumenical days. We walked with one back to the hotel. He was charming, friendly—and careful. Later, another told us that he had no doubts about his priesthood or the Church. "I've never wanted anything else," he said. "I've always been comfortable." It was clear that he had found everything he needed in this life and the next within the boundaries of the Church.

Our two episcopal friends were relaxing, emptying out, the way my father used to talk to my mother about his boss while soaking his tired feet in a bucket of Epsom salts after a long night at the bakery. These bishops were just letting their miters down.

"Write about the Blessed Mother, the new *Catechism of the Catholic Church*, and the abortion issue. And, oh yes, vocations," the older man said. "Vocations are always a good topic."

The younger bishop agreed, but some anger showed. "Ordaining anyone with testicles?" he asked rhetorically. "Why the plural?" He went on to cite a recent review of three seminarians by a seminary faculty. Two of the ordination candidates were rejected by a vote of ten to two; the third managed five votes but had seven against him. The bishop ordained all three.

Over a glass of Dewar's, the younger bishop cited another bishop who, in his effort to secure an appointment to a megadiocese that was soon to be open, is ordaining candidates with barely discernible pulses, men who have lost most of the dots on their dominoes. "Rome sees the ordination figures and puts a star on his page," he said.

"Some pastors are desperate for help," he continued. "But they're refusing to take some of these newly ordained because they're just one more problem. But Rome is impressed."

"It helps to talk about vocations, too," the older man said. "It would help if you wrote a book about it."

"You wouldn't believe how some bishops count," the younger man said. "They see the ordination figures, but what they do with them is something miraculous. They turn them to their own purposes. They just don't *want* to admit to the problem. It's easier to criticize those who have developed the data."

"Write about family values," the older man said with a smile. "That's in at the moment. Just be sure that the family unit has a working father, non-working mother, and, of course, children. And whatever you do, don't write about women.

"Oh, and if you're already an auxiliary or ordinary, issue an edict condemning something, one practice or another that is viewed as an abuse. Rome likes edicts. They give the appearance of authority. A good one currently would be that all religious instruction is to be brought in line with the new catechism."

We were gathered at a meeting, a good-sized one that involved hierarchy, regular clergy, religious, and laity. The atmosphere was cordial. The agenda did not involve power. All antlers had been shed. These two bishops were welcomed at every session. They differed from a growing number of their fellow bishops; their smiles reached up to their eyes.

It was a good conference. The best conversations came when corks were pulled and sealed bags torn while someone went down the corridor with the ice bucket. The sessions—at which the bishops drew applause when they entered—had good substance but tended to end like the final speeches of the treacly Miss America contestants. Statements were issued about saving the whole world. None of the bishops in attendance offered a statement. Curial-minded bishops have little to worry about from such conferences. But there was some hope that the energies released would at least ease the pangs of their xenophobia.

"Rome is moving guys all over the place," the younger bishop said. "They don't pay any attention to bishops' provinces anymore. They moved a guy from Boston to Green Bay and another from Boston to Fort Wayne-South Bend. They moved another guy from Lafayette, Louisiana, to St. Paul-Minneapolis, one from Rome to Rockford and another from Rome to St. Louis. It's a control thing."

The American Church has 33 archdioceses and 150 dioceses. The Official Catholic Directory for 1993 listed 11 cardinals, 60 archbishops, 382 bishops (including 105 auxiliaries; 103 retired) working in 183 dioceses that embrace a Catholic population of 56,398,696. The bishops are responsible for the spiritual welfare of 22 percent of the population of the entire United States. That's a lot of power in the hands of a few aging men who are prisoners to a model with many cultural limitations.

"They say it's not a plot," the younger bishop continued. "They say that they're only trying to pick the best men."

"Are they telling the truth?" I asked.

"Of course not!" he answered with a laugh.

The older bishop was adding to his list of current criteria: "Learn a foreign language. Preferably Italian. Take a sabbatical and go to Rome and study there. While there, visit curial offices frequently and tell them what you're doing.

"If you're in a chancery office, write tailclip letters to your fellow priests. Be sure that one copy gets to the right people so that they'll know you're a good cop. And don't miss installations of fellow bishops. Get there and shake hands."

The meeting we were attending had gathered a lot of experienced and talented people. "Wouldn't it be wonderful," the older bishop said, "if we could make this group available to the bishops. It's not that the bishops don't have information. We try to consult. Just look at the consultations on our pastorals on peace and the economy and on catechetical instructions. We do a good job of listening. But we're afraid. We're afraid of the people in the bishops' offices. We're afraid of those who want to be bishops. We're afraid to listen because the laity might come up with something that the bishops don't want."

Dominican theologian Edward Schillebeeckx confirms the fear. What bishops say and do in public is guided by "fear and the thought of what the Vatican might think," he wrote. "They do not have the courage to oppose the Vatican."

"The Vatican speaks a language that no one understands," he wrote. In *The Tablet*, London's Catholic newspaper, he called for new values "which can only be found in the Church and her message of the reign of God."

Lots of names of sitting bishops were floated across the table. The two bishops were kind to all. But there was some impatience at the waste of manpower even within their own ranks. "Just look at so-and-so," one said. "Perhaps the best-informed bishop on peace and justice issues. But he doesn't serve on the committee—not on any committees, in fact—because his views are too liberal."

There are over sixty permanent and temporary committees of the NCCB and its administrative arm, the United States Catholic Conference. The entire organization has little influence at the Vatican, which most likely would want to do away with all national conferences, but the committee structure defines who the top players are.

Bishops of major dioceses often lobby hard for seats on the more significant committees. It can mean that they control the committee's actions. It can mean that Rome has influence on a given committee through a more loyal bishop.

"Years ago," the older bishop recalled, "the cardinals sat up front at all meetings. They had open microphones and could interrupt at any time. Just a word of opposition from one of them and discussion ended. Now, the big bishops blend in with the others, but they still have an influence, especially on those who are still seeking advancement.

Another name was mentioned. "He's a good man, a good theologian, a virtual workaholic," one bishop said. "But he's scared. It gives him eczema."

"They really play hardball, don't they?" I observed.

The older bishop grew quiet. "Yes, I'm afraid they do," he said. "Yes, it's hardball, and it shouldn't be."

Then he brightened. "I should add," he said, "that it helps to visit the Shrine of Our Lady of Czestochowa or to offer to accompany the pope to Zagreb."

3

Patty Crowley:
Founder, Faithful Dissident

The eighty-eighth floor of a Chicago Gold Coast highrise is not the place one expects to find a widowed woman in her ninth decade who spends at least one or two nights a week in a shelter for abused and homeless women and her Sunday afternoons visiting female prisoners at the Metropolitan Correctional Center. Most of the other women of her vintage who live in the Hancock Building are dowagers, waiting for God, and thinking about their next bridge game.

Patty Crowley likes the monastic quiet of her three-bedroom apartment that literally touches the clouds. The Crowleys moved in when the Hancock was a rental building. Typically for them, they had just been turned away from a condominium they wanted when the condo association learned that the blacks who were among the dozens of children and students they took in were not domestics but would be living there. A nondiscriminatory rental unit was their only choice.

She owns the place now. It could be a showplace. There are touches of luxury; the furnishings are all quality. One wall bears a painting of Pat Crowley's great-grandfather, a man who married into the O'Brien family, founders of a paint and varnish company in South Bend. But Patty has chosen a functional home-workplace. There is too much furniture, including at least a dozen dining room chairs, which Patty needs for the many meetings she holds for one cause or another. On occasion, she has packed 100-plus people into the place. There are loads of books and the walls are lathered with pictures of an extended family. Her bedside book was a recently released life of Paul VI in which she and her husband figure significantly. (More about this later.)

Her bedroom doubles as her office. The bureau holds boxes of index cards of potential donors to her beloved Deborah's Place. (More about this later, too.) "Patty could run General Motors," an admirer said years

19

ago. She combines dedication with organization. She is a woman who makes decisions and is capable of living with the consequences of her decisions. One gets the feeling that she would welcome a closer relationship with the institutional church—a relationship she once enjoyed. "We used to know every priest in Chicago and elsewhere," she said. "Now, I don't know any of them." But she can live without it.

"After Pat died," she said, "I felt the need to be with a group. So we started Genesis. In the beginning, a priest used to come to open the meetings. Then, when he left, the next priest showed up only at the end. Finally, we had no priest at all. Now, we have our own meetings. It works fine."

Patty Crowley has always lived rather upscale. Her family, the Carons, owned a successful spinning company outside Chicago, where Patty was born in 1913. At first, her father was a salesman for the company, located in Rochelle, Illinois. But Patty never really lived there. Her mother didn't like the country. When her younger brother contracted rheumatic fever, the family moved to Chicago, presumably to insure better medical care. She has spent years in the suburbs, but it's clear that she enjoys the city. It seems to energize her.

Patty attended Sacred Heart Convent in Lake Forest, and later Trinity College in Washington, where she received a liberal arts education that included a year in France. "I had very little connection with my parish," she recalled. "I was in private school. At First Communion and Confirmation, I felt like an outsider. I didn't like that."

Her husband, Pat, was cut from much the same cloth. His father was a moderately successful lawyer whose firm won the famous Joe Jackson case—the one involving the infamous Chicago Black Sox—in 1919–1920. The firm seemed to hold its clients because it was a friendly place, unlike the crisp style and cold demeanor of the more driven firms. Today, over two decades after Pat Crowley's death, the firm still carries his name—a clear sign that it remains respected.

Patty and Pat were born just a few blocks apart but didn't meet until one of those *Tre Ore* devotions at Chicago's Holy Name Cathedral in 1934. Pat, an undergraduate at Notre Dame, was taken with her but forgot her name. By the time he tracked her down, she had returned to college in Washington.

At Trinity, Patty had taken one course with the legendary Msgr. John A. Ryan, a social ethnician from nearby Catholic University of America and the director of the Social Action Department of what was then called the National Catholic Welfare Council. (It is now the National Conference of

Catholic Bishops and the United States Catholic Conference [NCCB-USCC].) Patty didn't even know who Ryan was—she had been told that the course was a real slowball. Instead, Ryan introduced her to the great social encyclicals of Leo XIII and Pius XI. He pricked her conscience. Later, Msgr. Ryan met her on the train back to Chicago. He bought her dinner and his influence was set. "He opened my eyes to the other side," Patty remembered. "My family was against unions. They were staunch Republicans."

Patty and Pat were married in 1937, a year after she graduated from Trinity. Looking back, she marvels about how things were then. "We just got married," she said. "There were no preparation classes, nothing like that. We had been raised to attend Mass and to not eat meat on Friday. Oh, we went to the occasional meeting, but there was no formal marriage preparation. We got ours in a bar at the Bismarck Hotel. The priests did everything."

Pat was working at Chicago Title and Trust and attending Loyola University's Law School. Soon after graduation, he joined his father's law firm where he would practice the rest of his life, if he wasn't involved in some movement or other. He wasn't a very practical lawyer; he always forgot to turn his meter on. Mostly, he handled corporate work. "But he was always doing everything for nothing for everyone else. I can tell you that," Patty recalled with some trace marks of resentment.

Patty Crowley is not a bitter woman. It's just that she has a highly developed sense of life's ironies. Both she and her husband have been used by both people and institutions. There have been more letters and calls asking for help than there have been expressions of thanks. Patty can still smile—even laugh—about it. Her laugh, in fact, is expressive and contagious. Always an attractive women, she now faintly resembles the legendary actress, Helen Hayes. In spite of serious hip surgery a few years ago, she now walks briskly without a cane. She swims regularly in the pool in her building. She is not indifferent to her health but doesn't talk about it. It's important, but she doesn't burden her friends with the wearisome details. She just takes care of herself.

Pat Crowley was a dreamer like his father. His law practice put bread on the table. He represented the legal interests of a varnish company that his mother's family owned and of Caron International—but he was much more interested in social causes and matters of the spirit. He made money. The Crowleys lived well. But if he had directed his energies toward only power and money, they would have lived a far more comfortable life.

"We just went ahead," Patty stated nearly sixty years after their marriage. "You just took children as they came." Patty had six births; she lost two of them, one following a miscarriage and another that died after only three days.

In 1943, the Vatican issued *Mystici Corporis Christi*, an encyclical that seemed to anticipate the very things that the Christian Family Movement would later embrace. Even before that, Patty and her husband were learning about Canon Joseph Cardijn of Belgium and his Inquiry Method. Its basic ingredients were "See, Judge, Act." It became the formula for the Young Christian Workers (YCW) as early as 1925.

One of the disciples of the YCW, a German Holy Cross Father named Louis Putz, came to the University of Notre Dame just before World War II. In 1941, Putz met Msgr. Reynald Hillenbrand, the rector of Chicago's major seminary. Hillenbrand returned to Chicago with the Inquiry Method and taught it to other priests and laity, including a former seminarian named Paul Hazard. ("Paul had to leave the seminary in 1933 because of a bad back," Patty recalled with laughter. "Then, he got married and had eight kids!")

In 1943, Hazard started a discussion group for businessmen. "It was just a group of men sitting around a table in Pat's office," Patty said with a bit more irony. "The men were leaving home, going away from their families without their wives, to talk about marriage," she recalled. "But that's the way it was in those days. The women were expected to stay in the background."

"I hated it," Patty recalled a half-century later. "I had only been married five years or so, and I kind of liked the guy. Now here he was, going out to meetings every night to talk about marriage!"

The years that followed World War II saw the expansion of the suburbs. Msgr. Hillenbrand had been removed as rector of the archdiocesan seminary in 1944 and appointed pastor of Sacred Heart Parish in Hubbard Woods, a posh northshore suburb. Many of the couples relocated there.

By 1946, women became involved, but only as a separate group under the leadership of a priest, Fr. Gerard Weber. "Sometimes, I could have shot Fr. Weber," she said. "But he was good."

At first, Patty refused to join. "We were a group of women talking about social issues while the men met separately to talk about marriage issues." She couldn't quite articulate her anger; the issues were too new. But they could be summarized by her recollection of driving to meetings with Pat at the wheel and Msgr. Hillenbrand in the front seat, while Patty sat in the back.

She and Pat were going to write a book on marriage. But the clergy objected. In those days, books were written by clergy and approved by the

Church. Not long before World War II, the Chicago church had declared that the rhythm method of birth control was morally wrong. "It was that way," Patty said. "Paul Hazard had put out a forty-page book on the rhythm method. But both Paul and the doctor who devised the rhythm method were declared in error. We never even thought or talked about other methods of birth control."

But things changed. By 1948, the men and women were meeting together in a meeting format that included Gospel, liturgy, and social action. The goal of the Catholic Action group, as it was then called, was to make the neighborhood a more nurturing place. It was among the first of the small Christian communities that are sweeping the country today.

"You didn't plan these things," she recalled. "They just came to us and we accepted them."

She remembered a Father Delaney, who had just returned from the Philippines and who was now doing family renewal days. "We had never heard of such a thing," she said. "We thought they were wonderful. We talked about marriage, about getting along and all that.

"We began going from parish to parish, trying to get names of people who were going to get married. Most parishes wouldn't give us any names. They thought we were going to try to sell them flowers or something like that. My own sister was getting married at that time and she and her husband didn't like the idea of this preparation, either. But that was the beginning of the pre-Cana Movement."

By 1949, the loosely organized movement had changed its name to Christian Family Movement (CFM). The theological basis remained the encyclical on the Mystical Body. "Hillenbrand was devoted to it and Pat loved it," she said. "Pat would have a martini at night and then go on and on about the encyclical. I didn't know what he was talking about, but it was the first time that I realized that we had a role in the Church."

Working out of Pat Crowley's law offices, they inspired small CFM communities in 100 cities. In Chicago, the group linked up with the Family Life Council out of Msgr. Edward Burke's office in the chancery. Again, the tensions involved with authority and creativeness were still evolving. The clergy could often be repressive but, just as often, they were the catalysts in making the movement work.

Pat Crowley was elected executive director; Patty's name was not even mentioned. It was still that way, but Vatican II and a host of other currents were still years away.

By 1950, they were ready for their first convention. It was held at St. Procopius College (now Illinois Benedictine) in Lisle, Illinois. (Another irony:

the husbands and their largely pregnant wives slept separately; Catholic colleges weren't ready for cohabitation yet, even for married people.)

"Both groups were in dormitories. It was awful," she recalled. "The next year, we tried Loyola University in Chicago, but the Jesuits would not even let us in. Pat had gone to the University of Notre Dame. He did his undergraduate degree there. His family was from South Bend and he knew Father Cavanaugh, who was then the president. [John J. Cavanaugh, C.S.C., was president of Notre Dame from 1946–1952.] We also knew Father Hesburgh. [Theodore M. Hesburgh, C.S.C., succeeded Cavanaugh in 1952.] He was a young priest then, but he had stayed at our house. Through him, we got Cavanaugh to allow us to live coed on the campus. So, we met often at Notre Dame until it got too expensive.

"Those were great meetings. We really got into issues. In 1957, I think it was, we took the whole year on the race issue. We had speakers like Eugene McCarthy [former senator and presidential candidate] and Monsignor Pietro Pavan [head of the editorial team that wrote *Pacem in Terris* for John XXIII]. People came away from these meetings and decided to dedicate their lives to social justice."

The conventions met mainly to write programs. Hillenbrand insisted on a structured program. That was his style. Others wanted something unstructured, with each unit doing its own thing. "It was a man named Clem Lane who was a member of AA that settled the issue. He introduced us to the AA handbook and the Twelve Steps. It proved prophetic. It put structure into the program.

"We advertised in Catholic papers. Then, if we got a response, we would come and visit. We called ourselves the 'Christian' Family Movement, but the bishops always referred to us as the 'Catholic' Family Movement. Some bishops wouldn't even let us in their diocese, but that was only a few. In Chicago, Cardinal [Samuel] Stritch gave us full-time chaplains. That was a wonderful thing if you consider that our numbers weren't that big.

"We drove all over the country, eventually reaching the west coast. We always wrote ahead and asked for hospitality. We never stayed in a motel or hotel. When we went to South America, we slept in some unusual beds. We were going to write a book about the beds we slept in."

Gradually, the issues expanded, in spite of occasional finger-wagging from chaplains who were threatened by their pace. CFM groups helped needy families to move; "adopted" a single mother of two; helped handicapped people; bought subscriptions to local papers for servicemen away from home; did a housing survey to explore the potential for low-cost housing, etc. There were almost as many causes as there were members. "We had to be concerned with different areas of life, not just married life," she said. "I liked the broader ideas. They appealed to me."

By 1956, CFM boasted twenty thousand couples. It would eventually reach one hundred thousand couples. In that same year, Patty and Pat toured the world—Honolulu, Tokyo, Hong Kong, Manila, Saigon, Singapore, Bombay, Beirut, Jerusalem, Cairo, Rome ("We got three minutes with Pope Pius XII"), Paris, and Dublin. The following year, they covered Spain and Latin America. CFM spread faster than a fast-food franchise.

It wasn't all a ribbon-cutting fantasy. They met resistance. These were pre-Vatican II years. In the United States there were bishops, priests, and laity who wanted nothing to do with CFM.

Four decades ago, nothing much functioned in the church without a desk at the chancery office. Some critics saw CFM as bourgeois, even elite. Others viewed its social action agenda as tinged with communism. The Crowleys—comfortable, upper-class, educated—were an ideal target for some critics.

Again, CFM's mail drop was out of Pat Crowley's office. Often, visitors simply dropped in and, although it was close to five o'clock, the wonderfully impractical Pat would invite them to dinner. Visitors came from Japan and the Philippines, from Nigeria and New Zealand. The Nigerian was a student; the priest from New Zealand would later become a cardinal. "We often had twenty people to dinner," she recalled. "When Pat and I went to Tanzania in early 1974, he wondered aloud if its president, Julius K. Nyerere, had ever been to our house. We did keep a guest book, and, sure enough, when we checked it, there was his signature."

In spite of some clerical concern, the Crowleys remained determinedly ecumenical. They put an Episcopal priest and a Presbyterian minister on the program committee.

Just before this period, the Crowleys began taking in foster children. The last of a dozen foster children was Theresa. She arrived in 1955 and never left. The Crowleys adopted her.

Later, they began accepting European students. It was a response to appeals from the Church to help Western European children, mainly from Germany and Austria, to get an education. Later, they took in dozens of largely Third World college-level students. Most worked out, but cultural moats separated some from the Crowleys. Some students refused to perform even the simplest household chores in exchange for their board, room, and often tuition and clothing. Patty's own children didn't simply seethe; they told their parents. But Patty felt that some inequity was part of the bargain. "I guess we had twelve to fourteen foster children and thirty to forty foreign students," Patty recalled. "I never really counted them." Although any formal program ended years ago, Patty had one student living in her apartment as recently as 1993.

By 1964, Pat and Patty Crowley were perhaps the best-known couple in Catholic America. Still, they were surprised and thrilled when asked by Paul VI to be part of a fifty-seven-member, worldwide Commission for Studies on Problems of Population and Birth Control. They were one of only three couples—the others were French and Canadian—to sit on the panel which was composed of theologians, economists, demographers, philosophers, doctors, canon lawyers, etc.

The Crowleys clearly didn't see themselves as experts. "I still don't know how we got on the list," she recalls with a laugh. "It had to be CFM. But we just didn't even know people who practiced birth control. We knew some who practiced rhythm, but they all had children."

They gathered outside Rome in March, 1965. (More ironies: At the opening session, husbands and wives were assigned to separate sleeping accommodations. Paul VI welcomed them with "Dear Sons." And, although they didn't know it at the time, not one of the married women was capable of bearing a child.) "There were actually seven women in the whole group," Patty said, "including the three married women. We were told not to say anything about the separation of the men and the women. We were dutiful Catholics, so we said nothing. But Pat must have made a wisecrack to the *Ladies' Home Journal* about the separation. In any case, it ended up in *Paris Match*. The pope must read *Paris Match* because by the next session each couple had an apartment."

The Commission had actually been formed by John XXIII. There was never any real agreement on how many took part. The Vatican is pretty casual about such things, partly because final decisions are reserved to one person. Patty's figures show seven on the original group. Fifteen were added later—all males, all theologians. The Crowleys were part of the third round of picks, bringing the group to fifty-seven. "At least that's what is on my list," she recalls. "But some cardinals arrived later. The group could have been seventy."

"It was funny," Patty recalls with good humor. "Everyone there was an expert, except us. They didn't know what to do with us. So much of the time they put us with the theologians."

These were heady sessions, lasting about a week each. When Patty and Pat realized that the other delegates were experts in their disciplines, they decided to return to the next session with letters from their "experts"—the couples of CFM. They contacted the sociology department of the University of Notre Dame and asked them to prepare a questionnaire that could be mailed to CFMers. "Remember," Patty said. "These were people like us who followed the Church's teachings on birth control.

"The responses we got were heartbreaking. The letters were filled with pain and tension."

The Crowleys also found that birth control was only an issue in America and Ireland and in countries where Irish priests had gone. Europeans thought that the idea was ridiculous because everyone was practicing some form of birth control. They saw it as a matter for individual conscience.

The Crowleys had always supported the teachings of the Church. For their part, since 1947, when Patty nearly died following surgery, they knew that they could have no more children, but the letters they brought to the meetings were filled with anguish.

Later, the Crowleys would testify before the Birth Control Commission that, according to the thousands of letters they had received from three thousand devout Catholics in some eighteen countries, almost without exception, rhythm had bad psychological effects. In a remarkably frank chapter of John Kotre's *Simple Gifts: The Lives of Pat and Patty Crowley*, the Crowleys reported they had told the Commission that, while rhythm might be useful for developing discipline, no one believed that it fostered married love or married unity. Instead it substituted tension, dissatisfaction, frustration, and disunity. Further, the physical and psychological implications of rhythm were not understood by the male church.

There were four sessions, two of them just ten days apart, over a period of about eighteen months. "It was tough on the children," she said. "We were away a lot. We brought the kids over between one session and drove around a bit. Cardinal [Alfredo] Ottaviani presided at the sessions. He was an old man then. He used to fall asleep and so we had to stop the discussion.

"There were problems in translation," she continued. "There was no simultaneous translation, just interpreters. It could get difficult. My French was only passable and Pat didn't speak a word."

According to Peter Hebblethwaite, author of a masterful biography of Paul VI, the summary report on rhythm that the Crowleys presented was placed on the desk of the Commission's secretary, Fr. Henri de Reidmatten, O.P., but there is no evidence that it got to the pope's desk. In an ironic twist, another member of the Commission did not hear the evidence submitted by the Crowleys. He did not attend the final sessions of the Commission, partly

because his senior episcopal colleague, Cardinal Stefan Wyszynski, primate of
Poland, had been refused permission to travel out of his country. He remained in Krakow out of loyalty to his friend. He was Cardinal Karol Wojtyla,
who would become John Paul II. The future pope was perhaps better prepared to address the issue than other clerical members of the Commission. In
1965, he had written a book, *Love and Responsibility*, which had been well received by theologians such as Henri de Lubac, O.P. But he was absent on
May, 1965, when the Crowleys presented their report. According to
Hebblethwaite, the future pope also missed two scripture scholars who told
the Commission that the Bible had nothing to say about birth control.
Onan's sin was not "withdrawal" but the refusal to continue his brother's
line. One can only speculate on what he might have said over a dozen years
before being elected pope.

Patty believes that the poignant letters changed the direction of the
discussion. When they left the final meeting, they were convinced that
Paul VI would permit some form of birth control. In their closing session
of June, 1966, the Commission had concluded that contraception was
not intrinsically evil, that *Casti Connubii*, an encyclical on Christian marriage issued by Pius XI in 1930 which forbade all forms of birth control,
was not irreformable, that the Church was in a state of doubt, and that it
could change its position. In fact, following the last session, the co-pres-
ident of the Commission, Cardinal Julius Dopfner, and its secretary, Fr.
Riedmatten, presented a report to Paul VI that concluded that the
Catholic position on birth control "could not be sustained by reasoned
argument."

The Crowleys presented the letters they had received to Paul VI. "We
put them in a large white folder. God knows where they are now. There
are copies of most of them at Notre Dame."

Patty and some other members of the Commission naively thought
that their report would be the sole document on the matter. "I've read
every word of Peter Hebblethwaite's book," she said, "and I am just
learning that a lot went on after we left. Hebblethwaite reported that the
distinguished theologian Bernard Haring was alarmed by the activity
that followed the submission of the Commission's report. More conservative clergy urged the pope to re-think the recommendations, not on
their merits, but because any change in papal teaching would weaken the
authority of the pope. Conservative bishops such as Cardinal Alfredo
Ottaviani and Archbishop Pietro Parente of the Holy Office saw the
Commission's work as authority being taken out of their hands. Further,
they felt that the Vatican II document, *Gaudium et Spes*, which pointed

in the direction of responsible parenthood, did not have the authority of an encyclical such as *Casti Connubii.*

Whatever the case, the Commission was never consulted again. "We didn't even get a thank-you note," Patty recalls. Clearly, their recommendations had now become grist for the Vatican's political mills.

Two years later, in 1968, at 4:00 A.M., a reporter called the Crowleys and asked their opinion of *Humanae Vitae,* the encyclical that reiterated the traditional teaching on birth control. They were stunned. Pat answered simply, "I can't believe it."

The Crowleys had maintained a discreet silence on the Commission's recommendations, partly because they didn't want to send the decision the other way. They knew that Paul VI, a theological conservative, would agonize over the decision. But they were confident that he would permit some form of contraception. While they believed that their evidence had turned the tide, they didn't know that their "psychological" evidence was simply not a match for those who viewed it as unscientific and inferior to any theological reasoning.

What hurt them even more was the reaction of their hundreds of priest friends. The clergy closed ranks. Some priests severed all relationship with them and cut themselves off from CFM. "I tried a couple of times to talk with priests. After all, we had changed our minds. Perhaps they would, too. But I never succeeded," she said. What hurt Patty more so than Pat was that, while the clergy would not address the issue of birth control directly, they avoided the Crowleys and CFM as if it had initiated the practice. Patty saw this as hypocritical. "To this day," she said, "not one of my priest friends has discussed the matter with me. And since 1968, I've never heard the issue brought up at the pulpit."

Msgr. Hillenbrand, their close friend and adviser, severed all connections with the Crowleys. (At Pat's request, he did return in 1974 to give him the Last Rites of the Church. "Only after he asked me if Pat had been anointed already," Patty recalls.)

It hurt. It still does. Even before the release of Paul's encyclical, the Crowleys had written Cardinal John Cody, archbishop of Chicago. They informed him of their appointment to the Commission and asked to work with him on this and other issues through CFM. Cody never responded. When Cardinal Joseph Bernardin became archbishop in 1982, Patty wrote again, this time reflecting her pain over the reaction to *Humanae Vitae.* He responded four months later with a noncommittal letter. "I don't think he likes me," Patty concluded.

Humanae Vitae divided the Christian Family Movement. However, earlier, the sixteen documents of Vatican II and the encyclicals of John XXIII, *Mater et Magistra* and *Pacem in Terris*, had divided the membership even more. The conservative wing of CFM had viewed John's teachings as borderline socialism. The younger members, down to 3 percent among those couples under twenty-five, found *Humanae Vitae* too harsh a burden. Circulation of *Act*, the CFM publication, began to dwindle from its peak of forty-one thousand.

A year later, the Crowleys began to withdraw from their leadership role. By 1970, they resigned. They continued their CFM efforts through new ecumenical and international CFM groups. It was another irony: CFM had been inspired by an encyclical—*Mystici Corporis*. Now, nearly twenty-five years later, another encyclical—*Humanae Vitae*—would almost bring about its demise.

In the years that followed, the Crowleys pursued their work for the Church and society. Their home continued to be a gathering place for the celebrated and the lowly. (One night, their apartment was so crowded that they unwittingly invited an encyclopedia salesman to join them for dinner.) They remained involved with CFM, especially its international arm, and got very involved in the presidential campaign of peace candidate, Eugene McCarthy. Soon, their apartment was filled with politicians, peace activists, folk singers, and religious people of all stripes. It was a complete turnaround from a promise Pat Crowley had made to Patty's mother in 1937—not to get involved in politics. Marietta Caron had held politicians—especially Democratic ones—in low regard. In 1928, Pat had worked as a teenager for Al Smith's campaign. But Smith, the first Catholic presidential candidate, had been defeated by Herbert Hoover. In 1960, Patty, now a confirmed Democrat in spite of her family, had worked vigorously for John F. Kennedy. When Kennedy won, the Crowleys asked him to address the CFM meeting at Notre Dame. But it was too close to the election and the young president declined.

The 1968 Democratic Convention was held in Chicago and was disrupted by a riot. McCarthy's backers were viewed as the instigators. The reaction was predictable. McCarthy lost the nomination to Hubert Humphrey. McCarthy tried again in 1972. Pat never lost faith in him. The Crowleys' experience with CFM had raised their social conscience to a level that few pragmatic politicians could sustain. They were able to bring some issues forward—the same issues on which they challenged CFM members and the Church. In their political efforts, one heard echoes of their work with the Catholic Interracial Council, Catholic Scholarships for Negroes, American Indian Center for Chicago, Catholic Labor Alliance, the Human Rights Commission of Illinois, and a number of other groups that were changing the Church from piety to social concerns.

But the McCarthy experience may have served only to distance the Crowleys more from an institution that was closer to the old Democrat philosophy of the late Richard J. Daley. Daley was a decent, honest politician with a social conscience that reacted more slowly. He often called Pat Crowley, who did legal favors for him, but they were never close. Pat's idealism created a distance.

In 1971, Pat was diagnosed with cancer. He lived for three years before dying in their Hancock apartment with Patty at his side.

For the next two decades, Patty Crowley continued a bewildering variety of personal missions. For twenty-five years, she maintained a smoldering silence about *Humanae Vitae*, partly because no one had asked her to speak or to write. She was finally asked to write her reflections for *Conscience*, a publication of the Catholics for a Free Choice. Patty has genuine reservations about this group. She feels there is a quantum difference between the birth control and abortion issues. But she wanted to make her point, including the fact that abortion was never mentioned during the Commission's meetings. *Conscience* printed her article but edited it considerably.

When the *National Catholic Reporter* printed her entire article, she got a larger response, including two bitter letters from priests who informed her that she was going to hell. "I still burn when I hear that birth control is a dead issue," she said. "Yet the pope goes everywhere and mentions it. The *New World* [Chicago's archdiocesan paper] still mentions it. The archdiocese still has a family planning office. Yet, no one will really talk about it. It's so hypocritical."

Over twenty-five years later, one can still sense the anger in this intense, dedicated woman. "When Pat was alive, I could talk to him about it," she added. "Now, I don't have anyone." Perhaps that is why she is speaking out more.

She continues to host Genesis, a discussion group for women, in her apartment. "After Pat died, I found myself very much alone. I found that I needed a group. So, we started Genesis. We met seventeen weeks in a row. Imagine! I called it a consciousness-raising group. Now, we don't meet as often, but they still come in from the suburbs. We used to have a chaplain—Fr. Jim Jakes—but after he went to another parish, the priests dropped away. So we get along fine without them. Why, when we had Sr. Teresa Kane, the nun who spoke to the pope, we had a hundred women here!"

"We don't expect that people will believe everything they hear. We just ask them to listen and form their own conscience. I think in that way we raise consciousness."

Patty remains a lector, commentator, and eucharistic minister in Holy Name Cathedral parish where she met her husband sixty years ago. She brings the Eucharist to the sick at Northwestern Hospital. When asked, she speaks before groups who barely remember CFM. She uses the occasion to challenge them. At a recent meeting of the First Friday Club of Chicago, a group of business people, she signed up listeners to help rehabilitate apartments in a housing project. "You asked me what you can do. Well, here it is. Come, sign up!"

Her primary mission now is Deborah's Place, a facility for battered and homeless women. It's directed by her oldest daughter, Patricia, a Benedictine nun since 1958.

She organized Deborah's Place partly because she was weary of serving on boards who expected nothing of her but her fund-raising ability. "I wanted a group where members of the board would do the work that it said it was doing," she recalled. It wasn't easy. Although her friend, Father Jakes, offered her space in Immaculate Conception parish, where he was now pastor, a private school group which was renting the former Catholic school objected strenuously. "They didn't want these women around their dumpsters," Patty reflected sadly. They lost a second place which wasn't up to code. Now they are in a third home on Chicago's teaming Milwaukee Avenue and planning a fourth and final home in a former religious article store.

The group receives support from Patty's parish as well at the local Episcopal and Presbyterian churches. Patty has now resigned from the board. "With Patricia as executive director, there would be a conflict of interest." Besides, Patty is opposed to groups that rely on the energies of one leader. "They generally die with their leader," she observes.

Now eighty-one, she is a tireless fund raiser and organizer for Deborah's Place. She spends at least one night a week at the shelter and is actively trying to gather $1 million to renovate the building they have acquired. Her Sunday afternoons are spent in the women's section of the federal prison in Chicago. (Another irony: "I asked the prisoners what they wanted to do and they answered, 'Play Bingo.' So Patricia and I play Bingo with them.")

Presently, she's working with a journalist on a history of the Christian Family Movement. She wants to get the CFM between covers in the hope that it will inspire still other Christians who want to "see, judge, and act."

"I stay in the Church," she said with a measure of distance not remotely in sight fifty years ago. "It's as good or better than the other churches. But I see it differently now. If I miss Mass now, I have no qualms. I never would have done that years ago.

"I still have a hard time going to church. If they would just get up and say that birth control is intrinsically evil, then they wouldn't be so hypocritical. I've never spoken out on abortion, but if they were wrong about birth control, maybe they're wrong about abortion, too. Oh well, maybe they want to kick me out. Maybe they will!" (She laughs.)

"Oh," she adds, "Trinity College invited me to talk on *Humanae Vitae*. I hope they don't get in any trouble!"

She laughs again. Patty Crowley can still laugh.

POSTSCRIPT: John Paul II, who loves to canonize, says that he hopes to canonize a married couple some day. Thus far, only one couple are in the canon, an obscure thirteenth-century pair named Elzear and Delphine who lived together for twenty-five years without consummating their marriage. Authorities are now investigating the cause of Louis and Azelle Gurin Martin, parents of St. Therese of Lisieux. But they, too, would not have conceived Therese and her sisters if the parish priest hadn't counselled them to procreate. Allegedly, they had remained celibate for at least a decade.

Patty Crowley would scoff at any suggestion that she and Pat would be good candidates. They are prototypes of the new laity in the Church. From unpretentious beginnings, they became the most influential couple in the American church of the fifties to the seventies. Clearly, they must rank with the late Frank Sheed and Maise Ward, another couple who had an impact.

Perhaps the day will come. For now, Patty Caron Crowley would just as soon live the Beatitudes.

4

Tom Roeser:
Loyalty to "The Great Perhaps"

———•◦•———

"**I** like Tom Roeser," one of his old friends said. "But he gives me indigestion."

Tell that to Tom Roeser and he laughs knowingly. He delights in the fact that he leaves people dyspeptic, but he objects to being described as a curmudgeon, a characterization linked to ill-tempered people, full of resentment and stubborn notions. Roeser is right. He's more of an iconoclast, one who likes to overthrow popular ideas or institutions. However, true iconoclasts enjoy imploding traditional "icons" or institutions. Tom Roeser seems bent on preserving them.

Columnist Jimmy Breslin has written that, as a devout liberal, one of his recurring dilemmas is that he often finds some of his fellow liberals insufferable while he genuinely likes the conservatives who give him indigestion. It's that way with Roeser. He is a genuinely nice person. He is the neighbor to whom one would give his house keys when going away on vacation. He would loan you his best drill bits—or a favored book. He'd never tell you, but at any given time, there's probably someone he's helping with a serious problem.

Some liberals would find people hungry and have a meaningful discussion about them. Tom Roeser would cook up a pot of soup.

Tom Roeser is Blaise Pascal. At least he would like to be. If one has an affinity for reincarnation, the Pascal-Roeser connection would give one pause. Pascal is his idol and mentor. The seventeenth-century French scientist and religious philosopher had just the combination of high intelligence and painfully realized faith that Roeser treasures.

Pascal was born in 1623. Before the age of sixteen, he produced a pivotal scientific paper on conic sections, dealing with the intersection of a right circular cone and plane, which generates one of a group of plane curves, including the circle, ellipse, hyperbola, and parabola. By nineteen,

34

he had devised a calculator that could lay claim to being the precursor of the computer. (One of today's computer languages is named after Pascal.)

Pascal worked on the elusive theory of probability and contributed to the advance of differential calculus. In physics, while still a young man, he formulated Pascal's Law which states that pressure applied to a confined fluid is transmitted undiminished throughout the fluid. (Practical applications are found in most hydraulic machines.) He also helped to invent the barometer.

Roeser's own life is far removed from science. He is a liberal arts major and political scientist. But his interest level in broad-based studies remains high. He attended college during the days when studying Shakespeare involved reading all thirty-seven of his plays, not simply snippets from a half-dozen, a commonplace practice today.

Born in Evanston, Illinois, in 1928, he still attends classes at the University of Chicago's Continuing Education Program. (Most recent course: on Pascal's *Pensées*.)

Roeser would stoutly defend a certain level of cultural elitism. He would call for a standard to which people might aspire, not an egalitarian environment that encourages an influx of mediocrities who study only present or recent past writers of their own gender, ethnicity, or sexual preference. He reminds one strongly of the late William Henry III, *Time*'s theater critic, who wrote many stories about American society. In the weeks before his death, Henry completed *In Defense of Elitism*, a book that decried the assault he perceived on the attributes he valued most: "respect and even deference for leadership and position; esteem for accomplishment, especially when achieved through long labor and rigorous education; reverence for heritage, particularly history, philosophy and culture; commitment to rationalism and scientific investigation; upholding of objective standards; most important, the willingness to assert unyieldingly that one idea, contribution or attainment is better than another."

Henry's creed may be a bit too effete for Roeser, but he would accept it, particularly if it could be recited in a smoke-filled room or over a well-seared steak. Further, Roeser would have added a faith dimension. In a world where even sources such as *Current Biography* often omit the religious affiliation of their subjects, Roeser's brag sheet states clearly that he is a Roman Catholic and that he was named a Knight of the Equestrian Order of the Holy Sepulchre of Jerusalem by John Paul II.

William Henry III argued that an overweening anti-elitism has debased higher education. Roeser would likely agree and add that the Catholic Church is debasing its heritage by diluting its teachings and its disciplines, settling for a faith as thin as John F. Kennedy's. Like much of today's education, Roeser sees church membership for most Catholics as no proof of faith or commitment but simply a rite of passage. He would prefer a leaner Church adhered to by those who follow its bylaws. He would like a church with a reading list. Unlike some liberals who want to drop Confirmation as redundant, Roeser would retain it as necessary to complete the grace of Baptism. He likely sees Confirmation as a booster shot that gives Christians a special strength of the Holy Spirit to spread and defend the faith boldly.

Some years ago, Roeser and I were adversaries on an evening talk show over WGN Radio in Chicago. Two priests were also part of the panel. Roeser challenged them more than he did me. While we expressed concern over the dwindling number of priests, he questioned whether today's priests' corps should be trimmed and disciplined to march in step with John Paul II, a man he regards as one of the top ten popes.

According to priest-sociologist Andrew Greeley, conservative Catholics account for only about 7 percent of the Church's population. Although often stereotyped as blue-collar, six-pack believers, Catholics tend to be more liberal than other religious groups on many issues. Further, loyal Catholics, conservative or liberal, are not necessarily docile. "They don't leave the Church," retired Fort Wayne-South Bend bishop, William E. McManus observed. "They stay and complain. They are loyal and disappointed."

Tom Roeser would agree with that sentiment, a rare concession to his liberal brothers and sisters in the Church.

Liberal-minded Catholics control much of what constitutes the day-to-day faith of most Catholics. They control education at all levels; they are generally in charge of groups like the Confraternity of Christian Doctrine (CCD), Rite of Christian Initiation for Adults (RCIA), the pre-Cana and Cana Movements, Christ Renews his Parish (CRP), and others. Parish liturgy committees are generally in the hands of moderate to liberal Catholics as are most of the social services. Women virtually run the weekday church, presiding at liturgies in the absence of a priest, giving "reflections" (read *homilies*) and bringing the Eucharist to the sick and elderly. Liberal publishers easily outsell their counterparts.

While parish priests tend to be moderates or liberals, a growing number of bishops are virtually bar-coded as conservatives before their appointments. The Church's administration controls its finances, seminaries and cemeteries, diocesan newspapers, and any significant authority. Because of a compulsively prudent hierarchy, conservatives continue to exercise an influence far out of proportion to their numbers. (Should John Paul II live to the millennium, he will have appointed virtually all the Church's over four thousand bishops, all of them carefully vetted for unquestioned loyalty and a branch manager's mentality.)

Chicago's Cardinal Joseph Bernardin, a moderate, and Milwaukee's Archbishop Rembert Weakland, a more outspoken moderate, may be the only major prelates in the U.S. who plea repeatedly for some form of theological detente between liberals and conservatives. Both pay a high price for their efforts. More typical of the new model is San Diego's Bishop John Brom who, when John Paul's apostolic letter ("On Reserving Priestly Ordination to Men Alone") appeared in May, 1994, issued a preemptive strike against dissent. It was a memorandum to his staff that read in part: "Anyone who even thinks of dissenting should resign with integrity." Such directives leave little doubt that the pope and his appointees will not hesitate to use their decrees punitively. Washington's Cardinal James Hickey has already ordered that all teaching materials in his diocese be brought in line with the new *Catechism of the Catholic Church* and Peoria's Bishop John Meyer has directed that all involved in the teaching of religion either bring their teaching into line or withdraw from teaching. The circle draws tighter and tighter.

Tom Roeser is at home with much of this. His political experience may make him more nuanced than the hierarchy. He has lost as many battles as he has won. He can live with liberal thought; his theology isn't tied to power. But his mind is a mailbox of carefully sorted slots with little room for new addresses.

Roeser's German-American father was a gifted writer who didn't like journalism. Instead, he supported his family by selling package travel tours to ethnic groups and colleges, including St. John's in Collegeville, Minnesota, where Roeser would later matriculate. The business evolved into a heavily Catholic clientele.

When Tom was ten, his father took the family to Europe. They were in Austria during Germany's takeover and young Tom had the dubious privilege of standing at his hotel window and viewing Adolph Hitler, goose-stepping in front of his troops.

World War II put an end to the travel business. His father opened a small insurance office which, somehow, never seemed to sell any insurance. Tom, an only child and intuitive reporter, wondered endlessly about why insurance sales or claims were never discussed over the kitchen table.

He soon realized that his father was an FBI mole, monitoring people who had pro-Nazi sentiments. His undercover work inevitably brought him in touch with just such people and the tightly knit neighborhood in St. Juliana's Parish began to buzz. Roeser's father was tagged as a pro-Nazi sympathizer.

At school, Tom was awarded the Good Citizen Award by the American Legion, but the gossip was running so high that the group seriously considered taking the award back. It was a difficult time for Tom. He wondered himself if his German-speaking father was working for the Nazis.

With the loss of his father's travel business, the Roesers' fortunes fell and they could not afford a Catholic high school for Tom. Further, the McCarthy-like paranoia was still running high and Roeser's mother thought that he could benefit by some "secular" thrust to his education. So, he attended Taft High School, then a highly regarded public school.

About this time, an FBI agent came to dinner and confided to Tom that his father was a special agent, working for the government. "He told me that my father was a patriot," Roeser recalled with great relief.

The college years were at St. John's, a small Benedictine liberal arts college in a monastic setting. Roeser loved the place. He still considers himself a 'Benedictine. He graduated in June, 1950, with a B.A. in English.

A few weeks later, the Korean War ignited. Tom, a long-time asthmatic, tried to sign up for the marines but was rejected. His grateful parents threw a graduation party and presented him with an electric razor.

"I wanted to get out of town at this point," he said. "I tried to find a job at the City News Bureau in Chicago but had no luck. Eventually, I found myself back in Minnesota working for the *St. Cloud Times*." He liked the job. The small city of twenty-five thousand was one he could get his arms around. At first, he did just sports and obituaries but, soon after, started covering politics. Soon, he became the unofficial but *de facto* political editor.

Still in his early twenties, Roeser began traveling the state with Hubert H. Humphrey (1911–1978). The late senator, vice-president, and two-time candidate for the presidency was perhaps the best-known politician to come out of Minnesota. He was mayor of Minneapolis while Roeser was in college. In 1948, he became the first Democratic senator elected from Minnesota. Tom Roeser genuinely liked the talkative senator, an ardent New Dealer and a strong advocate of civil rights. It is one of the seeming contradictions that mark Roeser's life. Almost instantly identified with conservative causes in politics or religion, he often advocated ideals not normally identified with Republican or conservative philosophy.

While the political trips were exciting, his salary kept him somewhere between poverty and destitution. He supplemented it by playing piano in a local bar and by doing freelance interviews for the Associated Press which paid him twenty dollars for a significant one.

One day he had an opportunity to go out to the airport to interview Eleanor Roosevelt (1884–1962), widow of Franklin Roosevelt and arguably the most effective first lady in history. A vigorous humanitarian, she became the first first lady to give a press conference in 1933. "I didn't even know what to ask her," he recalled. "She spoke about the human rights charter. I got a fantastic story. She wrote the story for me."

Roeser's Roosevelt story got a lot of attention. Such stories always add to any writer's brag sheet. He got to write more than he expected. The experience earned him a position as director of communications for Governor Elmer L. Andersen, "a sort of John Garner Republican," Roeser recalled. When Andersen lost his bid for re-election, Roeser was hired by the Minnesota Republican Party which hired him as a research-publicist. Ironically, these were the days when Arizona Senator Barry Goldwater was the conservative Republican candidate for the presidency. Roeser's camp hated him. "We considered him a primitive savage," he said. "His people told me that they'd kick my ass."

"At twenty-eight, I was an important person," he said with unaffected self-satisfaction. "I was a moderate Republican, doing what I liked. I was idealistically happy."

He became good friends with Eugene McCarthy, a congressman from 1949–1959 and Minnesota's other senator from 1959–1971. The friendship is typical of Roeser's catholic reach.

In 1964, Roeser returned to Chicago and joined Quaker Oats. Just a year after Hubert Humphrey's unsuccessful second bid for the presidency—this time against Richard M. Nixon—Roeser took a leave from his position in order to form the nation's first unit of government dedicated to fostering minority enterprise. It was a job he knew well since he had been promoting minority entrepreneurship since he joined Quaker Oats. He had also supported Dorothy Day and her renowned Houses of Hospitality. As assistant secretary of commerce, he gave President Richard M. Nixon's team, led by White House aide John Ehrlichman, a strategy that coordinated the 116 government programs which could be utilized for minority entrepreneurs.

Having done his job, Roeser did something that nicely fit his philosophy but which was politically incorrect: he recommended the abolition of his own federal agency, an absolute no-no in a government that likely still has a bureau for inspecting covered wagons. "I ran into a buzz saw," he said. "Nixon really had a southern strategy which didn't want my program." The challenge to the permanent bureaucracy led to his reassignment to a liberally-identified position as director of congressional relations for the Peace Corps, an invention of John F. Kennedy.

With the exception of his years in Washington, he would remain with Quaker Oats for twenty-seven years, retiring in 1991 as vice-president. During his years with the company, Roeser did much to change its image. "Those were the days when we had Aunt Jemima, a black slave on our box," he said. He immediately got involved in urban affairs, bringing such African-American leaders as Andrew Young into the Quaker Oats executive offices to meet with top management.

Since retirement, he has been president of his own corporate relations firm, as well as a writer, lecturer, teacher, and a commentator on public policy. On election nights, he can be counted on to be an analyst for NBC-TV, Chicago. He remains the political commentator on the right for the Chicago *Sun-Times* and has been doing an afternoon talk show on politics for one of the major radio stations in Chicago.

Roeser is the perfect radio and television personality. He speaks in the first person, using declarative sentences and the present tense. If there is a subjunctive mood, Roeser reserves it for spiritual pursuits. The electronic media abhors a vacuum; reflective pauses are viewed as speech defects. His points of view are in place, framed on the walls of his mind, and backed with what is obviously copious reading.

Taking on Tom Roeser is not unlike taking on religious conservative Michael Novak or political conservative George Will. He occupies the conservative chair on a nationally syndicated radio program of analysis, "Inside Politics."

Roeser may be as quick-minded as his hero, Pascal. Typically, when a well-known local politician had a dispute with a local radio station over his afternoon talk show, Roeser was able to replace him on a moment's notice. Give him an hour's preparation and he could interview God.

Roeser was the first corporate government relations executive. He admits to but doesn't much like terms like "political action committee representative." He was named a Kennedy Fellow at Harvard. He later received a Woodrow Wilson Fellowship at Princeton and, still later, took the course he designed to many private colleges across the nation. He has lectured on public policy at Northwestern University's Kellogg Graduate School of Management; St. John's College, Oxford; the Wharton School of Finance; and Loyola University of Chicago. Presently, he is an adjunct professor of public policy at the University of Illinois, Chicago.

In 1654, at thirty-one, Blaise Pascal experienced what he described as a "conversion." He abandoned basic science and turned his attention to religion for the remaining eight years of his life. Tom Roeser experienced no such conversion, but it's clear that he has moved gradually to the right on most issues.

Here the parallels get blurred. Even as a young man, Pascal came under the influence of Jansenism, especially after his sister entered the Jansenist convent at Port Royal which served as the center of the movement. His affiliation would strengthen the movement but, years later, would draw ridicule from Voltaire.

Cornelis Jansen (1585–1638) was a Dutch theologian whose teachings were deemed heretical by Pope Urban VIII in 1642. Jansenism emphasizes predestination, denies free will, and maintains that human nature is incapable of good.

Jansen wanted to reform Christian life along the lines of a return to St. Augustine. His teachings stressed personal holiness and held that the soul must be converted to God by action of divine grace. In its extreme form, Jansenism believed that God predestines from eternity the salvation of certain souls. This is posited on the basis of God's omniscience and omnipotence and can be linked easily to the doctrine of divine providence and grace. St. Augustine's interpretation of the doctrine has been the fountainhead for most subsequent versions. It's an easy heresy to slip into because it wills the salvation of all souls but holds that certain souls are granted a special grace that in effect foreordains their salvation. The damned may be said to be reprobated to Hell only in the sense that God foresees their resistance to the grace given them. Jansen's emphasis on it brought his teachings into conflict with the Church; but predestination proved popular with some strains of Catholicism, Protestantism, and even Jewish theology, which embraced predestination in the general sense that everything ultimately depends upon God.

Jansenism was driven out of France by Louis XIV (1638–1715), but it survived within the Church, especially among the clergy. It infected the seminary and religious order culture for centuries, taking the form of extreme scruples about most moral problems, especially with regard to the Holy Eucharist. It never quite caught on among

Protestants, since Jansenism held that one must be Catholic in order to be saved.

There are Catholics alive today who may not be able to quote its gospel but who might volunteer that one trip to the confessional is good for only one trip to the communion rail.

Whatever the case, Pascal's reputation, together with that of Jean Baptiste Racine (1639–1699), perhaps France's greatest playwright of the period, proved a great booster shot to Jansen's rather gloomy teachings. When Antoine Arnauld, a noted Jansenist, was attacked by the Jesuits, Pascal championed him in a series of witty, irony-laden Latin essays called *Provincial Letters*. His *Thoughts: an Apology for Christianity* has become a philosophical and religious classic that is still in print. It is here that Pascal and Roeser come closest. Roeser would likely dismiss the predestination teachings—as did Pascal—but he would likely cite St. Augustine even before St. Thomas Aquinas.

Pascal states his belief in the inadequacy of reason to solve man's difficulties or to satisfy his hopes. Both men would preach the final necessity of mystic faith for a true understanding of the universe and its meaning to man.

Pascal wanted to restore austerity and discipline to the Church. His writings, like Roeser's retorts in a debate, offer a wealth of insights based on personal experiences and psychological perceptions.

Pascal believed in "the God of Abraham, the God of Isaac, the God of Jacob—not of philosophers and scholars." At one level, he seems anti-intellectual, but he rescues such thoughts with "Man is a reed, the weakest in nature, but he is a thinking reed."

There is an underlying pessimism and faintly melancholy feeling about Pascal. So with Roeser. "We shall all die alone," Pascal wrote. Roeser might add that a period of suffering before death must be expected.

Tom Roeser's sense of human nature and his ironic humor would resonate with Pascal's observations that "All human evil will come from this: man's being unable to sit still in a room." He would laugh with Pascal at his observation that ". . . if all men knew what others say of them, there would not be four friends in the world."

Pascal's religion was centered on the person of Christ as Savior and based on personal experience. Although he was courted strenuously by the Jansenist community at Port Royal, he was never wholly one with them. Three centuries later, Tom Roeser would be courted by Opus Dei, the ultra conservative cult-like group that was founded in Madrid in

1928 by Msgr. Josemaria Escriva, who was beatified with unseemly haste in 1992, and which now has over 76,000 members and 1,459 priests throughout the world. (Roeser's oldest daughter is an active member.) While Roeser admires their theology and their goals, his exposure to them ran against his grain. "They talked incessantly about Escriva," he recalled. "I came to hear about Christ." With his customary candor, he told them just that. He was never asked to attend another meeting.

It's likely that Roeser would be slow to join any religious group. He would lose his edge.

Pascal's deepest experience was that of man's tragic situation between greatness and misery. To escape from it, Pascal believed that man plunged into distractions. Once weighed down with distractions, only faith can free someone. There is an element of risk in a life of faith. Roeser seems to echo these sentiments. He sometimes refers to the deity as "The Great Perhaps," a borrowing from the French comic genius François Rabelais (1490–1553). He has his doubts. But if there is an emphasis on the will, faith stands a chance of survival. Like Pascal, he views man as full of natural error which cannot be eradicated except through grace. Despite a strong attraction to the intellectual, one gets the feeling that, like Pascal, he can be moved by devotions and simple faith. "Whoever knows Jesus," Pascal wrote, "knows the reason for everything." Roeser would agree.

Roeser believes that life is a struggle and that sin is as real as the weather. "I'm a natural law man," he says, explaining his moral code. He likes his truths plain and simple. Jesus is both God and man. Christ is present in the Eucharist. Kings may give up their kingdoms, but the pope cannot abandon his. It is Pascal on instant replay. "You should read him for an hour," Tom said. "You'd see."

In 1959, he married his wife Lillian, an Irish-American Chicago native, then an active member of Young Christian Students and a volunteer for the *Catholic Worker*. "We went through all the pre-Cana and Cana," he remembers. "We had four children. No birth control"—and he meant it.

Roeser lives in suburban Park Ridge in an upper-middle-class parish of 3,500 families. But he often attends the Latin Mass at Chicago's St. John Cantius Church, sometimes presided over by the archdiocesan chancellor. He is comfortable with the Latin and the liturgy.

Tom Roeser's conservative mindset was not the product of a midlife crisis or the kind of philosophical shifts experienced by Cardinal Joseph Ratzinger or American Catholic thinker Michael Novak, both of whom were once considered liberals. "My father was quite religious, almost scrupulous," he recalled. "My mother was Irish; she wore her religion proudly.

"The Church isn't a Rotary Club. It's not an affirmative action group. I believe, for example, that the role of women in the Church is well-defined, and I'm comfortable with it. If we allowed women priests, we would end up ordaining a load of ex-nuns.

"I couldn't join Opus Dei. I don't want to be caught in a strait-jacket. I can't equate Escriva with the Trinity. But I think they can be good spiritual advisers. Spiritually, I'm a Benedictine and the Benedictines don't talk about Benedict the way the Opus Dei people talk about Escriva. However, on the other hand, an awful lot of sins have been committed in the name of Vatican II."

It is likely that he would reject the excesses of some conservative publications such as the *Wanderer*, partly because it would offend his intuition for good reporting. He might agree with their sentiments on a given issue, but it's likely he would find their accusations unhealthy and unproductive.

In common with many conservatives, he has a fierce loyalty to the pope but a low regard towards his bishop. He considers Cardinal Joseph Bernardin a "disaster." (Bernardin is considered a moderate, a prudent man. He is the highest ranking active bishop in America. The Vatican regards him as an oil can, a man to settle problems that develop among the hierarchy. But his stock in Rome has slipped, partly because of the influence of more conservative megabishops such as New York's Cardinal John O'Connor, Boston's Cardinal Bernard Law, and Washington's James Hickey. The East Coast has four cardinals; the Midwest only one. Rome still views it as mission country, and, while the eastern church has shown little growth in years, it still has the power and the cash. However, Bernardin remains well-liked by many lower-ranking bishops and most of his own priests.)

"He is not an advocate for what the pope has spoken," Roeser said of Bernardin. "Look, I like Archbishop [Rembert] Weakland in Milwaukee or Archbishop [Raymond] Hunthausen [former archbishop of Seattle]. They're liberal, but they speak up for what they believe. But Bernardin is linked to Rome with a rope of sand. He's good at easing conflicts—maybe the best since Cardinal [James] Gibbons [archbishop of Baltimore 1877–1921], but he's a Hamlet. He has a masterful sense of politics, but he always emerges on the side of the left. There is no instruction in the moral virtues."

"Are we in schism?" he asked rhetorically. "I don't know but, aside from John Paul II, the Church doesn't stand for anything. Since Jack

Kennedy, Catholics are being assimilated into the mainstream. We've lost our sight. We've gotten fat.

"I hear stories of a Catholic high school distributing condoms or of women calling Catholic Charities and learning about the pill. Catholic Charities has become an outreach of the federal government."

Roeser delivers his thoughts with quiet concern. He is no conservative of convenience. He is a man in genuine pain because the things he holds sacred appear to be slipping away. "Oh, we conservatives have some nuts on our side," he said, "people seeing apparitions and all that. But we will face much tougher circumstances in the future. We may have to go underground."

It's clear that Roeser does not always have an easy time with his spirituality. At times, one gets the impression that it may cause him a measure of Job-like depression. And, while he can roll over his less articulate and nimble-minded opponents in religious debate, one sometimes gets the feeling that he is hurt by their ripostes. (During one radio show, he once said that he found one of my retorts "personally insulting." Although I had not intended it as such, I must have hit a soft spot.)

Roeser is no dry-mouthed penitent. He enjoys life. He reaches for the bread basket within seconds after he has settled his ample frame at the restaurant table. With confidence born of experiences that have earned him an ample double chin, he will order a couple of scotches, a steak with a side dish, and a wedge of cheesecake—all at a luncheon while surrounded by people of weaker faith who are eating like John the Baptist. He does it with a style that can put one at ease.

He clearly loves to talk and does so in well-organized paragraphs. Unlike many liberals who simply don't read conservatives, he knows what the liberals are saying. He frequently involves himself in causes such as the Better Government Association and a Catholic foundation that deals with drug abuse, alcoholism, and AIDS—organizations more identified with liberal pursuits. But he views his faith as an emotional and intellectual anchor. He's no Jansenist, but he does believe that suffering is part of our lot in life and that it must be accepted.

"The heart has its reasons which reason knows nothing of," he said, citing his spiritual ancestor, Pascal. "Just say I'm a restorationist," he added with a smile. "I want to restore guilt."

5

Ed Moffett:
Pu Shumbu (Priest)

———◦•◦———

If I told you how beautiful Nina Sullivan is, you would lick the words right off the page. She came to our home for dinner in August, 1994, and filled the place with her grace and beauty.

She told us that she was returning to New York to get married in just seventeen days, but she took the time to visit and tell us about what she knew of Ed Moffett. She had met him only twice, both times when she was just a teenager, but her parents, Joe and Anna Sullivan of Mattituck, New York, were among Ed Moffett's closet friends. Her parents spoke of him so often that she viewed him as an uncle.

He was a family icon to Nina. He loved her and her brothers so much that he even cleaned up his language when he visited them. Moffett had a mouth on him that could peel paint.

Ed Moffett was one of those mythic characters found occasionally in church annals. They are always larger than life, and even the ordinary details about them appear in bold print. Gradually, incidents in their lives turn into legends. They are people unafraid to make enemies and thus have quantities of friends. Moffett was unvarnished and unfiltered—the kind of missioner that may have angered others, but even those he angered found themselves envying him. Moffett never perspired; he sweated. He had central heating. He drank and swore and fell in love. He gave his life for a church that may have wished that he would go away. "Holy, sweet Jesus! I loved that man," another missionary said after Moffett died.

I was going to write a book about him; he deserves one. But this will have to do.

First, however, I've got to tell you about Nina's parents, Anna and Joe. It was through Joe that I learned much of what I know about Ed.

Nina Sullivan is the Amerasian daughter of an American Maryknoll priest and a Korean nun. Her blended features reflect a stunningly beautiful

46

combination of Asian and Caucasian genes, together with intelligence and charm that people would expect only of a genie.

Joe Sullivan met Nina's mother at an orphanage in Pengyong, called P.Y. Do. (*Do* is the Korean word for an island.) The mission is on a rocky mountain tip of an island in the Northern Yellow Sea, a few miles off the coast of North Korea and over 170 miles north and northwest of Inchon and South Korea.

The Catholic Foreign Missionary Society of America, better known as Maryknoll Fathers and Brothers, helped to staff an orphanage there that took care of 170 children of lepers. The orphanage was run by the Catholic Leprosy Service of Korea, which had been founded by a legendary Maryknoller, Fr. Joseph A. Sweeney.

Korea has not been kind to its lepers, at least no kinder than other countries since New Testament days. Sweeney had worked among lepers in South China and Korea since 1932. He could tell stories of them, living next to burial grounds in huts made of old coffin boards, eking out a miserable existence by planting tiny vegetable patches in hollows too wet for graves. These were rat-infested places where at night the rats gnawed at the feet of the bedridden lepers, who had lost all feeling in their extremities.

Joe Sweeney and Ed Moffett, who was twenty-seven years younger, worked in China until the Communists expelled the missionaries. It wasn't the first time Sweeney had to leave China. A nun who had been a missionary there for eighteen years and who had been evacuated from Hunan by the American air force toward the close of World War II, informed me that she had met Sweeney in 1945. He had somehow evaded the Japanese. She traveled as far as San Francisco with the tall, homely, woman-shy priest, who was then down to 150 pounds. One story had it that, after expelling Sweeney, the Chinese had put all the lepers at his mission in a boat, towed them to deep waters, and sank the boat. Sister Mary Carita remembered the story, and a chapter from an untitled book also mentioned the tragedy.

Sweeney returned to Maryknoll's headquarters for rest and recuperation. It's likely he met Ed Moffett there. "Moff" would have been a seminarian in 1945, three years from ordination.

Years later, it seems, both men were imprisoned in China before being expelled. Another letter from a former Columban missionary who knew Moffett from their days in the Philippines—more about this later—recalls that one of Moff's parishioners in China had sneaked a piece of bread and raisin wine into his cell. Father Ed Moffett said Mass, lying on the floor.

Later, Sweeney and Moffett were reunited in Korea where Sweeney founded the Catholic Leprosy Service, an organization that went out across Korea in mobile clinics to minister to patients where they lived, rather than dragging them in and piling them up in asylums and colonies. When Moffett came to Korea, he was assigned to administer an orphanage for the children of lepers who were forbidden by law to go to school. The orphanage had been founded by Sweeney.

It was at that orphanage that Joe Sullivan met Anna. He was there with Moffett when Sweeney, in Moffett's dramatic words, "developed a pain in his gut." Sweeney lived until November, 1966, when he died in Moffett's arms, after extracting a promise from him that he would continue the Catholic Leprosy Service. Sweeney was seventy-one. To hear Moffett tell it, a week in Sweeney's life would have cleaned out purgatory.

Stories of Sweeney and Moffett are all big-screen, technicolor, three-hanky. It would take years to separate fact from fiction. One missioner told me that I'd have to go to Korea to unravel much of it. Accurate or not, no one questioned the dedication of these two big, sweaty men. Both had a capacity for laughter and liquor that would break a Vatican official's heart.

Twenty years after Sweeney's death, I visited Maryknoll's recruitment and development office near New York's Grand Central Station. The priest on duty told me that I was "asking about two of the giants." I heard much the same at Maryknoll's Chicago house and at their headquarters at Maryknoll, New York. If legend gets confused with fact, chances are the true stories outweigh the legends.

Sullivan worked with Moffett in the mid-sixties and early seventies. He was there in 1966 when Moffett hung a huge picture of Sweeney on the wall of the orphanage. It's not likely that the Vatican will canonize Sweeney, but Moffett surely did. In his letters to me, he frequently called him "the saint."

Sullivan and Moffett were at Penyong Island when the North Koreans captured the American ship known as the *USS Pueblo* in 1968. The small ship and its eighty-three-man crew was seized in the Sea of Japan on January 23. Its crew was declared spies and held in captivity until December 22. The action put the orphanage in a war zone. It turned P.Y. Do into a hotbed of CIA activity.

Again, legend and fact get muddy. There are those who claim that Ed Moffett—and perhaps even Sullivan—had links with the CIA. If they did, the bonds were conceptually akin to those forged later by the famous Dr. Tom Dooley, medical missionary in Vietnam, who was said to have cooperated with the CIA in exchange for vital medicines for his patients whom he treated without regard to political affiliation. It's entirely possible that Moffett, a flag-waving patriot with strong anti-

Communist sentiments, could have supplied the CIA with information. If he did, it's certain that he did so in exchange for supplies for the mission and that he got the better end of the deal.

Approaches to work in the missions have changed dramatically since then. They were changing even in Moffett's time, as the documents of Vatican II took effect. But Moffett never quite made the adjustment. Moffett wore his cassock. He evangelized and converted, although he did respect the ways of the Orient. Basically, he would have to be classed as "old school." What saved him from being perceived as a dictator was that he drew most of his inspiration from the Gospel.

Some time after the *Pueblo* incident, the people at the mission were told to evacuate. Moff and Sulli's response was the classic missionary one: "The shepherd stays with his flock." By this time, they had built a hospital, tuberculosis sanitarium, an old folks' home and a number of other services. There were twenty-five to thirty Korean nuns, including Anna, who was to be Nina's mother.

The military was flying in C-130s and C-47s, as well as C-36s, to bring in tanks, Korean marines, and to evacuate over a dozen American advisers. Moffett and Sullivan were able to evacuate the sisters, doctors, nurses, and some local politicians. The planes landed and took off from the beach as soon as the tides were out, but soon there were only five planes left and the Korean marines were using their M-16 rifles to control the crowds of refugees who wanted to get on the planes before the Communists descended from the North.

"Holy shit, Sulli," Moffett yelled. "Do you realize that this is the last transportation out of here?" Moffett had spoken in English, but it seemed that everyone had come to the same conclusion. The people panicked, including the South Korean marines, who used their American-issue rifles to shoot their way onto the planes. The departing planes just plowed through the crowds. According to Sullivan, "The people were hanging from the open doors, landing gears, or any other part of the plane they could grab."

Moffett and Sullivan went back to the orphan kids who were now without their nuns. They told them that they would all work together to survive but, that if the Communists came, the kids were to vanish into the villages. Moffett told them that they were never to acknowledge that they knew Sullivan or him, no matter what they saw being done to them.

I never did learn quite how Sulli and Moff survived, but they managed. The mission held. Chances are, the American forces intimidated the invading North Koreans and they backed off.

Sullivan eventually experienced burnout. "I was in danger of losing my humanity," he told me. "I was sick in mind and body, totally exhausted. I felt I had no faith. There were times when I thought I must die. I had no strength, no courage left. I was exhausted by my own torments."

Sullivan's situation was not an isolated one. Ed De Persio, a former Columban, wrote from South Carolina that missionaries often suffered from depression and stress. Further, in the process of recovery, a number of them became romantically involved. "It's some kind of natural reaction, almost a reflex," he said. (The Irish Columban Fathers in Korea, perhaps more inhibited than their American counterparts at Maryknoll, used to call them "the Marrying-Knollers.")

At the height of his burnout, Sullivan went to Moffett and told him that he was leaving the priesthood. "Moff asked me where I was going," he said. "I didn't even know. But I had some contacts in Vietnam and thought I'd go there to look for a job."

Moffett was disappointed and hurt. He was from the old school. One made whatever compromises one had to make, but one didn't leave the priesthood. Moffett's religious faith was often tested. He saw so much suffering that he had his dark nights of the soul. There might have been times when he was tempted to leave the Church, but not the priesthood. Sullivan's departure would fracture a friendship that would take a decade to repair. Yet, years later, when some priests were criticizing Sullivan for leaving, Moffett bellowed: "You guys should be ashamed of yourselves. You should thank Joe for what he gave the Church. The gentle Jesus whom you claim as your Lord would have changed water into wine for him." Pure Moffett melodrama.

Sullivan approached Sister Anna and confided that he was leaving. She had been a sister for thirteen years, most of them working with the orphans. Their relationship had been obvious to everyone at the mission, but it was always entirely appropriate. In fact, a driver on the island had once said to Sullivan: "Father, that nun is in love with you." Sullivan, as naive as many priests, was surprised.

He had to repeat himself three times to Anna to make her understand. She wept and then said quietly, "I will go with you."

Moffett used his clout to fly them out on an American plane the next day. He declined to marry them. In some ways, Moff was the Woman at the Well, but the rules were tattooed on his conscience.

Joe and Anna met alone at the mission chapel and pledged themselves to each other. They exchanged a rose which the Sullivans have to this day.

The military plane brought them to Seoul, where they lived in a virtual hovel for four months while Anna's visa was being processed. They survived on a few dollars that Joe earned teaching English at a Korean language school.

One day, while Joe was at work, the Korean CIA broke into their room. They questioned Anna for hours, beating her badly and tearing her few pieces of clothing to shreds. They thought she was a spy from North Korea and that Joe was a G.I. on some subversive mission. They left only after Anna showed them pictures of her in her religious habit.

The experience shattered Joe. He sent Anna home to her parents to rethink the whole matter.

After a month, a little messenger girl delivered a note to him. It came from Anna and it requested that he meet her at a tea room that they had frequented. "I was starved just for a glance of her," he said. "I would have given my soul to be with her just one more time."

Anna was sitting with the little messenger, a relative. She was dressed in her religious habit. In a series of episodes worthy of a Shakespearian tragedy, she told of how a Korean priest and several Korean nuns had tried to kidnap her and return her to the convent.

"She asked me what my plans were," he said. "I just looked at her. I was tongue-tied. The tension just built. I wanted to yell at her that she should never have left the island. She was so beautiful and so Korean."

Anna resolved the issue in a typically Korean way. "Husband," she said, "I asked you a question and you did not answer me. Have you changed your mind?"

They arrived in America with twenty dollars. Joe got a job as a substitute teacher. He was still clinically depressed. "I was excommunicated from the Church, excommunicated from Maryknoll, excommunicated from my family," he wrote. "There was no support system. I was often denied employment simply because I was a priest."

But his experience in Korea had put a little piece of steel into him. When he first arrived there, one old missionary had told him, "One or two years in Korea will clean the shit out of you." The pain and suffering he witnessed there became his standard for the years that followed.

Sullivan wondered about his faith and his vocation. He recalled that the Dalai Lama had once asked Thomas Merton if ordination vows symbolized the beginning or the end of a person's spiritual journey.

It took a year to find full-time employment. For the next twenty years, he worked as a probation officer in Long Island's Suffolk County. He also labored as a part-time potato farmer and flounder fisherman while he and Anna built a home, raised much of their own food and foraged for clams, oysters, mussels, scallops, and fish along the shores of Long Island.

There were three children. The Sullivans sacrificed everything to insure a quality education for each. Gradually, Joe's faith returned, but it was never quite the same. "Only a remnant remained," he said, "but that remnant was like a new creation, a new person."

During those years, he was asked to be part of a group that called itself "The Joint Committee at Maryknoll." It was composed of active and resigned priests who wanted to explore what they still had in common and to absolve one another. The Sullivans became active in their parish and Joe joined a group called Human Understanding and Growth Seminars (H.U.G.S.) that did about ten seminars each year for high-school kids. Joe, the probation officer, helped them with the dehumanizing issues of drugs, alcohol, racism, poverty—and wealth. He also organized retreats for former priests at a Passionist Monastery on Shelter Island.

He was a priest again. It happens to a lot of them. They would never go back to active ministry, but they never really leave.

One day, while working their one-acre property on which they planted most everything they consumed, Joe witnessed a light plane go down, just a few hundred yards away. Nina recalled how his arm rose instinctively in the gesture of absolution.

During those years on rural Long Island, Ed Moffett visited twice. The strained relationship had long since healed and Moffett's life had changed. Typically, he overwhelmed the kids. He gave each child a hundred dollars each time he came. "Pure, Moff," Sullivan would write later. "He laughed with those who laughed and he cried with those who cried. He starved with the starving and he ate when there was plenty." God knows where he got the money.

Moffett would literally take off his own clothes to bury someone who had died in rags. After years in the Far East, he had become so thoroughly oriental that he shared the belief that one was truly poor only when one died alone and without decent clothes.

In the years that followed Moffett's resignation from active ministry, Joe and Anna and their sons visited Moffett and his family in Korea. They found him changed only a little. He had lost some more hair and some weight, but he was still St. Peter.

They stayed in touch until Moffett's death in 1986. "It was the first time I ever saw my father cry," Nina remembers.

In April, 1993, Joe Sullivan suffered a massive heart attack and died within hours. There were sixteen priests on the altar at his funeral. Sulli would be pleased with that. In his Irish-Korean culture, such tributes can heal the leprosy that too many souls acquire in their search for holiness.

Sullivan and I had corresponded several times following the appearance of my article on Moffett in the *National Catholic Reporter*. But when Nina came to dinner, she brought the longest and most revealing letter. It was hand-written, ten pages long, and unfinished. Joe had never mailed it. He might have felt that it pulled back the curtains too far on his—and Moffett's—life.

When Moffett himself had died earlier, one former Maryknoller wrote: "For some crazy reason," one priest said, "I thought he would live longer, probably because he seemed to be feeding half of Korea."

The "feeding" was the reason I met him. I was working in development at Northwestern University in Chicago and freelancing for a number of publications, one of which was the *National Catholic Reporter*. I did an essay on church fund raising that somehow got to Moffett.

In 1985, he wrote me a sprawling, eight-page letter, describing his promise to Joe Sweeney to keep the Catholic Leprosy Service, especially the orphanage for children of lepers, from closing. I would learn later that Moff had hand written thousands of such letters over the years.

Moffett's letter was a masterpiece of blarney and pleading. He had kept his promise to Sweeney with help from bishops, priests, relatives, friends—even the military, from whom it seems he swiped anything that wasn't under guard.

The German Leprosy Relief Association was particularly generous, sending between $22,000 to $36,000 each year for nearly fifteen years. But in 1982, the Association informed him that, because Korea is now considered a developed country, they had decided to divert their funds to more needy areas.

Maryknoll tried to help but no longer had a priest to staff the mission. It needed between $25,000 and $35,000 in new income in order to survive.

With a characteristic sense of drama, Moff had waited until page 6 of his letter to inform me why he couldn't "turn to Joe and Mary Catholic in the States to save these little ones."

With equally characteristic openness, Moffett told me that he had been suspended from the priesthood for fathering a child. Following the customary practice in those days, Maryknoll had offered to support the mother and the baby but only on the condition that Moffett leave Korea and go to the Sudan.

"Grace," he wrote, "but no guts." He stayed in Korea.

Moffett was a believer in the rules that governed priesthood. He applied seven times to the Vatican for laicization from the priesthood and permission to marry. But each time the request was rejected for "insufficient reason." The Vatican would set aside his ordination, but would not give him permission to marry, especially to a local woman. The response encapsulated the institutional church's attitude toward both what it viewed scandal and how it regarded women.

Finally, Moffett played his best card—clout. He wrote his good friend, Tony Bevilacqua, bishop of Pittsburgh (now Cardinal Anthony J. Bevilacqua, archbishop of Philadelphia). The bishop, a canon and civil lawyer, got the rescript and Moffett immediately had the marriage blessed. Together with his wife and family, he returned to the Sacraments.

Moffett was that way about rules. He broke them, but he believed in them.

By the time the rescript came through, there were eight children. Four were from his wife's first marriage; three were the Moffetts', and another was an adopted child. "There is always room at the table for one more pair of chopsticks," Moffett said when they adopted Brigette. She would later take sick and Moff, with his pre-Vatican II devotional style, would promise God that he would give up his favorite beverage—Scotch —for the remainder of his life, if she would be spared. Note well: he limited the promise to one form of alcohol, merely his favorite. He was a man of faith but no fool. He knew his limits. He also promised to erect a statue of the Blessed Mother in his back yard in Korea. Brigette got well and Moffett proudly displayed the statue to the Sullivans when they visited.

MOFFETT'S LIFE HAS BEEN PATCHED TOGETHER from letters that arrived following his death. I visited Maryknoll and spoke to some missionaries who knew him. Sister Barbara Hendricks, former president of the Maryknoll Sisters, sent me a few clippings about the Korean Missions that she had gotten from Fr. Jack Corcoran, former regional director in Korea and now vicar general of the Maryknoll Society.

Ed Moffett was born in New Jersey in 1922 and raised in a tough section of Newark. Apparently, he spent some time in the seminary for the Columban Fathers, another missionary congregation with Irish roots. According to Ed De Persio, who was in the Columban seminary with him, he was asked to leave because of some physical condition. "There was a lot of double-talk in those days," he wrote. "We were told he would not be able to survive the rigors of mission life. That's as good an example of medical malpractice as you might find." Moffett, it seems, was as hardy as a Michelangelo carving. He was big, strong, and athletic. Poor health was the diplomatic way of dealing with any departures in those days. Vocations were viewed as "calls from God" and any other reason for leaving was viewed as putting one's hand to the plow and turning back.

De Persio recalls one incident from their seminary days well over a half-century ago. His mother, brother, and sister found themselves stranded in Newark one winter day. Moffett brought them all to his home and put them up overnight. It was typical of him—a sign of things to come. He could never say "no."

Moffett then entered the prep seminary for the archdiocese of Newark and, after a short time there, the idea of being a missionary returned. He entered Maryknoll.

"Anyway," De Persio concluded, "the Maryknollers took him in. They were always more adventuresome."

Moffett was ordained in 1948 and missioned to Wuchow in China. He was there only three years before being imprisoned by the Communists. Later, in one of the stories he told over and over, he claimed that his first reaction to the imprisonment was that he could see a headline in every paper in the United States proclaiming: "Moff got shot." As a matter of fact, according to Jack Corcoran, the Communists did take him out a couple of times to shoot him. "They were bluffing," Corcoran said, "but Moff didn't know it until he heard the click of the trigger and realized he was still around."

When he was finally released, Moffett had lost about ninety pounds. He spent a little time back in the States, getting his health back, and was then assigned to the Lipa diocese in the Philippines. He opened a new mission near Manila and expanded it for about six years.

Joe Sullivan used to say that Moffett was a lover of humanity, a Christian through and through. "He had no messianic hangups," Sulli recalled. "He was nobody's savior and he never tried to pass himself off as that. He was a very human person."

Perhaps it was that humanity that got him involved—and in trouble. The details aren't important but, while in the Philippines, he became involved with a woman and Maryknoll had to pull him out. "There are worst things," one cynic observed. "For example, *not* being involved with a woman." Allegedly, she was related to a high-ranking prelate and that might have been the crime.

Maryknoll brought him back to the United States for promotional work and perhaps a period of reflection. But Moffett had already become partly Oriental. He had to get back.

He put in for Korea and asked for the toughest, hardest challenge the society could find. He ended up at P.Y. Do. He had learned one language in China, another in the Philippines. Now, he would try to master a third.

Archbishop Paul Ro of Seoul told Moffett about P.Y. Do. Thousands of refugees, it seemed, had fled North Korea and settled there. There were only about eighty Catholics and they hadn't seen a priest in a long time.

South Korea isn't a big country; it's only slightly larger than Indiana, with mountains in the east and harbors and islands to the west and south. It's crowded. Indiana has just over 5.5 million people; Korea has 44.6 million living in much the same space. The country is only 11 percent Catholic.

For two years, Moff lived in a tent. He made very little headway. He was viewed as a foreigner.

"One day," according to Corcoran, "someone rushed to Moff and told him that a boy had fallen into a 'honey-bucket pit'—a euphemism for a giant hole where villagers emptied human waste.

"No one would go after him," Corcoran continued. "Moffett jumped over his head right into the awful stuff and pulled the boy out. It was too late. The boy didn't live, but the people now realized what tremendous concern he had for them."

Things improved after that. He eventually built a home for 150 kids and established a school for both the orphans and the other poor kids on the island. He introduced western medical practices. God knows where he got all the drugs but he gave the people aspirins, sulfa drugs, and penicillin and saved thousands of lives. He built a hospital. People began to view him as a man who raised people from the dead.

With the exception of a few decrepit military vehicles, there was no transportation on the island. One Moffett legend recalls that he "borrowed" a jeep from the local U.S. military commander. When the colonel discovered that his jeep was missing, he sent an enlisted man to retrieve it. The next day, Moff was seen carrying an aged woman on his back through the streets of P.Y. Do. The locals saw it, raised a fuss, and the jeep was returned to the mission.

When Ed thought that the people could use a bus, he wrote to the City of New York and asked for an old one—one that was out of commission. He was turned down—something about not being able to ship a bus to Korea.

Again, witness Moffett in action. His next letter was to Michael J. Quill, head of the of the Transportation Workers' Union, the voice of the city's subway and bus workers and a sworn enemy of the politicians. Moffett and Quill were cut from the same cloth. "Mike," he wrote to the Irish immigrant union chief, "I can understand the problems you have negotiating with that city bunch. I wrote a letter and asked them for a used bus—not a new one or anything. I felt so bad because they couldn't even find it within themselves to cough up a used one. I just want to say that I support you, Mike, because I know what you're going through with those guys."

Quill wrote back immediately and said: "Father, you'll have your bus."

Moffett's letters to New York's politicians and to Mike Quill were just two of thousands that he would write until the day he died. When he needed a medical school for postwar Korea, he wrote to John F. Kennedy. He knew how to push buttons and he believed in what he was doing.

The American soldiers stationed on the lonely island loved him. Often, when they grew terribly homesick, Moffett would invite them to dinner at the mission. They would forget their loneliness for a little while and, chances are, Moffett would get some goods in return. For Moffett, helping the needy wasn't something his government should do. They owed it.

During the period when the U.S. Air Force had its base on the island, they began losing big drums of oil. The base commander turned to Moffett and said: "Father, I don't mind losing the oil; we can live with that. I'm just trying to figure out how they're doing it."

Moffett suggested a plan. He quietly told the commander that the fishermen had virtually nothing to do during parts of the year and suggested that they be hired as security guards. "I'll just bet you that the stealing will stop."

The C.O. did—and the stealing stopped. Moffett would learn later how the locals were stealing the big drums, but, chances are, he never told the military.

Moffett had so many of the American soldiers doing volunteer work at the mission that the C.O. got miffed. He asked aloud just who was the commander on the island. The C.O. had his air base, but Moff ruled the whole island. "They're taking more orders from Father Moffett than they are from me," the colonel grumbled.

He was probably right. One day, word came down that the late Raymond Burr of Perry Mason fame was going to visit the island. The C.O. gave orders that the actor was not to be brought anywhere near Moff's compound. But, of course, the word got to Moffett and, as Burr's plane was coming in, Moff jumped in the jeep he had swiped and raced for the beach.

The commander was in full dress; the soldiers were lined up in ranks. There was even a small band.

Jack Corcoran was there. "As soon as the plane landed, Burr started to come down the ladder," he recalled. "Moff strode right up in front of the commander, stuck out his hand and said: 'Ray, I'm Ed Moffett. I'd like to have you come up and have a drink with me.'"

Burr spent the next three days at Moff's place. He never did get to the military compound. He became another of the donors to Moffett's leprosy fund.

Like most charismatic leaders, Moffett could be a dictator. Mother Teresa doesn't serve on committees; Moffett would mock them, too. Typically, sometime in the late sixties, a young priest who had been vaccinated with the zeal of the Pentecostal Movement, was sent to help him. Moff generally said two Masses each day and another at an outstation. He assigned the new priest to the outstation.

"Let me go into the church first," the new priest said.

After time at prayer, the young Pentecostal returned to Moff and said, "I think it would be better if we got a little prayer movement going at the outstation first."

"Who told you that?" Moffett asked.

"The Lord," said the priest.

"Well, I'm the king around here," Moffett said, "and if the Lord is going to be here and talk to anybody, it's going to be through me to you."

Moffett befriended the South Korean military as well as the Americans. When the Korean ships came to P.Y. Do for refueling, Moffett would hold an open house for the crew. In return, Moffett got medical supplies and medical help. He cultivated friendships with senior officers, some of whom later moved through the ranks to top positions in the South Korean military. It meant that he could travel to Seoul and call upon the nation's top brass. They would send personal cars to pick him up. He loved it.

He began to refer to himself as "chief" and his people as "the troops." He lived simply, in a little room, sleeping on an army cot. But there was no mistaking who was in charge.

The model Moffett represented is now a thing of the past. Missionaries now try to blend in, encouraging the people they serve to take leadership roles. Moffett practiced his priesthood differently. It wasn't that he saw himself above the people. He welcomed Korean farmers to his home with as much enthusiasm as some of his highly placed political friends. However, he was a man for his time. His style might cause problems today.

He had started his mission with eighty Catholics. By 1971, his parish had fourteen thousand parishioners on three islands. His catechists were uneducated people and not always trained to present-day standards. But he trusted them and they responded.

Father William O'Leary, another Maryknoller appearing in Fr. Edward Miller's book, *Maryknoll at Work in the World*, recalls arriving at an island off P.Y. Do. It had only four hundred people—all Moffett's. It was pitch dark, but the people had all come to the shore. They held lanterns and were singing hymns of welcome. The simple fishermen, reminiscent of Old Testament figures, were wading into the water to carry the priests to shore. They would not have their priests get wet.

"We heard confessions," O'Leary said, "and then concelebrated Mass. We went back to our boat at four in the morning. It was one of the most emotional experiences I've ever had."

Dan Charboneau of Poway, California, is another former Maryknoller who spent ten years in Korea. He resigned from active ministry in 1971 and returned to the United States. He relocated to Seoul in 1978, this time with his wife and family. It was during this second tour that he met Moffett again.

Back in Korea, Charboneau held two successive jobs with major U.S. companies. His family lived just a few blocks from the Moffetts. "We saw each other every day," he recalled. "We played handball three times each week. We ate and drank together in a private air force club. Once in a while, we partied with a group of Maryknollers who could still laugh with us. We laughed and cried a lot in those years."

Following his departure from active ministry, Ed Moffett had moved to Seoul and became the executive director of the Korean-American Foundation. Moffett may have held the job for some seven to ten years before being fired by a physician whom he had known for some twenty-three years. Moffett had saved his hide many times during those years, but his clout had been on the wane since the death of his sponsor, Park Chung Hee.

General Park Chung Hee came to power in 1961, when the country was only sixteen years old. He rebuilt South Korea and its economy. Two years after forcibly taking office, he was officially elected president in 1963. Park was clearly a favorite of President Kennedy and it's entirely possible that Moffett, living on his island just a short distance from North Korea, was writing letters to Kennedy. During JFK's two years in office, there is some evidence that Moffett wrote to him about a medical school for South Korea. The United States was accepting government-sponsored Korean students into their medical schools, but many were not returning to Korea following their education. Moffett wanted a school on Korean soil.

General Park ruled South Korea until October, 1979, when he was assassinated by Kim Jae Kyu, head of the Korean CIA. The killing signaled a period of instability. It appeared to mark the end of much of Moffett's influence.

Dan Charboneau's position with one of America's conglomerates ended when he uncovered a scheme to bribe Korean officials for nuclear power plant jobs. He was fired, harassed by the police—even detained in jail—before deciding to return to the States, lest his family be hurt. Typically, Moffett stood by him throughout his crisis.

They said a tearful goodbye at Kimpo Airport in August of 1984. They kept in touch by phone and letter but didn't see each other again.

During a trip to New York in search of grant money, Moffett was mugged at knife point by two thugs outside the New York Hilton. The incident shook him badly, more than those he had experienced at the hands of the Chinese and North Korean soldiers.

He made a deal with Charboneau: If anything did happen to him, Dan would look after the Catholic Leprosy Service. After Moff's death, Dan found a Maryknoller, Fr. Ben Zweber, to look after the mission while Dan continues to raise funds in the United States for the orphanage.

Moffett got another job at the medical school he had helped to build. He was the equivalent of associate dean for development, a position he held until his death.

I didn't know that Moffett would haunt me from his grave. We had only exchanged a few letters. Yet, on the day he died, I got a call from my friend, Marty Hegarty, a resigned priest who coordinates an organization of about 1,850 resigned and active priests, religious, and laity. He had gotten a call from a former missioner named Phil. A priest from South Korea, a man Moffett had helped through the seminary, had called him.

It was then that I wrote the article about Ed Moffett and his patron saint, Joe Sweeney. It was the article that brought all the letters.

The letters were loving memorials to one of the most colorful and most loved men I've ever encountered. Five years later, I was still meeting people who knew him. A former paratrooper-chaplain who had been stationed in Korea remembered him as if he were his brother. Frank

McCarthy, now retired from active ministry and, like Moffett, married with children, recalled that Moffett was loved by his people. "He could con you out of your money or anything else you had," McCarthy said. "But it was always for his people."

THE RIPPLE EFFECT HAS CONTINUED. Eight years after his death, Moffett's spirit brought Nina Sullivan to our door. "I'm not certain why I'm doing this," she said over dinner. "I just felt that I had to."

Father Thomas Egan, former regional superior in Korea and now vocation director for the society, allowed me several hours during my visit to their Oriental-style headquarters near Ossning, New York. He spoke of Moffett as if the man lay buried in their own cemetery. Maryknollers aren't small-minded.

Charboneau wrote a long tribute to his good friend. "In a great house, there are vessels not only of gold and silver," he said. It captured what others said: Moff was a flawed saint, the kind not being canonized much these days.

"To know him, you would have to tune in on the whole man, and the picture was not always pleasant. Moffett had a way of deflating ideas or people. If there was a softer, more nuanced way of turning aside an idea, Moffett didn't know it. He could ridicule others' thoughts, especially if they didn't tie with his experience. He often did so with language that in itself would be offensive."

He was apolitical. Yet, he hobnobbed with politicians and generals, always with his own agenda in mind. "He would have made a deal with the devil if he thought it good for his people," Charboneau said.

Moffett's hero was John XXIII, not because he was pope but because John had such human qualities. (The late pope was known to have forged hundreds of passports to permit Jews to escape certain death at the hands of the Nazis. Moffett would have applauded that.)

"We're having a Mass in honor of John XXIII," he once told the base commander at P.Y. Do. The commander had another event that conflicted with the Mass. Moffett gave him only one choice: "You're invited to the Mass," he said. The C.O. didn't dare schedule anything that conflicted. He knew where the people would go.

Archbishop Paul Ro once praised the men of Maryknoll. He said they were good men, good missioners—men who loved the people. Some loved *too* much, he hinted. He wasn't citing Ed Moffett but the observation fit Moff like a glove. His humanity was out there for all to see. He denied nothing. He left an indelible mark on the people. Long after he left the active priesthood, the people continued to call him "spiritual father."

Charboneau recalls that he could be vulgar and gentle, stubborn, misguided and loyal. He had boundless confidence but, somehow, never quite trusted himself. Clearly endowed with enormous street smarts, intellectual discussions just put him to sleep. "Either shit or get off the pot," has been attributed to him as a standard reaction to endless discussions.

He loved to tell stories, often over and over, but the entertaining way in which he told them made them more bearable.

When he entered a room, it grew brighter. In fact, he often took it over. Yet, there could be both diplomacy and intrigue. There were black cars with secret service men picking up Moffett in the dark of night. There were flights in army helicopters and secret missions for Korea's president.

Moffett was both diplomat and bag man. A bishop who met him in Guam, where Moffett apparently went to consult on the new hospital, found him with a canvas bag stuffed with American dollars. "God knows where it came from," the bishop said years later. "But he offered me some in case I needed it."

Modern missionaries don't fault Moffett. They view him as a breakthrough missioner. But much of what he did wouldn't work today. Contemporary governments wouldn't jail him; they would simply withdraw his passport and put him on the first plane out of the country.

Moffett, like other earlier missionaries, had been called a "red-haired devil"—a favorite term for Caucasians. It's likely he reveled in it. Today, however, they would address him as "Father" and turn him away.

His last years were spent at Chung-Ang University where his big dream—a college of medicine for Korea—was taking place. As development director, he had begged for two years and gotten very little. Some at the university were wondering aloud why the "old geezer" was kept around. (He was barely sixty.) And then he came in with a $6 million grant from the United States Government. He loved to tell that story.

A Korean newspaper referred to him as "a bridge person." "He would have loved that," Charboneau said. "He would have wanted nothing more to be said about him—*pontifex!*"

A woman named Carol Granstrom, whom Moffett had never met, wrote from central Florida after my column appeared. "I've been wondering why I'm staying with the Church," she said, "and you jumped right off the page with your article about Moffett. It told me why I should stay."

At Maryknoll, after my interview with Tom Egan, Jean and I were introduced to a half-dozen retired Maryknollers, now living at headquarters, waiting for God. They didn't know Moffett; they were all older than him; they had served in other countries.

"But we knew of him," they said with admiration and not a trace of pettiness. "He was one of the giants."

6

Barbara Blaine:
"I could no more not be a Catholic than I could not be a Blaine."

The parish priest had molested her from age thirteen to age seventeen. When she said it must stop, he just smiled and said, "OK." He walked away. Clearly, the "special friendship" he claimed they had meant nothing to him. Yet Barbara Blaine says today, "I could no more not be a Catholic than I could not be a Blaine."

Barbara Blaine sat in the back of the crowded, paneled courtroom at Chicago's Civic Center. "It's an interesting, complicated case," she said in tones that reminded one of one of those cable TV court programs. In fact, Barbara Blaine is now a law student at DePaul University's downtown campus, just a few blocks from the Daley Center.

It was a messy, angry, uneven case, as dirty as a priest's ear. It involved the alleged sexual abuse of a seven-year-old first-grade boy in a parish school during the 1987–88 school year. The defendants in the $7 million civil suit were the pastor of the parish and the former principal of the elementary school. No criminal charges had ever been lodged against the pastor or the principal. But the boy's parents, devout Catholics and practicing attorneys themselves, were determined to gain justice for their son.

The case encapsulated virtually every possible issue that attended nearly two dozen sexual abuse cases that surfaced in the Chicago church in the last half-dozen years. With twenty priests removed from active practice because they might pose a threat to children, the faithful were almost immune to shock. Although only two priests had actually been sentenced, the archdiocese had spent some $4.5 million in a single fiscal year on law suits, settlements, and treatment of cases involved with the sexual abuse of minors. The expense equalled all that had been spent in

64

the entire seminary system for the previous year. Every day, it seemed, a cock could be heard crowing somewhere in the vast archdiocese.

The archdiocese had to win this one. It had to show its dispirited priests' corps that it would back its clergy if it believed them innocent.

It wasn't a clean-cut case. It had grown out of all proportion since the time the boy's parents had brought the incident to the attention of the parish school board. The pastor lacked likability. He was seen as rigid, authoritarian. Yet at least two priests who claimed to know him well said categorically, "He just didn't do it."

The archdiocese reacted badly to the initial charges. Its Rambo-like tactics disgusted both clergy and laity. Allegedly, the private investigators for the archdiocese had knocked on neighbors' doors, asking loaded questions about the private lives of the alleged victim's parents. Priest-columnist Andrew Greeley was outraged by the tactics employed. Jason Berry, author of *Lead Us Not into Temptation*, perhaps the best general book on clerical sexual abuse, had detailed the less-than-honorable tactics of the lawyers representing the archdiocese.

Blaine had witnessed the pattern before. Cases that could have been settled by sensitive, pastoral response were turned into ugly legal battles. Ironically, the archdiocese that had done more than any other diocese to address the festering problem of clerical sexual abuse appeared to speak quietly and to carry a big stick.

"This case is not indicative of how I spend my life," she said. "I deal with survivors, people who are hurting. I deal with adults who were sexually molested as kids. This case does not reflect my experience. As a matter of fact, this is the first such trial I have attended. I'm here because I'm a law student and social worker. My focus is on healing. You could say that I try to mop up the mess."

The accused pastor sat looking painfully alone among his all-female defense team. The few pews for spectators were also largely filled with women who appeared to come from his parish.

Only one other priest attended. No one from the chancery was in the courtroom, although they admitted that they were paying the lawyers. Some critics claimed that the archdiocesan attorneys were quarterbacking the case. It's unlikely that they were signing legal fee checks without some supervision.

"It's getting into a pissing contest," one reporter said during a break. The archdiocese challenged everything. The hair-splitting was tedious, often pointless. "I don't think this should be a contest," the amiable judge reminded the lawyers frequently, but the challenges continued.

At times, testimony moved so slowly that it was difficult to gauge the direction of the case. The process was tedious and slow; the plaintiff's testimony was often dull and impenetrable. John Grisham fans would have fallen asleep; Perry Mason viewers would have changed channels. If the archdiocesan quarterbacks thought that female lawyers would soften the defense strategy, they erred. The women came off as cold, cynical, derisive. But they were ruthlessly competent.

The seven women and five men of the jury appeared to be affected by the "drone factor," a axiom that holds that the more one has to listen to, the less one hears. They tried hard to sustain interest but sometimes looked weary and distracted. Some took notes, but it was clear that they were having trouble separating the wheat from the chaff.

"The plaintiff's expert witness is a pompous ass," one reporter remarked. An expert on what a child's art reveals, the psychologist droned on and on about what the alleged victim's drawings said about his experience. On cross-examination, he only expanded upon his diagnosis in spite of warnings from the judge to confine his responses to "yes," "no" or "I don't know."

BARBARA BLAINE, Bachelor of Science in Social Work and Bachelor of Arts in Theology from St. Louis University, Master of Social Work from Washington University in St. Louis, Master of Divinity from Catholic Theological Union of Chicago, must have wondered about the merits of obtaining a fifth degree in order to practice law that resembled a production rather than an honest search for truth. She works with people abused by priests, most of whom have not brought legal charges or filed suits. The vast majority of the victims she has organized have not received a penny for healing; they haven't had the pyrrhic experience of seeing their molesters do some jail time; they haven't experienced the dubious comfort of a financial settlement in exchange for their silence. Some victims have received counseling, paid for by the offenders' keepers. But most are still seen as the enemy. Most can still point to their molesters, still presiding at Mass, still enjoying the respect of the people to whom they minister, and the protection of the bishop or religious superior who somehow can recognize rape in a housing project but not in a rectory.

Barbara's own life experiences had verified to her that truth was as elusive as angels' wings. The priest who had sexually molested her from the time she was thirteen until her seventeenth year, called her his "special" friend.

"I came from a big family," she said. "There were eight kids, raised in a very loving, traditional Catholic home. My parents lived for their kids.

"Studies of sexual abuse victims show that they tend to be people who get picked by their abusers. There's some evidence that they come from large families where there may not be enough attention to go around. In large families, parents cannot be with every kid for every minute. Perhaps some victims are looking for more attention.

"I'm a twin. That may have something to do with it. I've always felt like the inferior twin. My sister Marian was the 'good' twin. Somehow, she always seemed stronger. One thing is certain: Chet would never have tried this stuff with Marian.

"We weren't identical twins. Many days, we didn't even dress alike. Yet, sometimes we would fight over a single dress, refusing to change until our father had to get after us.

"We find we're the same in many ways. Within twenty-four hours after I received my master's in divinity from Catholic Theological Union at Chicago, she got her master's in nursing administration from the Medical College of Ohio. I guess we're both lifelong students."

Barbara has had twenty years to reflect upon her experiences. For a decade she said nothing, like a daughter who had been raped, fearful of telling her parents because of the torrent of arrows it could unleash. Since 1985, however, she has been talking. Gradually, the wounds are healing. The pain that gnawed at her soul has been turned into healthy action.

"Maybe I *was* seeking more attention. Chet Warren was a popular priest in my hometown of Toledo. He was a member of a religious order, the Oblates of St. Francis de Sales. I met him through my family when he came to the parish. I was only in second grade. In no time, he knew every kid in the school. He was always hanging around the kids.

"You know how it is. Kids want attention. When that attention comes from a priest, it's that much better.

"I've learned something else. Perpetrators don't necessarily worry about the gender of their victims. It seems to be the age that matters to them. And the offenders can be either heterosexual or homosexual. The studies show, in fact, that the majority are heterosexual."

The issue of sexual abuse of minors by clergy is a Pandora's box. Studies of offenders often uncover patterns of depression and addiction. The downward spiral begins with depression, followed by addiction— generally alcohol—which serve to unleash pent-up inhibitions. Offenders appear to suffer from a basic personality disorder that, once underway in their emotional system, causes them to act out.

Blaine's observations are more pragmatic. She is focused on healing the wounded and stopping the abuse. "I suppose that depression and drugs can have something to do with it," she said, "but there's not necessarily a connection between alcohol and abuse. Perhaps it simply breaks down inhibitions."

Blaine appeared less interested in the emotional chemistry of abuse that makes some clergy so combustible. "My concern," she said, "is that priests have been doing it and that they've been doing it for a long time. Their bishops have known about it for a long time and have done nothing. It took Jeanne Miller [founder of Linkup, a nationwide organization that catalogues and exposes sexually abusing clergy] to keep reporting it. She broke it open in Chicago. That's the only reason the Church now deals with it at all."

Blaine is still angry, although her emotional health has vastly improved. Her abuse began twenty-five years ago when she had just turned thirteen. It carried an enormous amount of baggage with it, leaving her with unfocused, irrational anger, depression, migraine headaches, psychosomatic ailments—even thoughts of suicide. "It affects everyone in the family," she added, "even before they learn that anything has been going on. It shows up in the behavior."

"I always tried to be a 'good' girl," she recalled. "We were a close-knit, loving family. My father was an engineer and my mother was a homemaker who worked part time at a local college, partly in the hope that she would get tuition remission when the kids started college.

"I went to St. Pius X Grammar School and to Notre Dame Academy, a rather conservative high school. I volunteered in the parish, all the usual things, playing the guitar, stapling parish bulletins, stuffing envelopes.

"For almost as long as I can remember, I wanted to work for justice. My parents were involved in the old sodality movement. It was called Christian Life Communities [CLC], a group run by the Jesuits.

"We weren't poor but with eight kids we lived modestly. I think our first and only real vacation as a family was to Niagara Falls. There was another trip to Iowa to a CLC convention where we met other kids and I learned about issues such as hunger, racism, and war.

"I wasn't a great student in high school. Just average. I was under constant stress, trying to keep my parents, my teachers, and Chet happy. I didn't think I was smart. I was always apologizing for everything under the sun, always saying 'I'm sorry.'

"I remember having trouble with French. Chet knew French fairly well. He promised to help. Needless to say, he used to just run through my homework and then he would molest me.

"He was so well-regarded, so close to God. I had to obey him. I knew *he* was right, therefore *I* was wrong. Something bad in me was causing the holy priest to sin. That's the rationale a young victim develops."

Attempting to identify the characteristics of a sexual abuser can be an exercise in frustration. The empty-eyed drifter who also sexually abuses his victims is hard enough to spot. But the well-educated, articulate predator with a surface personality is almost impossible to identify. Many appear to be more talented than the run-of-the-mill clergyman, doctor, or teacher. Thus, it is always something of a shock when "the best teacher in the school" is removed because he sexually abused the quiet, honor roll student who found the offender's humor or iconoclastic views attractive. It gets even more complicated when the offender is introduced as one who represents God. Sadly, the image of the priest is so highly polished that it can fool even the most cynical and wary. For a teenager, the halo effect is blinding. One seasoned observer pointed out, "It's hard to think of a better system for the production of abusers than the seminary system."

"A load of us entered the seminary at thirteen," one middle-aged priest observed. "We put our emotional growth on hold until we were ordained twelve years later.

"It isn't that we weren't weeded out. Hell, only about 10 percent of us made it through. It's just that it could have been the wrong 10 percent. An awful lot of guys who left look back on their seminary years with great fondness. As seminarians, they could achieve and grow in important ways until their testosterone kicked in. Then they left without a whole lot of damage to their psyche. They were protected during some critical growing years.

"But among the guys who stayed were some who had fixated at thirteen. Somehow, after ordination, the rest of us picked up where we left off and muddled through to some sort of maturity. But these guys didn't grow. With an emotional age of about thirteen, they went after victims the same age. If they were confronted sexually by a mature woman, chances are they'd crap in their pants and run."

The priest's diagnosis is probably oversimplified, but it comes closer to the reality than the carefully researched but bloodlessly academic studies that graph the problem while doing nothing about it. Too often, the system becomes a cocoon for the potential abuser. The seminary with its highly structured routine of prayer, study, sports, and chores can become a kind of emotional summer camp.

Another layer of abuse comes into play once the victimizer is away from the cyclopean eye of the seminary system. In a benighted effort to cover up, the Church protects offenders. The compulsive need to protect the institution causes the administrative church to become an accessory to the crime. Morally and legally, the institutional church is no different than the U.S. Navy brass who squelched the infamous Tailhook scandal.

"I went to the Church in 1985," Barbara recalled. "I never filed charges, never tried to make this a damage case. I just wanted justice. I wanted treatment for myself and I wanted Chet exposed.

"I honestly believed that the Church was going to come around, that it would do the right thing. Instead, I was treated as the enemy. I learned that Chet had been reported to the Oblates as early as 1970 but he was left in ministry until 1993. When he was confronted, his excuse was that this was a period when everyone was being affectionate.

"My allegations caused a rift in the parish. To this day, there are people who deny that he did anything, even though other victims have come forward. I really thought that the Oblates of St. Francis would do something. Instead, I found that they had gone to the bishop, consulted lawyers, and turned this into an adversarial situation."

Blaine is calmer now, the result of years of slow healing and good therapy. But her anger still boils up in the face of incendiary questions and the absence of any real closure. It took her nearly ten years after the abuse ended to gather the courage to report the matter. Now, nearly a decade later, the matter remains unresolved. Typically, a letter to her bishop, James R. Hoffman, ordinary of Toledo since 1980, written in February, 1994, received no response until she sent a second letter in May of the same year. She has since met with the bishop and a representative of the Oblates. She has been told only that Warren's case "remains in Rome." In common with the attitude of many bishops, Hoffman places himself in the middle, seeing himself as the harried administrator, instead of pursuing the facts of the case and taking appropriate action.

In the growing body of literature regarding clerical sexual abuse, victim after victim has reported turning to her or his bishop for healing and closure. Instead, the response came in the form of challenges and legal threats. Now the conventual wisdom is to have victims secure a lawyer and inform the local authorities well before they approach the Church.

National statistics show that one out of three girls and one out of seven boys is molested by the time they are eighteen. (Only a fraction of these are by Roman Catholic clergy.) Barbara has concluded that the Church is quick to condemn other atrocities such as abortion, adultery, racism—even poverty—but that it has been comparatively silent on the issue of sexual abuse. After listening to hundreds of other victims, Blaine reported in a paper submitted as part of her requirements for her Master of Divinity degree at Catholic Theological Union at Chicago that, even with the best of intentions, the setting up and following of sound procedures have not produced the desired outcomes. She also concluded that offenders who have high-level integrity on other moral matters will lie on this one and that no offender—she makes no exception—should be returned to active ministry.

"After high school, I didn't go to college right away," Blaine continued. "In 1974, I joined a volunteer program that was sponsored by the Cincinnati Province of the Sisters of Mercy. In fact, for a while, I entered the community and lived with nuns of many different cultures while I taught high school, worked as a remedial tutor and singing teacher at a boys' school, helped pregnant women, and distributed food and clothing for the St. Vincent de Paul Society. But after a few years, I concluded that it was time to get on with my life.

"It seems to me that I was always involved in service work. During my undergraduate and graduate years in St. Louis, I spent three significant years with a lay and religious community.

"I don't know if all the religious and social activities I've been involved in trace back to some reaction to the abuse. I think it's much more than that. My faith is in my blood. It gives me life. It nourishes me. It's my hope for the future."

Blaine is driven. It could be a mixture of anger, faith, and commitment. Her pace has slowed in recent years, at least in terms of the variety of tasks undertaken. But she puts in a full day no matter what the cause, and, despite lingering insecurities, she can kick like a horse if the situation demands. Since 1984, she has limited herself to overseeing a Catholic Worker shelter for homeless mothers and children and to the administration and extension of the Survivors' Network of those Abused by Priests (SNAP), a group she founded in 1989. SNAP now has sixteen hundred members in nine centers. Recently, she moved to her own apartment on Chicago's North Side. "It's the first time in my life that I've lived alone," she said. "I think I've burned out a little by always putting other people's concerns before my own. I think I need some time to step away, to learn some law, and to get my life on course."

Barbara came to Chicago in 1983 with Pax Christi, an international peace organization. She supervised many of the operations for the national office, wrote articles, and represented the group at local and national conferences.

Within a year, however, she was drawn to the St. Elizabeth Catholic Worker, a shelter for homeless mothers and their children. She came into contact with Nina Polcyn Moore, one of the earliest Catholic Workers in Milwaukee and Chicago. Nina and her husband, Gene, encouraged her to become more involved in the movement.

She lived at St. Elizabeth House for a decade, overseeing the operations, recruiting, training and supervising staff, doing fund raising and case management. St. Elizabeth's clients included mothers suffering from drug and alcohol addictions and mental and physical illness. There were the usual HIV+ residents and battered women, as well as seniors raising children and those driven from their substandard homes by fires.

Barbara has Catholic Worker gospel in her veins. Its founder, Dorothy Day, is an icon for her. Her devotion to the Catholic Worker ideal is so strong that, following the example of Eamon Hennessey, one of Day's early disciples, she did not even vote until reluctantly coming to the conclusion that the political process was the lesser of two evils.

After ten years, she has softened many of her positions. The overwhelming needs of St. Elizabeth Catholic Worker caused to her alter her viewpoint. It is now less "What would Dorothy Day have done?" than "What would Dorothy Day do now?" However, it hasn't cooled her anger or sense of mission. Her purpose in spending three years in law school—bringing her to her fortieth birthday—is to acquire a degree and a license that will help her to lead indigent clients through the maze of laws that hold out the dubious promise of help. "Attorney" can be a magic word when whispered over a bureaucrat's desk.

Ironically, the anger that has raged within her ever since the day she confronted Chet Warren and told him that his abuse must stop has served to fuel many of her efforts for others. She was still in recovery from his last indifferent smile.

Barbara grew at the Catholic Worker. By 1989, she was named director. She shared her life with the residents much in the manner of Dorothy Day. The extended family of black clients taught her something about the generosity of the poor. "They were generous to a fault," she said. "It was difficult to teach them how to budget. They would go to McDonald's and share what little they had buying treats for others."

She realized, too, that St. Elizabeth's was managed by whites while the residents were black. It wasn't an intentional choice; but, if other cultures were going to grow, the structure had to change. At Barbara's suggestion, they hired African-American staff while she quietly withdrew.

She now continues to live what she calls "the simple life." She attends DePaul's law school in the evening division but goes year round in the hope of matriculating in three years. DePaul employs her in clerical work for six dollars per hour.

SNAP got underway when Barbara reserved a meeting room in a suburban Holiday Inn. She advertised the meeting and wondered if anyone would show up. Between fifteen and twenty came to the first meeting outside Chicago. (The Chicago chapter now has eighty members.) "I was amazed at the turnout," she said, "but even more amazed that their experiences were just like mine."

Barbara laughs at her addiction to learning. She is a good student made stronger by sheer hard work. She writes well, partly because she reads well. Her papers written at Catholic Theological Union at Chicago (CTU) reveal someone with both journalistic and academic interests. If she was once a timid, compliant victim, it no longer surfaces in her writings. She plunges into her papers, rarely allowing herself the luxury of an introduction. Her anger at the institutional church is still there and, although it isn't confined to their collusion with offenders, that emotion is just under the thin top layer of many of her topics.

One paper, dealing directly with the issue, reminds both her professors and potential members of SNAP that "the healing process is never complete." To those contemplating attending their meetings, she reminds that they will experience pain, that they will hear "unbelievable" stories but that the recollections will be respected and believed by the members.

SNAP meetings are closed, especially to the press. Anonymity is assured; attendees do not even have to use their true names. Participants are asked not to ask questions of others. The process works best if participants are allowed to reveal themselves. Even silence is accepted because "just listening is a form of healing."

By 1992, Blaine had heard the stories of over two hundred victims. (It's not that there are that many priest-offenders. Their numbers remain small. It's just that a single offender can have many victims, some as many as two hundred.) The stories were remarkably similar, even to the language and tactics employed by their predators—including the added sacrilege of having the victim go to confession.

"Not one of the over two hundred I heard had received a pastoral response from the Church," she concluded. Most shared Barbara's experience. She was vilified in her parish. Her loving parents felt the strain. "They felt a lot of guilt and they didn't want it to go public," she said. "But they also felt betrayed by the Church. Dad would get angry when the topic was brought up, but I came to realize that his real anger was with Chet."

Members of SNAP are still encouraged to make their secrets public. "It not only helps with the healing," she says, "but when the silence is broken, the abuse stops." For many, however, the stories are so old that they have hardened somewhere inside their soul and their offenders have slipped into the vast network of clerical sanctuary.

Some members of SNAP have brought suits against the perpetrators and their dioceses, but the number is less than 5 percent. In many cases, the statute of limitations has long since expired or the priest-offender has left active ministry.

SNAP is now working with potential new groups in thirty locations. Perhaps twenty of these will organize formally but the numbers can raise eyebrows. It's not unlikely that SNAP's membership could double—to over three thousand—in just a few years.

"I founded SNAP as a mechanism for my own healing," she said. "It took a lot of courage for me to reveal details of my abuse to a group of strangers. But I was even more surprised and encouraged when these other victims began to tell their stories. Their experiences were just like mine!

"By sharing our stories, we come to realize that we're not alone and that we are not guilty. The blame must be placed where it belongs, on the priests who sexually abused us and the Church that protects them.

"It's tragic that the victims often leave the Church while the abusers remain in, driving cars, living in nice houses, eating in the best restaurants.

"We share resources and information. We work together to educate ourselves about the effects of the abuse. We learn what it means to be healthy psychologically, socially, sexually, and spiritually. We learn how to rid ourselves of the coping skills that we had adopted during the abuse. And we learn about our legal rights and how to use them.

"We organize for political action to challenge the Church to better deal with the problem. Progress has been terribly slow in this area. In 1993, we did succeed in getting a three-hour closed-door session with representatives of the bishops. They promised action and additional meetings but nothing has happened. The National Conference of Catholic Bishops has formed a committee to address this matter, headed by Bishop John F. Kinney of Bismarck, North Dakota. But nothing has happened. They go back home and talk to their lawyers and then do nothing.

"But if we put our voices together, they can become so strong that they can no longer not be heard. We can go to the media. Push the bishops into a corner. Victims must be healed and offenders must be exposed. That's what we are about."

Blaine can get passionate, even messianic. But there is no denying the depth of her hurt and anger about her plight and that of other victims. "It sounds almost irrational," she said. "Maybe it is, but some of our members can't even get on a crowded elevator with a priest. When they see that collar, they revert to the role of the frightened teenager.

"We can't even use the Twelve Step Program. [The Twelve-Step recovery program was developed by Alcoholics Anonymous. Today it is used as a model for virtually all recovery organizations.] Those steps call upon a higher power. In most minds, this means God and some of our victims just can't handle that. It was God, after all, that their victimizers represented and quoted. It was God [victms] were threatened with if they told anybody. It was God that these priests were supposed to represent."

Barbara told a story that illustrated the ripple effect of this abuse. SNAP was holding a meeting in St. Louis. Some of the participants decided to go to a trendy pizza place not far from the Mississippi riverfront. "The place was done up in stained glass windows and some of the seating was church benches," she recalled. "We never got our pizza. We had to leave. Some of the group just choked up with the associations."

One of the saddest ironies is that the majority of the victims will no longer have anything to do with the Church while many of their abusers continue to occupy positions of respect and authority. As a result, some victims will not even attend a family wedding if it involves setting foot in a Catholic church.

The bitterness is compounded by the fact that victims continue to be treated as enemies. They continue to be lied to, even threatened, and worn down by the politics of delay on the part of bishops who spend more time with their attorneys than with their wounded faithful.

"The bishops have at least met with us," Blaine reminds. "They have at least come to recognize us as human beings. They've said that we would meet again, but we haven't met yet."

Meanwhile, Blaine continues to pursue her studies. She continues to emulate the life of Dorothy Day, a simple, unadorned life, but one that recognizes that accommodations must be made in order to make things happen.

SNAP continues to grow; and there may come a time when its goals are incorporated into the institutional church. Meanwhile, her life experiences have taught her that the institutional church does not always reflect the true Church. Her faith remains strong. Meanwhile, in one of her papers, completed for her course work at CTU, she cites Mary Pellauer, author of *Sexual Assault and Abuse: A Handbook for Clergy and Religious Professionals.* Barbara's paper calls for a shift in emphasis from the sense of salvation being relegated to the afterlife to a sense of hope and liberation in the here and now. She introduces Pellauer and her paraphrase of Matthew 25: "I was raped and you stood by me. I was battered and you sheltered me. I was abused and you intervened."

FOR BARBARA BLAINE, the trial of the priest and the principal was only incidental to her larger pursuits. But she followed it because it ties to her sense of justice, regardless of the outcome.

After weeks of testimony, the jury deliberated for little more than an hour before exonerating the priest and principal. Interpretation of the case by the media suggested that the young boy had been influenced by a movie that contained scenes which influenced his imagination. The family of the young boy is considering an appeal, but the pastor's countersuit for defamation was settled out of court. The pastor accepted a modest settlement and announced his retirement. He was close to retirement age. The principal has continued her countersuit against the family. The archdiocese needed to win this case but was relieved that it was over. "There was so much that we couldn't say," one official close to the case said. "There is too much of the past ugliness in it."

Meanwhile, during the 1994 meeting of the National Conference of Catholic Bishops held in Washington, SNAP identified several dioceses it considered dangerous for victims of sexual abuse. Chicago was among them, possibly because of this case and another that resulted in a priest going to jail. Reportedly, Cardinal Bernardin was angered by Chicago's inclusion. He believes that Chicago has been a pacesetter in addressing the problem.

7

Dick Westley:
"It really doesn't matter."

D ick Westley finds humor if it just casts a shadow. He has a saloon-
sized laugh to go with it. Dressed in an open-necked shirt and
leather jacket and sitting in a formica restaurant better known for its
deep-dish pizza than gourmet entrees, he could pass for a retired blue-
collar worker, rather than a professor of philosophy and author of nine
books. We lunched at Giordano's with our mutual friend, Marty, three
guys looking more like cops than men about to embark on a serious
conversation.

There was some church gossip, a few bawdy stories, and a basket of
chewy Italian bread to get through first. The waitress most likely thought
we were retired soldiers, coming together to share old war stories.

"Why do I stay?" he asked, echoing the question I had just asked
him. "You've asked me a most difficult question. I really think that the
whole thing is going down. The pope doesn't realize it, but he's driving
people away.

"If you say you're not going to stay, then you have to answer that
awful question: 'Where do you go?' I'm not going to become a non-
Christian, so why would I want to go to another Christian denomination?"

Dick Westley reminded me of an earlier book I had written which used
the title *Here Comes Everybody!* The title was taken from James Joyce's
description of the Catholic Church, a church that, based on its own principles, accepts everybody. In real practice, especially under John Paul II, it
has become parochial. "We don't live it now," Westley said, "but we did
under John XXIII. He was pope to the whole world, not just Catholics."

Dick Westley has been thinking about the "Why be Catholic?" question for years. His first book, *I Believe—You Believe*, appeared in 1974,
and a more recent work, *Theology of Presence*, published in 1988, devoted
a brief but cogent chapter to the question.

Westley had come prepared. He had excerpts from his *Theology of Presence*. It contained triumphal answers about the Catholic Church being the one, true church and about its sacramental system—especially the Eucharist. It even touched on papal infallibility.

"But a moment's reflection tells you that these things are not the essential elements which make the Church `Catholic,'" Westley said over his Italian salad.

"What characterizes Protestantism is division, not diversity," he continued. "After all, Catholics are a pretty diverse bunch themselves, much moreso than Protestants. The genius of the Protestant ethos is that it can break off and form new communities. Catholics have no such freedom. The genius of our religion is that, despite diversity, everyone is in, everyone is part of us.

"The Catholic dream is to have unity with diversity. We could literally think about the possibility that, one day, there will be Buddhist Catholics, Methodist Catholics, Lutheran Catholics—all with the freedom to remain Catholic even while disagreeing.

"Sadly, in recent centuries, we have interpreted the Catholic ethos as one of total uniformity rather than unity in diversity. And every time we do that, we have betrayed the Catholic dream. We have unwittingly adopted a Protestant perspective."

Westley speaks and writes with intensity. In conversation, he raises his somewhat raspy voice; in print, he italicizes and underlines words. His thoughts on issues are more nuanced than those on people. "Now," he says, "there's a bigger jerk than that other fellow!" He is particularly unsparing of careerist clergy whose personal agenda has little to do with a search for truth.

"We seem to be embarking on a very reactionary time in the Church," he continued. "John Paul II is interpreting the Catholic ethos in a very Protestant way. First he tried to silence dissent by women; now he's trying to silence theologians. He's been very heavy-handed with some of the best of our bishops and he has dismayed a lot of Catholics who were so energized by the dreams of Vatican II."

"Isn't there anyone who can shepherd the Shepherd?" Westley asks. "Just look at the years since Vatican II. There's been a complete reversal of the direction of that council. He's been relentless in his pursuit of an order that has already passed. Issues that used to be matters of healthy discussion among theologians and believers are now definitively settled unilaterally by pontifical fiat. We will soon be expected to take loyalty oaths. Episcopal appointments are closely monitored to insure that vacant sees are filled with pre-Vatican II types."

Westley has been addressing many of these issues for years. Ironically, he has many reservations about Vatican II. "Except for that one on the Mission of the Church," he says, "the other documents just give it to you one way and then take it back in another." But his anger at the appearance of *Pascendi Dominici*, the 1994 encyclical slamming the door to the ordination of women, really set him off. As usual with Westley, the reason for his upset ran deeper than the surface issue itself.

"Women's ordination is a thorny issue," he said, "but his refusal to even entertain the possibility of such ordinations means that the Church as embodied in the magisterium will not allow women into positions of responsible power.

"Actually, it's worse than that. You know, it's one thing to refuse to negotiate about power with women. It's another to refuse even to be reconciled with them."

Westley's emotional temperature rises. "Do you recall when that nun, Sister Theresa Kane, called for some dialogue on the role of women in the church? From that day to this, [the pope] has treated her as a non-person. He doesn't want to reconcile with her. He doesn't want any contact with her whatsoever!

"Look at the publicity he gets when he visits his would-be assassin in jail. Look how much people made of the pope reconciling with him. But there isn't a chance that he would speak to a gentle, caring nun like Theresa Kane. Evidently, someone can put a bullet into him and get reconciled. But Theresa is a woman! He should be ashamed!

"I think he's grown bitter about women. I think he views all but the most obsequious as his enemies. I think he's got a vendetta against women and that it's getting in the way of the Kingdom. I think it's a scandal and embarrassment to all who walk in the Lord!"

Westley speaks easily. He has had this conversation many times before. He can speak in whole paragraphs—the old-fashioned kind with topic sentences, development, and conclusions. A native of Milwaukee, he graduated from Marquette University in 1950, then spent four intense years at the University of Toronto, earning a master's degree and a Ph.D. in philosophy. They were heady years. He studied under Jacques Maritain, Anton Pegis, and Etienne Gilson, three philosophical giants.

The next four decades have been spent in the college and university classroom, first at Barat College in Lake Forest, Illinois, and, since 1968, at Loyola University of Chicago.

Westley loves the classroom. It's clear that his students both love and respect him. He is the kind of professor who still eats lunch in the cafeteria with the students. In 1980, he was named Outstanding Faculty Member of the Year—an honor that describes one as the best of some sixteen hundred professors.

"There's another reason why I remain in the Catholic Church," he said, "and this is very important to me. It's this: I've learned that God dwells in people and that, therefore, revelation occurs in human experience. The Church does not want to accept that, but its theology of incarnation is open to that."

Westley grew more intense as he got into his argument. "The worst thing that the Catholic Church has ever said is that revelation ended with the death of the last apostles. That's awful! In Catholic theology, revelation locates God in human life. But you just look at the new encyclical, *Veritatis Splendor* ["The Splendor of Truth," issued in 1993]. That thing could have been written by a Southern Baptist, a Bible Belt American! Why, he has cut the bishops and the theologians off at the knees. Now, we've got a Protestant pope and a Protestant encyclical!"

Westley can be flip, but he is serious. He chooses his words carefully. If there is a little hyperbole in what he says, it is inserted for the sake of emphasis. It isn't that he doesn't respect authority. Indeed, he is naively trusting about it. Westley would push to the front of the line to give assent to a teaching that was verified by reason and experience but only after full theological discussion. He reminds one of Cardinal John Henry Newman, who wrote "I drink to the pope. But I drink to conscience first."

"You know," he continued, "*Veritatis Splendor* is just like *Humanae Vitae*" [Paul VI's encyclical on birth control that appeared in 1968]. "Everyone knows that birth control is not an immoral act. *Humanae Vitae* is still around, but it's on the shelf. *Veritatis Splendor* will sit up there with the new Catechism. It will be used only to insure that bishops are orthodox. The pope has put bishops in a position where they have no room."

"Catholicism is about incarnation and universality," he continued. "And I don't see these two things in other religions. I guess I could be happy with the Buddhists, but in terms of what I carry in my head, I'm not a Buddhist. I'm a Catholic. I'm for incarnation and universality and for bringing the mind to bear on the relationship between God and human beings, not just a dumb faith that says 'Shut up and drink your beer.'"

Dick Westley lives and worships in St. Gertrude's Parish on Chicago's North Side, not far from Loyola's main campus. He and his wife, Ethel, have six grown children, now all adults. The Westleys have five grandchildren. His children don't practice their faith in the same way that Westley does, but, in his universal view, he sees them as Catholics and repeats constantly, "It really doesn't matter!"

"Vatican II crystallized and proclaimed this 'Catholic' dream more eloquently than had ever been done in the history of the Roman Church," he said. "But as the Church grew, this proclamation of the solidarity of all mankind under God made it more difficult for those in high places within the Church to answer the question 'Why be Catholic?'"

"But this is precisely the wrong time to leave the Catholic Church!" Westley said with great emphasis. "The Church is on the verge of becoming truly 'Catholic.' What we are witnessing now are the last desperate attempts by the Roman Church to abort a new life."

Westley is not the personality type one associates with dissent. He's at Mass on Sunday, attentive, vital, participating. Spiritually, he is very Jewish, believing God dwells within each one of us, not in some far-off spiritual place. He believes in a religion of incarnation. For him this means that God is with us in every aspect of our lives—"even our sexuality! Especially our sexuality! Human sexuality *is* spirituality!"

Westley saves his dissent for peer groups or for discussion groups whom he leads carefully through forests of conflicting views. Even among the ivory towers of universities, he walks carefully and respectfully. But he doesn't run from a differing viewpoint or, like an abusing husband, strike out when his control is threatened. He remains a philosopher who treasures the respectful exchange of ideas.

In recent years, however, he has bent his ideas against the walls of rigid institutional thinking that treats differing ideas as challenges to its authority. Westley has received letters from the local chancery office which do not respond to his proffered ideas but instead remind him of his obligations as a Catholic in a Catholic university and his failure to submit to the magisterium. The letters leave him bewildered and hurt.

Still, he clings to a reserve of humor. Informed that the term "magisterium" was first introduced by Pope Gregory XVI (1831–1846), the same pope who condemned locomotives as an invention of the devil, he laughs and recalls his first problems with the local church. It started under Cardinal John Cody, Chicago's bizarre archbishop from 1965 to 1982. "He used to call me 'Wyclif,'" Westley recalls with a roaring laugh. "'What about that guy Wyclif?' he would ask his staff. They never corrected him. They knew he meant me."

Westley appreciated the irony. John Wyclif (1328–1384) was an English reformer who believed that Christ was the only overlord of people. He was a champion of the people against the abuses of the Church.

Wyclif preached that the good offices of the Church were not requisites for salvation. Instead, he held that the Scriptures are the supreme authority. Cody's mistaking Westley's name amounted to an ecclesiastical Freudian slip.

"We've all had experiences with ecclesial authority," Westley said. "Maybe it was the pastor refusing to minister to a dying family member. Maybe it was a refusal to give Christian burial to a prodigal or refusing to baptize a child, or to marry a young couple. They are always painful but are administered by someone under authority.

"Cody must have worried about me, but he never did anything. But in 1984, when my book, *Morality and Its Beyond*, was published, I was called downtown. The book called into question some of the official positions of the magisterial church concerning moral matters. [The archbishop then was Cardinal Joseph Bernardin, who succeeded Cardinal Cody in 1982 and whom Westley holds in high regard.]

"It turned out that Joseph [his informal but respectful name for America's highest-ranking active archbishop] had gotten a letter of inquiry about me and my book from Cardinal Joseph Ratzinger. [Ratzinger is the Prefect of the Congregation for the Doctrine of the Faith, a powerful curial cabinet post that was once known as the Inquisition. The brilliant but rigid German is the second most powerful man in the church, a man who can—and does—suppress dissent with ruthless efficiency. An inquiry from his office can make chanceries quiver. He has brought down major theologians such as America's Charles Curran and Brazil's Leonardo Boff and drained the energies of many ordinaries who must spend days responding to letters that already contain the seeds of judgment.]

"I don't know who turned me in. I think it was a twenty-one-year-old kid who came to one of my talks. He probably took one of my handouts and turned it over to someone," Westley recalls. [The Vatican seldom reveals its sources. It subscribes to no Bill of Rights.] "Chances are, this kid got some help from Opus Dei. [See chapter 4.] I don't think he was smart enough to do it on his own.

"Anyway, I had this meeting with Joseph. It was very cordial. We like each other and we have respect for one another. But in the course of this wonderful conversation between fellow believers, he finally got around to the reason for our meeting.

"You think you can say things in direct contradiction to the magisterium," Bernardin said to Westley. "That makes it very hard for me. How can I be supportive when you do something like that?"

"It was said gently, not harshly," Westley recalled. "The cardinal was really interested in what I had to say in answer to this very important question. He wanted to know who I thought I was in contradicting the magisterium.

"I had asked myself this question hundreds of times during the writing of this book. Under what circumstances is it proper for a lay person to question the authority of the Roman Catholic Church?

"I told him this: 'If you think that's what I'm doing, contradicting the magisterium in my own name, then I don't see how you can avoid censuring me. But I assure you, this is *not* what I'm doing. The fact of the matter is that it's the magisterium that is out of control. Ever since Vatican I and the definition of papal infallibility, it thinks it can teach anything it wants, regardless of what the Spirit is revealing in the people. It has forgotten the traditional theological dictum that the teaching church can only teach what the believing church believes.

"'Authority is not a one-way street. In the past the magisterium always balanced its statements and was held accountable for them by the *sensus fidelium*, the communally funded truth vested in the believing people.

"'It is only recently that the Church has chosen to ignore the common sense of the people. It now makes itself the sole judge of Catholic practice. This really goes against our deepest traditions.

"'Yes, I dissent. However, I'm just trying to rehabilitate the *sensus fidelium* as a vital counterbalance to the magisterium so that it can't claim absolute power usurping all authority to itself.

"'All I said in that book was that we must bracket what the Church says on moral issues and look at what life teaches. The Church can't be the moral policeman to the world.

"'Just look at *Humanae Vitae*, the birth control encyclical. It's a beautiful document about caring for people in the world. But as a moral document, it's terrible!'"

Basically, that is what Westley told the cardinal. The archbishop responded by saying that Westley had a certain freedom to say things in universities, but that he couldn't speak that way in parishes. Westley didn't completely agree but understood. So, of his own volition, he agreed to stop speaking in parishes for a full year. "The year was my gift to him. I wanted to give Joseph time to think about it and frame a thoughtful response," he said.

Westley refused all invitations to speak in parishes for a full year. But he never heard from the cardinal. Chances are, the cardinal felt he had done his duty in speaking to Westley. He could report to Rome that he had brought Westley to task. There would be a memo to the file. Sacred behinds were covered.

If *Morality and Its Beyond* unsettled some, Westley's most recent book, *When It's Right to Die: Conflicting Voices, Difficult Choices*, was guaranteed to break some stained glass windows on the walls of the Church's mind. (It was released in October, 1994 by Twenty-Third Publications, Mystic, Conn.) In it, Westley is challenging the Church's position on euthanasia because he believes that present church teaching is only in partial conformity to higher authority.

"I don't want to appear arrogant," he said, "but I continue to believe in and operate under the principle of the magisterium allied with the sense of the faithful, the *sensus fidelium.*

"Don't get me wrong. I'm not talking about taking a poll to see who gets the most votes for a particular position. It is rather a matter of discerning just what it is that the Spirit of God is revealing in the lives and experiences of people of faith at this moment in history."

Westley believes that papal authority reached its high-water mark in 1950 with the release of Pius XII's encyclical *Humani Generis*, a finger-wagging letter that warned believers about false opinions that the pope thought were undermining Catholic doctrine. With this letter, Pius was saying that even the ordinary teaching of the Church could be subject to his authority. (In 1994, John Paul II said as much again with his brief but hard-nosed *Pascendi Dominici*, in which he not only closed the door to the question of the ordination of women to the priesthood but demanded that the faithful give both internal and external assent.)

Since 1950, any real effort to shut off dissent has only served to make things worse. The low point was reached in 1968 with the release of *Humanae Vitae*, which condemned all forms of birth control. In effect it wiped out the *sensus fidelium* and any real claim to authority which the Church had.

"The noose has been tightening ever since," Westley said with a great deal of sadness in his voice.

"You know, I like Bernardin," he said. "I wrote him during his recent troubles and told him that I thought him innocent. I urged him not to quit because we need him." (In late 1993, Bernardin was falsely accused of the sexual abuse of a minor when he was archbishop of Cincinnati. He was completely cleared a few months later when his accuser recanted.) "But he couldn't get elected dogcatcher in this church now. He's too kind and gentle. He's got enemies in Rome. He's too catholic in the same sense that I use the term—you know, 'Here comes everybody.'"

Months before his euthanasia book appeared, Westley sent a copy of the manuscript to Cardinal Bernardin. He was hurt when Bernardin's response pointed more to the magisterium rather than the issues raised by the book. He had hoped for a more reasoned answer. Perhaps the response came from a Bernardin staffer.

Dick Westley's argument for euthanasia calls for the Church to reach into its own pastoral compassion and to develop its own "liturgy of separation."

"We live in a dysfunctional world," he wrote in chapter 6. "There is a desperate need among people for ways to celebrate and render more hopeful two very painful experiences of separation: divorce and death. Up to now, both experiences have been made more painful by proclamations of disapproval.

"When marriages fail, we have no way for the faith community to publicly redeem that situation and send the parties on their way with renewed hope for the future. There is an awkward absence of a faith dimension to a divorce. This just isn't right.

"How wonderful it would be to have a 'Liturgy of Separation' to mark the ending of a marriage and to express the faith community's love and support and confidence in both parties as they begin the search for a new life."

Westley is fervent about the concept of God in our midst. "Our everyday experiences, being married, raising children, working at jobs— these are all experiences of God in our midst," he told Rich Heffern for an interview in *Praying*. He feels the same about facing death.

"The second experience of separation which cries out for liturgizing is euthanasia," he said. "It is not enough to condemn the act before it is performed and to proclaim forgiveness afterward. These prior condemnations insure that the act will be performed secretly and in private without the benefit of a loving faith community.

"By discouraging the participation of real believers in acts of mercy killing and euthanasia, you remove from the scene the people who are best able to do this thing in a godly way. You leave it to the more dysfunctional among us.

"I'm no supporter of Jack Kevorkian [controversial physician from Michigan who has taken part in an estimated twenty mercy killings at the request of the individuals involved]. But I respect what he's trying to say. People of faith have always understood that the absolute prohibition against mercy killing made for a very edifying abstract theology but one which failed them in the concrete. You know, even in the High Middle Ages—a Golden Age for the Church—believers found ways to do what had to be done."

Westley had been reading Kenneth Vaux (*Death Ethics: Religious and Cultural Values in Prolonging and Ending Life*). Vaux writes that "easy" deaths were commonplace through the Christian ages. Direct euthanasia was often practiced in the local chapel itself. The "Holy Hammer," made of stone, was kept in an old chapel in each district. When it was needed or requested, it was obtained and wielded by the oldest person in the village in order to crush the head of the dying person while all the inhabitants prayed.

"The days of the 'Holy Hammer' are gone," Westley said, "but it's time now to have an up-to-date version for those who choose to die, by their own hands or by the hands of others, in the presence of the faith community. It's time, too, for the Church and the community of believers to get into this process—to humanize it and to insure that when it happens, it will be done in ways that are the most skillful.

"I know that sounds outrageous now, but the day is coming."

Westley is fully aware that his position on euthanasia could get him in even hotter water. He laughs about his situation. "I am a philosopher, not a theologian," he said, mindful of the fact that local ordinaries are limited largely to theology when exercising their teaching authority. "But I teach ethics and that spills over into theology.

"I could take early retirement, but I like to teach and I'd like to stay until I'm seventy. They won't fire me. I don't know what I would do if they did. Hey, they just gave me a watch!

"Believe me, I am fully mindful of the highest ideals of my faith. I endorse them and remain fully committed to them as *ideals*. I'm not encouraging suicide or euthanasia. No, my quarrel lies elsewhere.

"An awful lot of Christians who espouse the life and death ideals of their faith think that those ideals require them to condemn the people who don't live up to their rules. So, those who are terminally ill have the added burden of being branded 'sinners' by their fellow Catholics and the Church."

Westley's notes reminded of the Jesuit priest, an administrator at the university where Dick has taught since 1968. The priest's mother is in a Catholic nursing home where he visits her regularly. "I don't like going there with my collar on," he said. "People see the collar and call out from their beds: 'Father, kill me. Please!'"

Westley's book directly challenges the doctrine that terms euthanasia as "intrinsically evil." His quarrel is not with people who work in hospice programs or other teachers such as Daniel Callahan (author of *The Troubled Dream of Life: Living with Mortality*). He has no difficulty with the "higher" or "nobler" ways of dying. His battle is with the pompous and religiously misguided and their incessant moral condemnation.

"Slavery was once accepted as an economic necessity," Westley observed. "Now it is viewed as disreputable and disgraceful. Now, we must compete with a life-support technology that is capable of keeping people alive indefinitely. Now, especially with the AIDS epidemic, we have come around a little. Euthanasia is now seen as a tragic necessity required to protect human dignity.

"We've got to take death back from the health professionals and the lawyers. It belongs to all of us, but most especially to people of faith."

Westley was finished. Out of time and the tape recorder had run out. He was ready to drive back home to prepare his classes and do his writings in which he says much the same things.

"Why be Catholic?" he concluded. "Well, the Catholic ethos is really the ethos of our time. Its dream of peaceful solidarity amid diversity is precisely what the world needs as we usher in a global village.

"If we really think about it and live long enough, we come to understand things which eluded us earlier because of our youth and the dogmatic posture of our religious teachers. When we reach that point, we can no longer be parochial. We can no longer say with conviction that someone *must* be a Catholic. It really doesn't matter!

"I remain a Catholic because that's my tradition, my roots. Where else could I go? In the end, it doesn't really matter what church I belong to but how well I witness the loving presence of God to all of humankind. Then, I am perfectly at liberty to be who and what I am."

N.B.: Some of Westley's observations are from earlier conversations and from notes he brought with him or sent to me following the interview.

8

The Currans:
"Something has been lost somewhere. There is nothing to go back to."

———◆◆◆———

Diane and Tom Curran may be among the most innately talented parents one can find. The family is so integrated that one wonders if they are real. However, repeated visits to their Downers Grove, Illinois, home only serve to confirm the initial experience. Diane and Tom Curran have an unfiltered, unvarnished marriage, one marked by casualness, honesty, and openness. This translates to their four kids. The interviews for this chapter were basically no different from other conversations in their home or at Chicago's Lincoln Park Zoo, where the family goes to picnic. The children kiss their parents before bedtime and before leaving the house. Problems appear to be solved at the most basic level. Voices are raised but only to a point. Asked what his response to a serious problem involving one of his sons might be, Tom Curran responded: "If that happened, he and I would have a very serious talk." Somehow, the tone suggested that it wouldn't happen.

I was so taken with the Currans that I reviewed the experience with a psychologist friend. He pronounced such families unusual in this present climate. He used words such as "reaffirming" and "supportive" and suggested that it drew its strength from a good marriage and an appropriate sense of values. He also pointed to their deep religious faith in spite of their strong reservations on some questions of doctrine.

The Currans live in a well-cared-for upper-middle-class house. Tom does the outside work. He's good at it. He raises flowers and herbs in a lush garden that hugs the house. Diane does the inside work. Both share cooking duties. The house is furnished with some good second-hand furniture as well as new pieces. It's arranged quite well. Diane has a touch. She's an artist.

Diane Kolaczek Curran works at home, mostly doing calligraphy, silk screen designs, framed pieces. She sells through distributors. Business is pretty good. The kids help with packing and mailing. She's wonderfully efficient. She once nursed two kids at once. She's well organized. There is still time left over to breed and sell an annual litter of their two pure-bred dogs, who double as well-behaved family pets.

Tom manages an art supplies store located in another suburb forty-five minutes from their home. Tom Jr., the oldest child, works as a recreation manager in a townhouse complex. He's a lifeguard and certified emergency medical technician. He is also a full-time student at the College of DuPage not far from his home. Young Tom drives his own car, a second-hand sedan that was his high-school graduation present. He has his own cellular phone, a gift from his girlfriend. Cars and phones are not luxuries to his generation. They are necessities. Tim, the second oldest, will seek employment as soon as he gets his driver's license. The Currans spend $2400 each year on car insurance for their three vehicles. But cars are a must.

Tom Sr. has been in retail sales since he finished college. It hasn't been easy. There have been failures in his own business and periods of unemployment. One particularly bad time saw him unemployed for six months. It wiped out their modest nest egg and resulted in a Christmas that saw a decorated tree but few presents. ("We were closer that Christmas than we ever were," Diane recalled. "Maybe we were," the oldest son answered. "But I missed the presents.")

Diane is ten years younger than her only sibling, a brother who lives in Alabama. Her family is thoroughly Polish. Tom is one of six children, five of them boys. His roots are Irish-American.

Emily Kolaczek, Diane's mother, lives with them. She's in her mid-seventies and in good health.

Tom Jr. has a girlfriend, Becky Wiencek, who is treated like another member of the family. She took time off at her job as a bank clerk to be part of this interview. (The bank was robbed that evening!) Becky attends DuPage with Tom. They are very close but sensible. Becky refers to Diane as "Mrs. Curran" even as she helps with chores. The formalities are part of a household etiquette that seems to hold the structure together.

I have known them for at least twenty years. Diane was one of my wife's art students at Loyola University of Chicago. She also worked at Loyola University Press, proofing copy and doing layout and design.

The interviews were conducted in the Currans' living room with all present. The openness of the family to each other may, in fact, be a measure of the family's outstanding emotional health. Their responses may suggest a family that has left religion and active practice. In fact, while Mass attendance may be spotty, they remain devoted Catholics, attempting to find a comfortable place within the structure.

Diane, mother, age 40: "When Tom and I were dating, we used to go to Christ the King Parish on the West Side. Sometimes, when we didn't feel like going to Mass, we would go to a restaurant around the corner. It was called King Edward's—so, if anyone asked, we would say that we went to the King. (*Laughs.*) I think our kids knew this but my mother must be hearing it for the first time. But we still felt guilty.

"When we were first married, before the children came, we used to go to Mass sometimes, but not others. But we still felt guilty, though not as much.

"Probably our first and biggest problem was with Confession. It has changed so much since I was a kid. I don't recognize it. As a kid, I walked eight blocks with my mom to the church. I would practice the Act of Contrition the whole way, to be sure that I got it right for the priest. It had to be a 'perfect' Act of Contrition. But by the time Tom and I got married, it wasn't that important. Now, it seems, one doesn't have to go to Confession before each Communion. That's the way we were taught.

"But when our first child came, we needed to have him baptized. We needed to get him used to going to church, plus we needed to feel a sense of community and of belonging. As the other kids came, it became more difficult to get them all ready for church. At the same time, church seemed to become more necessary for the older children. Tom is nineteen now and Emily is ten. There's a nearly ten-year gap between the oldest and the youngest. We felt that the older ones should be in church, but it was hard organizing it for the younger ones.

"The church began introducing crying rooms. I didn't know how to feel about them. I remember a priest that used to ask: 'What better sound than that of a child crying or singing in church?' Yet young mothers brought toys for their kids and sat in the crying room with them and talked about pre-school with the other mothers. There was no real Mass for them. They might just as well have stayed at home. We let our kids bring quiet toys to church but they had to keep them in their pockets. They were pretty good kids.

"Then, the Sacraments started coming for them. I got involved with the teaching of CCD. Some of it was good; much was bad. In fact, a lot of it was a waste of time. The kids really weren't learning what they were supposed to be learning. And during that ten-year period, as the four kids came of age for Communion, I watched the whole idea of Communion completely change. When I made my First Communion, it was very special. I remember going up and kneeling and the priest would go down the line. It was part of the mystery. It was special. It was that way with Tommy—even with Timmy—it was special. But by the time John made his Communion, it wasn't so special anymore. Anybody could come to Communion. When I was young, the priest put it in your mouth. Now, there aren't enough priests. People don't want to wait. Now lay people put it in your hand. It isn't so special anymore. By the time Emily made her Communion, it was just another day to have a party and to wear a pretty dress. There was no special looking forward to something that was going to be different in your life. Before I made my Communion, I remember looking at the grownups going to Communion. I couldn't wait for that day. You got to carry your prayer book and to wear gloves—it was special! With Emily, we were told that there could be no gloves or prayerbooks—not even a rosary. Now Emily doesn't even know what a rosary is, except what I told her about it.

"It has all changed so much. Everything we were told was special now no longer exists. We have two girl neighbors who were educated in Catholic schools from first grade through college. They had never heard the term 'venial sin.'

"Religion has changed. It was supposed to be a constant—something you could always turn to—a rock. Sure, the only thing that is constant is change. But do we have to go from hats and white gloves to tanks tops and cutoffs up to the butt?

"The sense of respect is totally gone because the sense of fear is totally gone. We think that we can better understand God and Jesus by bringing everything down to the human level, but we've taken everything that is mysterious away.

"What happened to all those things we believed in? Why did I not eat meat all those Fridays? Why did I give up something for Lent? Why did I go to church hungry on Sunday morning because I couldn't eat breakfast because it was part of the preparation? Now I don't even have to go to Mass on Sunday morning. It's not a sin any more.

"Now what do I tell my kids? Now even between the births of my children, things change all over again. That's my gripe!

"There is no sense of Christianity in my parish. I haven't experienced that feeling since my brother's wife was killed in an accident in Alabama. There are few Catholics down there. The parish is tight. People care. The sense of community showed through there more than it ever did here. Early in the morning, the doorbell rang and there were doughnuts; later there was lunch meat. Then, the moms would prepare dinner for the family. They were there not to talk but to offer support. Here, they would simply announce the name at Mass.

"When we came to Downers Grove, we decided to enroll the kids in the parish school. When we did, we found that we were often asked to bring up the gifts. I helped with art work. But, after we pulled the kids out of the parish school, we weren't asked to do much of anything.

"They built a new church with an entry space that is huge, but there isn't enough room in the church itself to accommodate those who come on big feasts. There isn't even enough parking. They retained only a few of the stained-glass windows and put the beautiful crucifix on the side.

"Now we just haven't been attending as often as we used to. And I can't ask the kids to go. I have too many questions. I suppose that I should go for myself and for God, but I have so many negative feelings when I go there that I ask, 'Why even bother?' I return from Communion and go to kneel down and there are no kneelers! One more thing has been taken away!

"I didn't understand the Latin, but I remember it and it impressed me. I can still quote it. But now, it's all gone. Why go there?

"I never went to Catholic school until college. I went to CCD until third grade when I walked out because the nun was continually telling us that the kids who went to Catholic school were the ones that would grow up to be doctors and lawyers and that the other kids—us—would rob banks and be good-for-nothings. I grabbed my coat and walked out. Sister screamed, 'Where are you going?' I said, 'I'm leaving. I'm not good enough to be here.' And I knew in my heart that the kids who went to Catholic school weren't any better than we were. The same words that came out of our mouths came out of theirs.

"I went to Forman High School, then I did a semester at University of Illinois in Urbana. I visited the Vatican after that semester and saw the Pieta. If ever I had a religious experience it was at the Pieta. Oh, we had to kneel down first to make certain that our skirts touched the ground or we couldn't go in. I remember seeing all these people and, after that, the only thing I can remember is standing in front of the statue. I can't recall how I even got through the crowd. The only experience I can compare it to is childbirth. I still get choked up thinking about it! There was love and joy—a real catharsis. How a piece of art could evoke such feeling! I knew then that I was a believer.

"I had little religious education in high school, but what there was of it was positive. I suppose I got more when I went to Loyola, especially when I got the job with the Loyola University Press. But even that was filled with change. We had to go through all the manuscripts and put all the Sacraments in lower case. Even the Bible wasn't capitalized! I guess that my religious schooling was just a series of changes.

"Loyola's religious education was cool. It was more like philosophy. I lost my fear of priests and found them to be human. Religion was taught more like history. There was a lot of discussion. You saw things differently.

"You know, I wish the Baltimore Catechism was back! At least you knew the answers!

"I met Tom before my senior year in high school. He had gone to Catholic grammar school and two years at a Maryknoll seminary in Missouri. He finished high school in a public high school. My aunt lived next door to him and I connived with his little sister to swim in her pool. I met him while swimming in that pool.

"We went to Loyola together. It was a good experience, not simply for its theology department but also its small class size. You had to do your homework! I majored in art; Tom in psychology. I graduated a little ahead of him so that I could go to work and we could get married. We were married in 1974.

"Our parish is always taking polls and asking questions. They get good responses from the people. They know the problems. They know where their people are in terms of liturgy, education, sexuality and all that. But they can't do anything about it. So nothing happens!"

Emily Kolaczek, grandmother: "I am really a little disappointed listening to all Diane said. I know there has been a lot of changes, but I was brought up to believe that you did what you thought was right, even to the point of going to Confession. I think I shook in my boots every time I had to go. We used to have to go up in rows, on the altar, where the priests just sat holding their hand up to the side of their heads. There was one priest who screamed at you. Everyone in the church knew what you did! We used to pray that we didn't get in his row. I didn't do that much that people would have a good time listening to it. But I was scared. Now, I believe that you stay with it and if there's some part you don't like, then don't do it, but don't leave.

"I welcome the change from Latin. Half the time I slept through the Mass because I didn't understand it. Now, I can understand and sing; I like it much better the way it is.

"I like the crying rooms. They keep the parents from being embarrassed. Half the time it isn't the crying babies. You only have to give them something to eat and they'll be quiet. It's the older brats that the parents can't control. The crying room is for sassy kids.

"I'm disappointed that Diane has decided to stay away from Mass. But she's a big girl. I don't miss the kneelers because I can't kneel anymore and I get very tired standing.

"Deep down, Diane will realize all this. She's not a worse person for what she's doing. I think she just can't make up her mind. It's true that the mystery has been taken away.

"I'm born Catholic in Chicago of immigrant Polish parents. I did grammar school and high school—a commercial course. College was out. It was the Depression.

"I had two children. Both good kids. I didn't want to go to work but I had to. A mother always feels bad when she has to work. She should be home with the children. I remember one day when Diane called me at work and said she had hurt her knee. Now when that happens, a mother wants to go home right away. But I couldn't. Diane didn't want to tell my mother—her grandmother—because she had a bad heart. I felt so bad!

"Now everyone has to work. Things are so expensive! Now, they need TVs and all that. When we were kids, we had breakfast and dinner together. Now, they just grab something and run. But I understand.

"I think the changes that they're making in the Church are good. I still can't get Communion from a lay person. I go to the priest's line. It just stays with you. The little things that Diane thinks about aren't that important. They shouldn't be that important.

"Oh, I like John Paul II! My brother-in-law who is a Carmelite priest went to school with him. I feel I know the pope. I don't agree with every point, but I like him.

"I don't mind married priests. After all, how can they counsel you if they know nothing about it? How can priests today tell you what to do?

"And why not women priests? I haven't seen an altar boy in our parish in weeks. It's all girls. Sure, why not?

"But that guitar Mass with the jazzed up guitar is awful. One priest said that we should come to Mass because we want to, not because it was a concert. It isn't the Church's fault when children come to church as if they were dressed up for a picnic. That's the parents' job. The Church wants to keep its people. They don't want to yell at them about how to dress.

Tom, age 19: "Lately, I've had too many problems with the Church. Too many rules. The Church should be there to support you, to help you pray, not to control everything else. They should not be there to judge you. Who's to say that if you pray on a Monday or a Wednesday that it's any different than praying on a Sunday. I don't see how some people, just because they abide by the Church's rules, are any better for it.

"The Church seems to say that all your love should go towards God. But I believe that one should worship oneself in a way because, without people, religion would not exist.

"People should spend some time thinking, expanding their minds, not just praying. I don't see how the Church should tell me when to pray or how to dress in church. I do pray, when I'm in the mood. The Church should be more lenient.

"There are a lot of things that I disagree with in the Church, but that doesn't mean that I should be shunned or told that I am going to heaven or hell or whatever they call it.

"A church wedding is very important to me because it's a tradition, but I think that the church should be there for the times when one feels the need to pray, as well as for weddings and funerals. But now it's locked most of the time and, if you want to see a priest, you need an appointment.

"The Church pushes into private matters that are really not its business. Birth control is one of them. I think children are something a couple should want, not the result of a mistake. As for sex before marriage, I can't understand why the Church thinks you're a better Catholic because you didn't have sex before marriage with the woman you love. The Church often doesn't know. They've never been there. They can't decide."

Becky Wiencek, Tom's girlfriend, age 18: "I agree with Tom. I was brought up in the Church and was told in CCD that, if you told a lie, it put a black mark on your soul. The priest who taught us CCD ended up in jail for sexual abuse. I still cannot understand how they could say that a lie can never be taken away. I can't understand how the Church can say to me that, if I love a man and I am going to marry him, I cannot have sex with him or else I'll be damned to hell. Yet that's what I was taught.

"I don't know how the Church can measure sins, such as mortal and venial. I haven't been to church in a long time, since Christmas [nine months]. Maybe it's because I was taught by volunteers. Maybe the priests would have said something different.

"The Church says it can help you, but I don't know how the priests can help you when they're not married. There are a lot of things in my life that I've already gone through that I don't think priests would understand."

Tom: "I would take advice from my parents or her parents before I would take it from the Church. I don't think the Church is open any more. Its doors are locked, unless there's Mass. I think that's foolish. The priests are just not there. If they want to make the rules, O.K., but then they should turn around and look at themselves and realize that they're not always there.

"I have the same feelings about the Church as my mother. I never really understood how I felt that way, but in college I've taken two religion courses and it has taught me a lot. I'm not saying that I'd convert to Buddhism or Judaism but a lot of the things I learned about Buddhism, about worshiping oneself first and working with one's mind and being kind to other people and making yourself a better person have a great appeal. I think it's a great mistake to ignore what these other religions have to say to us."

Becky: "I used to love to go to church, but now I agree with Mrs. Curran and Tom and the other kids. Something's been lost somewhere. I don't know what it is.

"Of course, if I had four children like the Currans, I would carry them to church and have them baptized and put them through CCD and their First Communion and have them confirmed. I would hope that they would go to church; learn the things that I believe. I don't want them to grow up to be compulsive liars. I don't know if I would send them to Catholic school.

"Religion is more acceptable now in school. It's talked about a lot. There was a time not long ago when Sunday was supposed to be a day when you had a hangover. Now it's cooler to have religion. That's the wrong reason to do it, of course, but now the kids are using words like "spiritual." Some of this might be just conforming, especially among those who are just a few years younger than we are. You know how it is: if it's cool to be a Catholic in 1994, then you're a Catholic. If it's cool to be Jewish in 1995, then you'll be Jewish. Our crowd isn't quite like that."

Tim, age 16: "I'm a junior in high school. I'm younger than Tom. I never experienced some of the things he did. I remember that my First Communion was special. I walked up there with a smile on my face. But then we moved here to St. Joe's and it all changed. The priest came in and taught us more about history than about right or wrong. But there were so many experiences in that school that should not have happened. When I have kids, I won't send them to Catholic school. The teaching in public school is ten times better. In Catholic school, you had to do your homework because of fear, but you didn't take the time to understand it. There was no bond with the children and that carried over to religion.

"CCD was a joke. They hired mothers of kids who had no background. It was the blind leading the blind. I often thought that the teachers were learning something themselves. In public school, I had great teachers. I had fun. In Catholic school, the kids seemed to take out the discipline on each other.

"Confirmation didn't mean as much to me. I went to CCD; got through it. I had my confirmation and it didn't mean anything to me.

"I don't hear much about religion now. I have no clue about what to believe or what to do. From my First Communion until now, I don't remember anything. I didn't absorb it. Confirmation meant nothing. I'm not going to be able to sit down with my kids and tell them anything."

Jonathan, age 12 "almost 13": "I've had my First Communion; no Confirmation yet. It's just another year of CCD. I'm in seventh grade. I haven't been to church much recently. We used to sing more. Now, we have a new church and we sang only two Christmas carols. The new church doesn't look like a church; it looks more like a barn. Inside, the whole sprinkler system is visible. The crucifix doesn't have Jesus on it. Parents do the CCD; they don't hardly know a thing about it. It's on a Wednesday. It's very impractical."

Diane: "It's terribly impractical. I have to pick up Emily, then deliver Jonathan. It used to be on Sunday morning. It was called Family Time. It was two hours or more. In that time, all the CCD was taught and Mass was fit in, including a special Mass with special readings for the kids. I thought it was a great idea to involve parents like that."

Emily, age 11: "I don't know that much about church because I don't go that much. I go at Christmas and Easter and those other times when we ought to. I don't exactly feel welcome there. There are so many rules to follow. You want to do it your way and they make you do it their way and that's not fair.

"As far as priests being mean, I know that we're supposed to go to them and tell them things that we did wrong and they're supposed to say that they understand, but instead they say mean things and they tell you not to do these things.

"I've always been in public school. Everybody's welcome to go to that school. And it's interesting. My teacher says that I'm not to leave the classroom unless I understand my homework or else come back at recess and she's happy to tell you. I hated CCD, never wanted to go. My CCD teacher was a volunteer mother.

"I was sort of looking forward to my First Communion. I don't remember much about it. I remember that I wanted to carry flowers and

a rosary the way my mother told me she did, but the CCD teacher said
'no.' Now, I know what a rosary is because my mother told me, but I
don't know how to use it. I just wore a white dress and a veil. It was just
a day when you could wear a fancy dress and maybe nylons for the first
time and have a party at your house."

(*Emily shows a shadow box taken from the wall in which her grandfa-
ther's picture is featured. It was obviously his First Communion day. There
is a prayerbook, rosary, piece of palm made into a cross, holy card, and bou-
tonniere. It is a family icon.*)

Diane: "It goes to show you how important those things were. I
still have mine. They're just precious. They're just things. But they evoke
memories."

Emily: "There isn't much talk about religion in school. I don't think
that the teachers are allowed to talk about it. It's not a religious school. I
talk to the kids in the Catholic school and I get the feeling that the
teachers are strict and that all they say is 'Don't!' and that at the end of
the day you get out of there. We like school at the school I go to. We
don't look forward to recess or lunch. We look forward to social studies
because she makes it so interesting."

Diane: "We're fortunate. We're in a good school district. The
Catholic schools just can't compete. I could never send my kids to
Catholic junior or senior high school. They just don't have the materials
that our kids need. Their science and math are inferior, not because their
teachers aren't good. The Catholic schools just don't have the materials."

Jonathan: "I went to Catholic school in kindergarten. Everything
was O.K. Then in first grade, I had two teachers. I don't know what I
did wrong, but one of them put me in the closet and turned the light off
and left me in there. I told my mother when I got home and I guess that
was the stick that broke the camel's back. The teacher told me that I was
no good and that God made a mistake when he made me." (*He cries.*)

Diane: "I never found out what he did wrong. But he came home
and wanted to kill himself. I know that he didn't make it up."

Emily, grandmother: "The teacher probably had PMS." (*Laughs.*)

Diane: "I went back to the school, asked for the kids' books and
walked out. I never once heard from the school or the parish. It was a
big turnover time in the parish—a principal and seven teachers—so
maybe that's the reason.

"It's all changed. There are no traditions to go back to. It isn't just the
Church. We have relatives and friends whose kids are being raised by others in day care centers. It's like Russia. Now, it seems, there are fewer
teachers as dedicated. And the nuns are gone. You know, I still think of

nuns as Loretta Young! (*Laughs.*) I really never thought about being a nun. My goal in life was to find a good man who could be a good father."

Tom, father, 43: "I'm the manager of Michael's, an art supplies store. We did $2.5 million last year, not bad for a place where much of the stuff sells for ninety-nine cents.

"Yes, I did spend two years with Maryknoll. They were a very radical order, but they decided that I didn't have a vocation. They asked me to take a few years off and then maybe return. They used to call me 'the Smiling Christian.' Years later, around 1975, I got a copy of *Fields Afar*, the Maryknoll magazine. On the cover was a picture of a bunch of guys coming through the seminary gates. It was captioned 'Today's Youth, Tomorrow's Priests.' And there I was on the cover! A married man with a kid! (*Laughs.*)

"In college, I majored in psychology with an education minor—a pairing that ranks right up there with an English-history combination. I got into retailing because I couldn't afford to go back for my master's in a practical field. College was good. The theology classes got me thinking.

"I've got to go back thirty or thirty-five years to where the Church was. There was a stability in the Church. It was the be-all and the end-all of the neighborhood. It was an intricate part of my life. There was a certain mystery, a certain awe—the buildings, the structure, the Latin Mass. There was a certain awe there that lent itself to believing in God. Like Jonathan said, the Christmas carols added to the season. Then, they started changing too much. It was very uncomfortable. The security and the awe aren't there.

"As a Catholic, I believe in the life of Christ. We can debunk a lot of things, but as long as you believe that you must treat others as they treat you, then life is good.

"Whether John Paul II is a problem, whether Martin Luther was right—all those things mean nothing. It all comes down to Jesus' law: Treat others as yourself.

"I respect John Paul. But I think I've had the upbringing and the moral training to make my own decisions. He's against abortion, for example. But if that ever came up in my life, I would have to look into my own heart and make my own decision. I don't believe in abortion, but I would have to think about it.

"I have reservations about the Church's teaching on birth control. But I think that some forms of birth control amount to abortion. I think that God created sex for fun as well as making children. Heck, Diane and I had four kids before we realized there was a connection! (*Laughs.*)

"I have a fellow working for me that sometimes works sixty hours a week. On top of that, he's an auditor for a motel chain. He's a great kid

—only twenty. He takes care of his mother. And he's gay. I hold nothing against him, but the Church condemns him. That's not right. And if he's using whatever he is using to keep himself around a little longer [i.e., condoms], then what harm is there to society?"

Becky: "If Jesus wanted everyone to love each other, why are there so many restrictions?"

Tom, Sr.: "I don't want to knock the Church. I could go back and find all sorts of scandals. But I don't want to do that. I just want to look at what Jesus said. I want to take what the Church teaches and weigh it against what I really believe: Love God; love your neighbor. The rest isn't important.

"The Franciscan nuns who taught me said that sins of omission were worse than sins of commission. They taught us that it was wrong to ignore a person in need—worse than telling a lie to your mother. I think of the thief on the right of the Cross on Calvary. He turned to Jesus and said: 'You're somebody and I'm sorry.'"

IT WAS TIME FOR DINNER. Lasagna by Diane and dessert cake by Grandma. There were ten people around the table. We began with Grace before Meals.

9

Margaret Traxler, S.S.N.D.:
"We want to be a part, not apart."

"If we don't follow the Spirit, we're simply taking orders from middlemen. We're hypocrites. We're ignoring the Spirit if we're just middle people. If we're taking orders from anyone—the bureaucracies of hierarchy, clergy, assemblies, whatever—we are hypocrites. We are obligated to follow the Spirit and take it where it leads us."

Sister Margaret Traxler, a School Sister of Notre Dame for over fifty years, speaks slowly and deliberately. She doesn't need to polish her sentences to make them sound slick. She doesn't give her listeners something in the beginning of a sentence and take it back at the end. She isn't looking over her shoulder. No one owns her.

Sister Margaret's thoughts come from something deep inside her, not from a policy manual. "Unfortunately, the bishops are not men who can think for themselves," she says with genuine concern for them. "They should be hurt to think that they are denying the freedom of spirit that every man has a right to expect for himself and of his ministry." She is genuinely concerned that the bishops have created their own moral universe, one detached from their own faithful. From her Maria Shelter in one of the country's poorest neighborhoods, she worries that the religious right—including many Catholics—are looking down on the poor and emotionally injured, seeing them as having no worth. From her office, she views the results of destitution while, not far away, a huge city and powerful country pursues a free-enterprise economy unconstrained by higher values.

"It's interesting that, since I was a Notre Dame sister, particularly in the last twenty-five years," she continued, "I thought that my order would catch up with me and my ideas. Not that I think I'm better. Their ideas are good. But I had different inspirations. I trusted my own, even though sometimes I was alone. But now, a few years ago, our sister international president said that we would choose the poor. They are our choice. And I thought, well, that has always been my choice. And each year, I did what the community allowed me to do—in fact, I was under obedience to do it—with their special permission and understanding. I choose the poor. Yet, it was only three years ago that I learned that this was their official position. I learned that they stand with the poor, trying to empower them, especially in education, housing, and the ability to raise their children in a way which would improve on their own life cycle. At that time, I knew what I have always known. Now, I know it for certain."

Margaret Traxler is a founder within a congregation that already has a founder. Religious orders occasionally need second and third founders to steer them on a course that echoes the charism of their original founder or that reflects what the founder would do now. She is a work-in-progress, reminding her fellow sisters and the communities they serve about the original goals of their congregations.

Regrettably, many congregations now have constitutions thicker than the New Testament. They have become victims of their own success, moving with their parishioners, patients, and students into the middle and upper classes. Many now conduct schools and hospitals that would turn away their founder from their rectories, convents, classrooms, and emergency rooms.

"My congregation has always allowed me to do what I have asked to do," the seventy-year-old sister said. "I think they were very noble in that. Now, they have defined this preferential treatment of the poor as a charism of the order. So I don't have to change."

Not that she would. Sister Margaret has heard different drums for most of her religious life. Initially, she was reluctant to be interviewed because she doesn't view herself as a Catholic on the edge. She believes her mission is at the center of the true church. "We all have a lot to learn," she said. "I'm the most needy of all. I try not to push my own agenda. My own mysteries are the Corporal Works of Mercy or the Spiritual Works of Mercy. That is my world and I'm at home in it."

Margaret Traxler's world is a nine-square-block area in Chicago's Englewood district on the city's South Side. Once a sprawling enclave of blue-collar and lace-curtain Irish, it is now an African-American ghetto of struggling poor. The crime rate is high. Random, drive-by shootings are common. Drugs are a major part of the economy. Children kill other children, largely at the behest of older gang members who control the turf much the way politicians once did.

Traxler does not despair of the area. "I feel safe here," she said. "Our staff members take walks in the neighborhood. There are block clubs to keep an eye on things. The local parish—St. Columbanus—is a good one and the pastor, Fr. Philip Cyscon, is a fine man."

We spoke in what was once the rectory of St. Carthage Parish. It is one of many parishes that closed following the population shifts of the twenties through the sixties. It was founded in 1919 to relieve the over-crowding at St. Columbanus. Its first pastor, Daniel H. Riordan, was one of the last of the F.B.I. (foreign-born Irish) priests to be part of the diocesan clergy corps in Chicago. He named the parish after St. Carthage, the bishop of Lismore.

St. Carthage began with some three hundred families, mostly second generation Irish. But from the day it opened, when Sunday Mass was still being celebrated at the old Triangle Theater, the first black families were moving into the area. White flight was underway. The adjoining area was once called Park Manor. The upwardly mobile Irish Catholics lived in spacious two- and three-flat buildings and sent their kids to the local Catholic schools. When equally upwardly mobile blacks tried to buy in the area, the homeowners in Park Manor entered into a series of restrictive covenants to keep the neighborhoods white. The covenants held until 1948 when the United States Supreme Court ruled that state courts could no longer uphold such agreements. A year later, the St. Carthage–St. Columbanus neighborhoods were the scene of some ugly race riots, largely frightened whites tossing rocks at homes recently occupied by blacks. It was not the city's or the church's finest moment. The white flight increased.

Membership peaked around 1930 with fourteen hundred families. In that year, the new pastor, Daniel J. Lanigan, built a Renaissance style rectory which would turn most bishops' hearts green. One story had it that Lanigan's mother had contributed generously to the structure, wanting her son to live in a style to which he had been accustomed in his youth. There is enough marble in the entrance way alone to start a small cemetery. In its prime, the house itself would have readily pleased one of the lesser Medicis.

Parish lore held that Lanigan was a kind man. He often opened the place to priests who were at loose ends with their bishops and needed a haven of peace. The great irony is that the elaborate structure, so care-fully constructed, has survived beautifully for sixty-five years, as if in anticipation of its present function. Its upper floor now serves as a convent for four sisters—two School Sisters of Notre Dame, a Dominican, and a Franciscan. The first floor serves as offices for the Institute of Women Today, an umbrella group founded in 1974 by Margaret Traxler, and embracing the Maria Shelter, the Vincennes Senior Citizen Center, Casa Notre Dame, facilities used by Catholic Charities, and a Head Start Program operated by the Catholic school system. In addition, some thirteen hundred mothers and children are given access to the shelter's counseling services as well as food and clothing.

Father Lanigan lived only a decade in his glorious rectory, but he left a building that would be the heart of an interfaith organization of women which has a special concern for incarcerated and economically deprived women and their children. The parish closed sometime in the early eighties, leaving behind only a dedicated secretary who somehow kept the senior citizens together.

Not long after Cardinal Joseph L. Bernardin was named archbishop in 1982, he gave the entire property to Sister Margaret's group. It's a good bet that it now does more for the community than the slowly diminishing parish had done. Bernardin remains a hero to Sister Margaret. He went against the advice of some of his counselors who were not adverse to having Traxler at St. Carthage but who wanted to charge rent her group simply could not afford.

"Oh, maybe I am on the fringe," Traxler continued. "Maybe so. But I would never give up my faith, because it's mine. It's my inheritance. And I think it's ignoble of anyone to expect any Catholic to be their kind of Catholic, whether it's according to the Vatican or some diocese or the spiritual life of some teacher. Each of us has a right to be herself or himself. It's pernicious of others to say that some people are only cafeteria Catholics. Why are they saying that? Who *are* they to say that?"

"I just got back from a trip to Rome," she continued in a quiet measured voice, but one that was weighted with emotion. "Honestly, if there is any similarity between what Jesus taught and what he did and said and what you see in Rome, I think it's a miracle of coincidence. The Vatican traffics in money making. It a place of art and great beauty. It's a place of old men or else men appointed by the Holy See.

"I was at the Synod on Religious Life. It was directed by men appointed by the Holy See to be their clones. I heard two American bishops give talks at the synod. The pope was present at these talks. These bishops were there at a Synod on the Consecrated Life and they talked about abortion. Talk about addressing the gallery! A talk about abortion to religious! But that's the way favors are granted: if they echo the platitudes of the men in charge. It was not inspiring.

"We had a thirteen-year-old girl with us. She and her family are converts. She's a great soccer fan. And afterwards, she said 'You know, they just don't get it, do they? This isn't about abortion.'

"That young girl doesn't know much about religious life, either. But she knows enough to know that it has nothing to do with abortion. So, maybe I *am* on the margin."

Sister Margaret led a group of nuns and laity in a low-key protest at the Vatican during the Synod on the Consecrated Life. On October 22, 1994, they gathered in the massive piazza outside St. Peter's and unfurled three banners. The first read: "The National Coalition of American Nuns." The second banner stated: "Women want to be a Part —not Apart!" The third banner, carried by Irene Thompson and Margaret Traxler read: "They are meeting about us—Without us."

They crossed the piazza singing "We shall not be silenced" to the tune of "We Shall Overcome." Halfway across the piazza, the group stopped for a minute. The police arrived and quickly informed them that they should leave. When they were too slow in responding, the police confiscated two of the banners. (The third one disappeared into the hands of a sympathetic bystander, who returned it to Irene Thompson.) The police then escorted the little group to the nearby police station where their names and passport numbers were recorded. (They had wisely left their official passports where they were staying.) After nearly an hour, they were released. A request for the return of their six-foot banners was denied. The Vatican police were bemused; they had never dealt with protesting nuns.

Reporter William Drozdiak, writing in the *International Herald Tribune*, observed that "the police who patrol St. Peter's Square could scarcely believe their eyes. American nuns marched into the cavernous piazza to carry their bold message straight to the windows of Pope John Paul II's apartment."

The protest dramatized one of the most controversial issues confronting the Roman Catholic Church—the pope's adamant refusal to alter the Vatican's male-dominated hierarchy and to empower women with greater rights, including ordination to the priesthood. Drozdiak's coverage pointed out that, while women make up more than half the world's 960 million Catholics and account for three-fourths of the membership of religious orders, they are excluded from virtually all positions of authority.

Only 59 of the 348 participants in the synod were women. American religious women were criticized as being "cultural imperialists." Eastern

European and Third World bishops, together with some conservative American bishops, were particularly critical. A French nun, Sr. Stephane-Marie Boullanger, stated that if priesthood is out of the question, the Vatican should open up senior administration so women "can reach the level of reflection and decision making and not just remain at the level at which orders are carried out." An African bishop, Ernest Kombo of the Congo, even suggested that women should be allowed to become lay cardinals. (There is no prohibition about lay people becoming cardinals although it has been over a century since a lay man did receive the red hat.)

Cardinal Basil Hume of Britain expressed sympathy for the goals on the women. "The criticism is that we are masculine led," he said. "The real question is how do we share power, because it's power that we're talking about."

After a month of listening to speeches—or "interventions" as they are termed—the bishops promised the nuns greater, if unspecified, participation in the conduct of the Church. The pope has at least a year to respond to the fifty-five propositions that were submitted privately to him. Most observers hold little hope for change. It's likely that only those religious from Third World countries, where they are treated much like Indian untouchables, will feel any difference. Religious such as those who belong to the United States's Leadership Conference of Women Religious are not looking forward to any changes. Indeed, they speculate that John Paul II will release another finger-wagging document, ordering American sisters back into their habits and their convents. "It's too late for that," one community president said. "The toothpaste is already out of the tube."

One American nun, Sister Doris Gottemoeller, head of the Sisters of Mercy of the Americas, addressed the bishops on behalf of over 97 percent of the sisters in the United States. Only two other American nuns spoke, both representatives of 3 percent of conservative sisters. Washington's conservative Cardinal James A. Hickey had used his clout to insure that the smaller group had the greater representation.

Women in religious life received great praise during the month-long series of speeches. Cardinal Bernardin observed in his intervention that women religious were undergoing "deep change" and that they had experienced "misunderstanding and tension." However, Bishop James C. Timlin of Scranton, a Vatican appointee to the synod, focused on "the aberrations and painful upheaval. . . the losses and uncertainties of recent years." According to James Torrens, writing in *America*, Timlin "was all for putting on the brakes: enough dialogue, enough experiment."

(This reporter visited the Vatican just after the close of the synod. While waiting for a Vatican official, I watched the colorful Swiss Guard snap to attention and click their boots at the approach of each priest as the minor Vatican officials departed their offices. Women religious passed unnoticed and unacknowledged. During an earlier visit, I witnessed the sad spectacle of a habited, female religious selling toilet tissue outside the Vatican restrooms. It will be a long time before the gap between those Vatican priests and that pathetic nun is closed.)

"The whole thing had its moments of tension," Margaret Traxler recalled. "But it was our humble way of teaching. We had thirty round tables of from ten to fifteen sisters each. They were in seven countries and were receiving our fax messages about the synod.

"It worked. Why, one bishop from Brazil, a man named Joseph Romer, said that the sisters of his diocese didn't know Christian Doctrine and that they were doing incalculable harm. Well, we faxed that to the sisters in Brazil and two days later the sisters in Brazil called upon him to prove his slander or else retract it."

Traxler knows how to organize. She is the founder of the National Coalition of American Nuns (NCAN), a group that works, studies and speaks out on human rights and social issues, which recently celebrated its twenty-fifth anniversary. It is a group that is constantly reminding its members and other listeners to "re-found" religious life. NCAN reminds its members that the state of consecrated virginity was once condemned by the institutional church because such women were not under the control of fathers or husbands. NCAN reminded its members that Archbishop Jan Schotte (now a curial cardinal) chided the sisters because they "were not cooperating with the Holy See" simply because they signed a letter asking for greater representation of women religious at the synod.

"We went to the press conferences at the synod," Traxler continued. "There were six or eight bishops answering questions. They talked around a subject, thinking that they were pulling the wool over our eyes. They avoided the questions they didn't know the answers to. There was one honest man there, Cardinal Hume of Britain. He was asked about the question of equal representation. He answered that he didn't know how the delegates were chosen but that certainly it was a question that deserved an answer. Now, there was a honest man.

"Hume understood the mystery of women. He sensed that the Church is ridiculous until it understands this.

"I think Cardinal Bernardin [another synod delegate] is very good. He's an honest man, a modest and humble man. But he can't do it alone.

The Canadians and the English are good, too. They seem to understand, as they do in their own government, the role of the loyal opposition. But the pope sees such opposition as disloyalty and dissent.

"Oh, those poor old men. They cannot read the signs of the times. Why one, a Filipino bishop—a Franciscan, I think—kept talking about cultural imperialism. He told me that there is no women's liberation movement in the Philippines. Soon after, I found at least four pages of women's groups in the Philippines. Oh, that poor man! He has learned to mouth the things the pope wants him to say.

"It's interesting. The pope has been taking on the Mafia these days. He has gone to Sicily and challenged them, risking his life. Yet, he's the head of a very colorful mafia."

Recently, Sister Margaret learned of the Community of Sant'Egidio, a group that was founded in Italy in the 1968 and that now numbers some fifteen thousand members. The community takes its name from the old Carmelite convent in a small piazza in Trastevere where its members began gathering over twenty-five years ago. They are now in several European countries as well as Africa and Latin America. Their first U.S. foundation has just begun in New York. The group is a contemporary mustard seed, pledged to live their lives in the light of the gospel and the service to the poor. It is now recognized by the Vatican as a Public Association of Laity, although it has a few members who are priests or religious.

Cardinal Carlo Maria Martini of Milan, bishop of the world's largest diocese with eleven hundred parishes, has written of them: "What impresses about Sant'Egidio is its unique integration of a profound sense of prayer and Scripture with an intelligent commitment to the poor and to difficult issues of social justice." The goals fit Margaret Traxler's vision perfectly.

Sant'Egidio has had its critics. They claim that it has erected parallel structures to existing ones rather than collaborating with other groups. However, as theologian Robert P. Imbelli, writing in *Commonweal*, states: ". . . by design, Sant'Egidio reaches out precisely to those not in the mainstream of parish life: the marginalized and the alienated. Their very charism consists in stretching established institutional boundaries."

"Groups like this are the signs of the times," Traxler continued. "They're coming here to Chicago, near the University of Illinois's Circle Campus. They'll attract young people and be a good counterpoint to Opus Dei."

Sant'Egidio is an ideal model for Margaret Traxler who has her own genius for well-organized chaos. She believes strongly that, while independence can cause a measure of confusion, it is essential to growth and gospel values. The Maria Shelter, which houses some fifty women and their children in what was once St. Carthage Elementary School, has its rules. But it is open twenty-four hours each day, seven days a week to receive women who have no place to go. Most of the residents come through agencies or the prison system, but referrals often come from the cops on the beat who can't penetrate the bureaucracies of other agencies. (The police brought one woman, who seemed to be lost, to Traxler's door. She was dressed casually and was carrying a back pack. "Oh, you're so lucky," Traxler told her. "We have just one more bed." As it happened the woman was a representative of a large foundation. She was in the neighborhood to check out the Maria Shelter for a possible grant. Traxler's initial response most likely assured the award.)

In 1992, Traxler found an unused convent not far from the Maria Shelter. "I begged Cardinal Bernardin for it," she said. "He answered that I didn't have to beg in order to do God's work. He gave it to us. So, we put on a new roof and installed a new furnace. Now, we are housing twenty women. They're poor but they're all working full time. They pay a nominal fee which we use to pay for food and utilities. Women can stay there for as long as two years."

Few things irritate Sister Margaret more than the assumption that the poor are lazy, shiftless, and indifferent. "We must take care of the poor," she says. "They are our family." She bristles at the notion that the poor are draining America's resources. In fact, welfare amounts to less than 5 percent of the federal budget, a fraction of what is spent on military weapons. The problem of poverty grows even worse as people continue to live longer and the new administration pledges to cut subsidies to the poor. The political rhetoric is salted with racism. It equates poverty with lawlessness and cries for more prisons. Meanwhile, while a free market economy has become the new religion, nearly 50 percent of those who go to bed hungry each night are children.

MARGARET TRAXLER WAS BORN IN ST. PAUL, Minnesota, and raised in nearby Henderson, where her father was a physician. She entered the School Sisters of Notre Dame in 1941 while in her late teens. She taught elementary school for two years before teaching high school and later college at Mount Mary College in Milwaukee. She enjoyed high school and college teaching. It gave her an opportunity to press for integration in the schools and to imbue her students with social justice.

She joined the Catholic Interracial Council and, later, when a position as director of education opened at the National Catholic Conference for Interracial Justice in Washington, D.C., she applied. She spent the next seven years in Washington working with one of her heroes, Matt Ahman, a prophetic layman who organized the first Conference on Religion and Race in 1973. The experience exposed her to a bewildering and depressing variety of social problems that only served to sharpen her spirit.

Now, just a few days after resigning as the chief administrator of the Maria Shelter and its allied programs, she reflected on her place within an institution that has been both cruel and kind to her.

"I can't understand Dorothy Day," she said. "She was so faithful to the bishops and I won't be. I will if they are leading according to the Spirit, but so many are not.

"Dorothy wouldn't take money from the government. We do. We get a third of our income from the government. We should. The people we take care of belong to all of us, not just to the Democrats."

In 1973, the United Nations declared the Decade of Women. Traxler decided that she would have to get something in place. So, she founded the Institute of Women Today and began her mission of helping poor women and their children. "We empower [a favorite term] women. We make it possible for them to get education, jobs and housing, and the training they need for independence."

In 1982, the institute founded Sister House, its first shelter. It is now an independent entity. Not long after, she acquired St. Carthage and the Maria Shelter was underway.

The entire operation is run by an ecumenical group of women—only two men are employed to do the heavy lifting of food cases at the food depository. On Wednesday mornings, the line stretches the length of Yale Avenue as people line up for boxes of food.

The shelter staff is a mix of professionals—Traxler's replacement as the new director is a clinical psychologist, for example—and former residents. The shelter gets three or four referrals a week, mostly from prisons, police, firemen, hospitals, and the Department of Human Services. The Head Start Program prepares the smaller children for the neighborhood public schools which bear the ironic titles of Harvard and Yale. "They are smart kids," Traxler said. "They really want to learn. It's hard to get them to take a shower in the morning because they are so anxious to go to school."

Now Margaret Traxler will revert to her job as director of the Institute of Women Today, a post she has functionally held for two decades. A major part of her job will involve raising at least $250,000 annually to keep the shelter and its affiliates going. She finds begging hard, but is true to her axiom about following the Spirit.

"You have to want this work," she said. "You can't be in religious life for forty years and then shift into this work. The Holy Spirit has to lead you. Besides, if you have ever been poor in your childhood, it's very hard to choose real poverty. That's why I don't like to say anything about other religious and what they are doing. They're doing the best they can do. Why, I was going to live over there [at the shelter] but I was told that I would never get other religious to live with me. And they were right."

Traxler's enterprise is officially disconnected from the church but it is not a hostile situation. Catholic Charities is involved in food distribution, and the Catholic school system works with Operation Head Start. Critics claim that the official isolation is caused by conflicts regarding birth control and abortion. Traxler denies this. "I'm not silent about how I feel about a woman's right to choose. I'm tired of all this fuss over abortion. Our women don't choose abortion; they want children. We don't do anything here that the Church would not approve of. We do have people of many faiths. We do lay out the options and leave the decision to each of them. Our nurse is a fine Catholic woman, an active parishioner in her parish, but she wouldn't come here until she knew that we respected a woman's right to choose."

Sister Margaret isn't certain about the future of religious life. Only this: that it will be men and women, married and single, working for the poor and basing their life on Scripture—much like the Sant'Egidio community. "The new congregations will be living low-profile lives," she said, "lives that are based on Matthew 25. ('Amen I say to you, whatever you did for one of these least brothers of mine. . .')

"Some [present-day] religious can't change. Change brings ambiguity and some are just too inhibited to do that. That's human nature. But new generations are coming.

"I can't see myself returning to the motherhouse. But who knows? I may become handicapped or ill. As long as I can work at a desk, I'd like to stay here. I just hope they'll save me a room at Casa Notre Dame. I could live out my days there. But when I die, I'd like to be buried with my sister [another member of the Congregation] at the motherhouse.

"The Holy Spirit is in charge. The Holy Spirit will change the Church and the world. Just now, I believe that I'm called to keep doing what I am doing."

10

Charles Schutt:
Marketing Jesus

C harlie Schutt would make Niccolo Machiavelli nervous. He is an ecclesiastical Dennis the Menace, a priest who can make his bishop lunge
for his crozier and start swinging it in circles, lest Charlie get any closer.

Charlie Schutt is also a spellbinding homilist. He can make the
Scriptures dance. He is a gifted liturgist and a priest who knows how to
work the curb after Mass. People call St. Clement's to ask when Charlie
will be on for Mass. Engaged couples ask for him to do their nuptials.
Before the final blessing at Mass, he introduces people, congratulating
them on their birthdays while he leads applause and the cited parishioner
giggles. He has a touch. Charlie Schutt may make his superiors nervous,
but his parishioners love him.

A few years ago, Father Schutt persuaded Cardinal Joseph
Bernardin, his bishop, to let him take a sabbatical in order to complete
his M.B.A. at Northwestern University's prestigious Kellogg Graduate
School of Management. Sabbaticals generally go to priests who are pursuing pastorally related subjects. Schutt's chosen field was marketing,
specifically marketing Jesus and the Church. In church parlance, it's
better known as evangelization. But his proposal didn't fit the rather
narrow definition of pastoral interests. Conceivably, a priest could get
time off to study the history of church vestments, but marketing methods, taught at one of the country's best business schools, fell outside
the ecclesiastical pale.

In fairness, Charlie got more time off than the average student-
priest. He did as well as those who go to Rome to study canon law and
who come home well versed in church law and politics—baby bishops
on the episcopal track. Two years is a long time in a church chronically
short of priests. Charlie really couldn't complain—and he didn't.

Schutt, who has left a succession of pastors searching for an old cincture with which to garrote him, got this sabbatical on condition that he support himself while learning about marketing. He does so with weekend help-out work at St. Clement's and by doing weddings and funerals at some of his former parishes. Church demographics show that parishioners often grow old with their parishes. Their children move away but the parents remain in their brick bungalows with the statue of the Blessed Mother under the bay window until they die. The process causes some parishes to have upwards of a hundred burials a year. For Charlie, the modest stipends help to pay rent and tuition. Northwestern's tuition keeps pace with its high academic status. Although he had some investment income and got some help from the archdiocese, his M.B.A. left him at least $5,000 in debt.

Charlie Schutt also waits tables at a neighborhood restaurant. For other graduate students, such efforts are both routine and laudable. But the notion of a priest waiting tables in a popular restaurant, patronized by parishioners and the occasional diocesan priest, rattles sensibilities.

Clericalism, or at least a clerical culture, has driven out the worker priest, once popular in France and a few other countries. In the United States, following World War II, one could find pockets of "Mass priests," especially in urban areas. They were generally rather poorly educated priests with few prospects in their home diocese, who had immigrated to the United States and found work as skilled laborers and Sunday Mass priests in ethnic parishes. European seminaries, especially those that crowded Italy, were terribly suspicious of well-educated candidates, unless they were well-connected. (Pius XII and Paul VI are good examples of the well connected; John XXIII represents the "worker" priest.)

Not many years ago, the Church ordained some priests *ad patrimonium sui*, loosely speaking, as their own boss, without being tied to a diocesan bishop or religious order. The vast majority were ordained ad titulum servitii ecclesiae, again loosely speaking, as servants of the Church or property of the diocese. It meant that they were tied to their bishop. The new Code of Canon Law, promulgated in 1983, has wiped out the former title. Today, all diocesan priests are linked to a bishop, generally their local one. Charlie might have had better luck as a free agent, but such souls don't enjoy the altar-to-the-grave care that the bishops' servants get.

The practice of accepting candidates with only a fifth-grade education said something about the low esteem in which the higher clergy held their profession. It also insured a measure of control. John XXIII was ten when he entered the seminary; Pius XII and Paul VI were teenagers but studied at home, amid upper-class comforts.

Regrettably, many of the Vatican's rules governing seminary education were devised in Rome with fifth-graders in mind. It severely hobbled American seminary education and culture.

In any case, a growing number of priests are now involved in weekday pursuits in secular professions. In Chicago, where Charlie waits tables, there are diocesan priests working as civil lawyers, psychologists, and professors. One is an executive of a cosmetic company. But Charlie Schutt, the waiter, unnerved some clerical observers.

It was Charlie's hope to work for the Church as a marketing professional. He could have fit well into an office of evangelization, but the other ingredients of chancery culture were missing. A high-ranking chancery official dubbed him "a loose cannon," a description that wounded Charlie, who is more sensitive that he would like to admit.

In 1994, Charles Schutt had completed a research project for his seminar under Professor Sidney J. Levy, one of Kellogg's big hitters. Schutt took a long look at the Catholic Church using the latest tools of qualitative market research. He wanted to find out what Catholics were buying about the Church and why they were buying it. He wanted to learn how the Church could better market its product to its target audience.

"I wanted to find out what people do when they get home from work," he said. "Why . . . they do the laundry," his mentor, Professor Levy, said, half in jest, half in earnest. Schutt was thinking of the myriad other activities in which people involve themselves—support groups, health clubs, encounter groups, political clubs, investment groups, book clubs, and the like. He especially wanted to measure the impact of his church against the plethora of spiritual groups—those who meditate, chant, practice tai-chi or any other activities that are competing for the American soul. "I wanted to ask why people involve themselves in these activities and groups," he said. "I wanted to know what they are buying and why they are buying—or not buying—it. And finally, I wanted to find out how the Church can better market its product to the spiritual consumer."

When applied to the Church, Schutt's language seems foreign. But that is precisely his point. It's possible that the Church has lost touch with the very mechanisms that move institutions toward a continued life.

Schutt used a variety of projective methodologies favored by business. The techniques were applied through in-depth and group interviews, mailed questionnaires, and about 150 projective research stimuli forms that were left in the back of the church.

It wasn't a perfect sampling but the respondents took it seriously. They were largely young Catholics, perhaps twenty-five to forty-five, who were not put off by the jargon of business or its information-gathering methods.

Technique "A" announced that the Church was dead. Respondents were asked to write an obituary. Some filled three pages.

The findings:

The Church had died following a long illness. It suffered from hardening of the arteries, malnourishment, stagnation, attitude-sclerosis. "She died in her sleep," one respondent concluded.

"They didn't see the death as something unexpected or shocking," Schutt concluded. "It was inevitable, yet preventable." The long-term causes were a fear of change, narrowing of vision, and increased deafness to pains in her body, combined with a closed mind and heart, an inability to take in fresh air, and a refusal to avail of modern treatment. "She refused all medicine and therapy, choosing instead to deny and to blame," they concluded.

The respondents stated more than once that the Church refused to either acknowledge any disease or illness and also refused any treatments. One respondent went so far as to state that the Church had really been dead for a while. "The Church has been dead for some time. But like Mrs. Bates of *Psycho* [a Hitchcock thriller], she has been propped up as if she were alive."

Again, they were serious. The obituaries also praised the Church as a loving mother, a force for good, a champion of the needy, a contributor to learning, a caring home. Some, indeed, refused to see the Church as dead. And virtually all were referring only to the institutional church.

There was very little bitterness found in the survey. As Schutt concluded: "There was much analysis about past situations and current conditions but always with an understanding heart and pen." There was much wry humor—vignettes of the pope calling a press conference to announce the death of the Church while still reiterating the institution's teaching on birth control.

Among the responses were several references to the fear that the Church had of its own people. Basically, the Church was viewed as an institution that needed to be dragged kicking and screaming into the twenty-first century.

Father Charles Schutt was ordained in 1977 after twelve years in the seminary system of the archdiocese of Chicago. Of German-Polish extraction, he attended a local public elementary school in St. Ferdinand's Parish, a mixed-ethnic, blue-collar parish of thirty-four hundred families that had enough clout to have a sizable clerical staff and a bishop as pastor for at least eight years. It was a parish ordained to produce vocations. Schutt was among them but states with warm humor, "I'm my mother's vocation."

At Quigley High School Seminary, he was immensely popular but always in trouble. Schutt has a twinkle in his eye that suggests a knowing manner, but part of his manner stems from a certain naiveté that gets him in hot water. Typically, as president of his class at Quigley, he was asked to greet the late Cardinal John Cody, who was making a rare visit to the school. On behalf of the student body, he presented the cardinal with a spiritual bouquet and a bottle of good Scotch. He was blissfully unaware that the cardinal had a reputation for drinking. The often paranoid cardinal took it as an insult. Schutt got twenty demerits (twenty-five meant dismissal) and a warning from the rector that became a chant in his life: "Don't you *ever* do *anything* without permission again!" In fact, Schutt was terribly hurt. He had paid for the Scotch out of his own pocket. Privately, he cried for days. He learned, too, the workings of a top-down church. Innocent or not, he had no defenders.

The survey's respondents were better educated, better employed, better housed that your average lunch-bucket Catholic. Most likely, the majority were women who, with unborn children inside them, will determine the future of the Church. Their responses echoed a population that has an almost endless list of other options which compete for their time. They can turn to yoga or tai-chi or join an ad hoc meditation group that doesn't finger-wag.

Yet the respondents failed to grasp the fact that they were the Church. They still saw leadership coming from the hierarchy. When Schutt suggested to the women that they "might consider boycotting Sunday Mass until the pope changed the ground rules on the ordination of women," they were mildly shocked. "Charlie, a woman can't cut herself off from the Eucharist just to make a point," one woman said. Yet her own anger on the ordination issue was near the boiling point. "You nearly crossed a line," another woman said. Charlie's response was that he was simply making a point about ownership.

Part of the lack-of-ownership feeling may be traced to their own views on their religion. Some admitted that attitudes had been inherited from their parents who likened religion to mountain climbing. Very few respondents stated that religion tied their lives together. Rather, in Schutt's analysis, "one almost got the impression that religion was a condiment for food flavoring or a particular exercise regimen."

The responses to the sentence completion section were pragmatic and direct. Thus, the Church should:

- allow women to be priests,
- allow clergy to marry,
- accept and bless the sanctity of homosexual relationships,
- encourage reproductive responsibility (contraception as well as abstinence.)

The same stems elicited responses that claimed that the Church was simply out of touch:

- The Church should come into the twenty-first century . . . should wake up to the reality of the times. . . should let go of patriarchy and grant all people dignity and equality. . . should see that it is losing people because of its undemocratic ways.

The typical churchgoer:

- is neither especially virtuous or bad, she/he is every person with all the virtues and all the warts. . . attends out of habit or obligation. . . has not been led to internalize the message of Jesus. . . does not realize what it means to be truly Catholic.

I dislike the Church:

- when it asks me to grovel. . . . because it is often hypocritical and closed-minded and self-righteous. . . . because it can be very stringent in its doctrine. . . . whenever I read another pronouncement from Rome about birth control, women's issues, etc. . . . when it is too clerical, too absorbed with power, too anti-women.

The remaining eight years of Charlie Schutt's seminary education were almost as bumpy. "It was a post-Kennedy era and a post-John XXIII era," he said. "I wanted to do all kinds of things. I thought of the Peace Corps, social justice issues—everything."

His first assignment, to a large suburban parish, lasted seven years. Like most priests' first assignments, it remains one of his favorites. "After St. Celestine's," he said, "the assignments came faster and faster. I went to St. John's in Streamwood because no one else would go there. The pastor was dying. In fact, he did die and I wound up in charge. It was a mess. There were twenty bank accounts and a bunch of permanent deacons preaching fundamentalism. I tried to change them, but they just didn't get it.

"Then, there was Our Lady of Mercy, a parish with forty different nationalities, followed by Sacred Heart in Englewood, an all-black parish, St. Raymond's in Mt. Prospect, and St. Martha's in Morton Grove. When I started my M.B.A., I looked for a parish that was alive and vibrant and had some young people who still cared about the Church. So, I came to St. Clement's. That's seven parishes in sixteen years!" (Most associates would be on only their third assignment by then; many would have been named pastors.)

"I was received very well at St. Clement's," he continued. "It's a wonderful parish, a place where I could search for connections between people's faith and their work lives. Sadly, I didn't find much connection. You know, religion is just life's software. I should have found something more there. We've got to strengthen that work-faith connection."

Schutt was well-received at Northwestern. "I came to know the other students. They understood that I was a priest. That didn't bother them. In fact, they told me their stories. It was a good two years."

The survey respondents evoked a strong desire to eliminate the negative aspects of their relationship with the Church. But with few exceptions their affiliation with the Church was pretty loose. "Their responses would be a challenge to the leadership of any organization," Schutt concluded. "Either the mission or purpose has not been adequately communicated or there are many messages regarding exactly what that purpose is or should be."

Even the message of Jesus was clouded. Most indicated that it centered on love. But their responses failed to focus the word "love" on a particular kind of behavior. There was a certain "New Age" aspect to the concept of love, one that is difficult to pin down.

When asked how they would act as image consultants for the Church, they suggested that the Church should emphasize its spiritual benefits, its awareness of the diversity of cultures, and its need to send a clear, unambiguous message about its central themes and purpose. "Get your message out there," one wrote. "The mainstream press thinks that the only good news is bad news. They're making the Church out to be an ogre and it's not."

Yet another "consultant" said: "Sorry, we can't work with your attitude of 'Let's have things the way they are. Just polish our image.' No hard feelings. Let's do lunch."

"The first thing you do is decide what you want to be," Consultant No. 11 wrote. "Either you are the stuffy, censorious, forbidding old aristocrat . . . or the extravagantly loving, colorful, forgiving and inviting mother you act like in other times. Make up your mind."

Charlie Schutt has found his church to be both censorious and loving. In recent years, it has become so monolithic that free spirits such as he is can find little breathing room. Ironically, the rigid style of earlier days gave more room for characters to develop. One only had to observe the external rules, it seemed. Priest candidates were on hold through all the years of their "training," as it was commonly referred to. Once in a parish, they had a certain free reign to develop their eccentricities. Today, an expanded structure to assist priests in their work and personal lives may be too tight, too dependent on "downtown." Presently, a pastor writing something challenging in his parish bulletin can expect a call from "downtown" for clarification. It is as if the Church had invented the "politically correct" language syndrome. Staff people at pastoral centers routinely follow up on every letter received, often simply to protect their own careers. The result is that a statistically insignificant group of arch-conservative laity can hold a chancery hostage.

During a Sunday homily, if Charlie Schutt says dramatically—and emotionally—"Let Jesus hide in the human heart. That's the last place they'll look!" he's likely to get a call about his loose cannon rhetoric. The irony is that dried-up priests who have read nothing since their seminary days can hold forth against the modernist heresy and hear nothing.

Charlie is the ecclesiastical equivalent of the Spanish *picaro*, the likable rogue. Even his superiors like him, though, at times, they would like to throttle him. Asked about him, one bishop just rolled his eyes and smiled, as if Charlie were Maria in *The Sound of Music*.

An intriguing projective technique used in the study gave the respondents a handful of "stems" on which to hang impressions. Thus, "If the Church was an animal, what would it be?" The main image was one of a lion—"powerful, pompous, feared and respected [but also] royal, dignified, confident." Lambs didn't come out well at all.

Asked what color the Church would be, the answer was white—suggesting everything from virginal to transcendent. As for a place, the answers—pardon the pun—were all over the map. One interesting connection was Guatemala—"magnificent landscape, horrible human rights record, embraces various cultures but oppresses the poor." However, at a discussion session Charlie held in the parish following the completion of this project, there was little support for this view. The young parishioners seemed to feel that the Church did more than its share of demanding peace and justice.

As an article of clothing, the Church emerged as a coat—evoking warmth, protection, and perhaps some prominence or position. As music, the answers were mixed, everything from Gregorian chant to the earthy sounds of *Carmina Burana*.

As a period of history, the Church most resembled the Renaissance, although some saw it as the Inquisition and the Dark Ages. As a store, it was described as Chicago's Marshall Field's—a massive seventy-two-acre downtown department store with branches everywhere.

As a feeling, the Church touched every emotion: agony, anxiety, trapped, stretched, powerful but also peace, quiet, somber, mystery, hope.

The Church is seen as a poor salesman. It would sell used cars, non-creative articles, and vacant lots. As a car, the images were uniformly big—dark and safe limousines. The buildings cited as examples of the Church as an edifice were all grand and prominent.

As furniture, the Church was described in warm terms as a couch or a large easy chair—a place for relaxation, sleep, dreams, good times, intimacy.

"Charlie's strong suite is liturgy," an admiring priest friend said of him. "His weak suite is . . . organization. He just can't finish things."

"This is a era of group decision making," he continued. "That process only frustrates Charlie; he doesn't organize well in advance; he sees solutions before his people do. Then he can become a real dictator."

"The people who come to hear him only on Sunday love him," the priest said. "But active parishioners who must work with him see him differently."

Schutt himself admits that he tends to get enthusiastic about things. For a while, it was Panama and the archdiocese's mission there. Then it was Carl Jung and, later, Joseph Campbell. Now it's marketing. He is a man of unlimited enthusiasms but, by his own admission, has difficulty settling down. He just can't sit still long enough.

For over six years, he has been in therapy in an honest effort to sort out the furniture that clutters his mind. His parishioners have been the beneficiaries of the process. His self-insights strike a familiar chord with his listeners, but he has trouble putting the insights into practice in his own life. He's a Pied Piper.

Schutt has a good understanding of who he is and what he should be. But he can't seem to make the change.

"He loosens up the soil," another priest friend said. "He's just not good at tilling it. He doesn't have the patience. But he's an enormous talent. I'm just not certain that the Church can make room for him—and that's sad."

Asked what would happen if the Church dated Jesus, the respondents concluded that the two had very little in common. The Church, it seemed, would be pressing its own agenda all evening. Indeed, it wasn't considered likely that the Church would even ask Jesus for a date. "At dinner, Jesus would probably order a healthy meal while the Church ordered beef Wellington and pie." Another suggested that after dinner, "We would probably attend a play about a schizophrenic mother."

Virtually all who answered the Jesus–Church date question painted a pretty grim picture. "Throughout the evening," one respondent said, "the Church kept telling Jesus what he had said and what he meant without letting Christ speak for himself."

"The Church had become too clinging and unsure," another respondent concluded. "The evening ended early. Jesus didn't even promise to call."

There was much more. Indeed, the survey was too long. Charlie would have gotten more responses if he had kept it shorter. But it's doubtful that he would have gotten the depth that he did from the 35 percent who did reply.

The implications drawn from the findings were a mixture of hope and despair. Among them:

- Although it has been thirty years since Vatican II, during which Catholics were told "the people are the Church," even liberal Catholics still see the hierarchy and the institution as the Church.

- The official Church is seen as "deaf, myopic, unfeeling and out of touch." Its credibility would improve measurably if it would listen more to the people in the pews.

- "Cafeteria Catholics" are not new. Catholics have always chosen what dogmas, teachings, and practices they will live out.

- The Church has been a vibrant and strong voice for the underprivileged, the weak, and the powerless, but it has been just as strong and recalcitrant in its inability to implement reform and justice within its own structure.

- The Church can no longer count on people coming to it for guidance. It is now just one of the competing voices pleading for the attention and contributions of the community.

- With all its weakness and duplicity, the Church maintains a preeminence and prestige in the hearts, minds, and imaginations of its members. Catholics still look to the Church for guidance on spiritual matters but not on pelvic issues.

- Reasons for belonging to the Church are "viscerally strong" and "intellectually weak." Catholics are attracted to the Church because of its rituals, pageantry, mystery, and transcendence, those intangibles that address sight, sound, touch, taste, smell, and imagination. (At the wrap-up session, however, respondents insisted that the emotional stems of the survey evoked emotional responses and that the Church was strongly intellectual.)

- Affiliation with the Church is local. The parish, not the Vatican, is the link.

- The Church's spiritual message is not communicated well. It is often unclear and unfocused. There is a definite lack of understanding, even for high-profile Catholics.

- The codependent posture and activities of its members continue to allow for a dysfunctional system in the Catholic Church.

ST. CLEMENT'S IS CROWDED on Sundays. It is filled with a mix of people high on the value food chain who would rather fight than switch, souls who are trying to balance their faith life and their checkbook. Some have given up hope but not belief. They seem to be telling the Church that she has turned an enriching process into a disabling process. But they still believe that it can bring people together to talk and to listen and to accept each other.

Charlie Schutt got an "A" for the course. Soon after he received his M.B.A. from Northwestern, he visited the pastoral center and spoke with Cardinal Joseph Bernardin about a job within the Church that would allow him to use what he had learned. "We're reaching only 25 percent of our target audience in Chicago," he told the cardinal. "There are things we can do."

The cardinal was gracious and caring but had nothing to offer. He knew Charlie well and the cardinal is a cautious man. "If I were a pastor, I'd love to have you as an associate," the cardinal told him. He even offered Charlie a clear shot at a parish. But Schutt has hopes of doing bigger things with his newly minted degree and the insights he has gotten through this study. They parted cordially.

After seventeen years in the priesthood, Fr. Charles Schutt is now on an indefinite leave of absence. A report on his study appeared in the *National Catholic Reporter*. It brought inquiries from two publishers and a cassette producer. Schutt hopes to round out the study and turn it into a book and a cassette series which he has tentatively titled *Marketing Jesus*. Meanwhile, he has found a job with a small consulting firm. It isn't likely that he will return to active ministry.

11

Arthur Falls:
Believing That "Catholic"
Means "Universal"

———◦•◦———

While Dorothy Day, perhaps the most influential American Catholic woman of this century, was "on pilgrimage," as she used to describe it, she visited a Catholic Worker house in Chicago, where she had spent much of her youth. As co-founder of the Catholic Worker movement, Day was a living legend to all who cared about social justice.

The details are sketchy now, but, while in Chicago, Day injured her arm. It required a brief hospitalization, so she was brought to a nearby Catholic hospital. The religious sisters who staffed the hospital were in a flutter over this icon who represented their most deeply felt values. She was New Testament faith personified. They would be honored to treat her.

Day was asked if she had a private physician in the area whom she might wish to consult. She replied that she had. So Dr. Arthur G. Falls was called and asked to come to the hospital's emergency room.

Dr. Falls came because Dorothy Day, along with Peter Maurin, the other co-founder of the movement, represented the Catholic faith as he had envisioned it. But he was concerned.

When he arrived at the hospital, whatever anxiety he may have felt shifted to the sisters. A role model had arrived at their hospital with a broken arm. Of course, they would treat her with great care and without fee. But her physician was black. No matter that he was Catholic and active in Chicago's Catholic Worker Movement. This Catholic hospital, in common with all others, did not allow black doctors on its staff. There was, after all, no real need. Colored doctors treated colored patients in colored hospitals. "They were there and we were here," Dr. Falls said. Segregation was so simple that even a bigot could understand it.

Dr. Falls's memory is fading. But, he remembered that after some discussion, he was permitted to treat Day, although a white physician had to admit her to the hospital. Except through an emergency room, physicians can admit patients only if they are staffed at a given hospital. In such cases, the physician on duty in the emergency room does the admitting. In this case, the procedure nicely masked the fact that Dr. Falls would never be staffed at the hospital and that none of his patients would be admitted. (White doctors could admit the rare black patient; never the reverse.)

It all went well and Day was grateful for the care and the fact that, with her broken arm, she had torn down a wall as thick as an Old Testament temple.

But her victory was short-lived. After she left the hospital, Dr. Falls waited a decent interval and then applied for staff status at the hospital. Such a designation means that he could refer and treat patients at the hospital that was justly proud of its crucifixes in every room. He was turned down. So were his black patients. "I could get a white patient in a Catholic hospital," he recalled years later. "But to do so I had to get a white colleague to admit the patient and do the treatment. The hospitals were worse than the churches and the schools."

"The time is not opportune," the official church used to say when confronted by these moral outrages. "The time was never opportune," Dr. Falls recalled with a hoarse laugh. "But let me tell you this. Segregation is always a conscious thing. It's not just a way of life or a cultural thing. Those who were responsible for it always knew what they were doing. And that included church leaders."

I thought that Dr. Arthur Falls had died. Church historian Steven M. Avella rescued him from obscurity by including him in an excellent history of the Chicago church, covering twenty-five years from 1940 to 1965, and focusing on the lives of two archbishops, Samuel A. Stritch (1940–1958) and Albert G. Meyer (1958–1965). Avella's book, *This Confident Church: Catholic Leadership and Life in Chicago, 1940–1965*, is a study of what he terms "a Catholic community in transition." It chronicles the phenomenal growth of what became America's largest diocese. It tells of seminaries packed with candidates, an evolution from a pious, liturgically impaired church to one of powerful liturgies and standing-room-only churches. It chronicles the birth of lay organizations, the link between unions and the church, and a host of other innovations. The Chicago church also introduced efforts at racial reform but, by and large, the record on race was not a issue that would make thinking Catholics proud.

Arthur Falls suffered in part because he was a Catholic ahead of his time. He was a forerunner of an ecclesiastical civil rights movement that would not flower fully until the sixties. There were efforts on behalf of integration as far back as the Civil War. Typically, in Falls' younger days, he was affiliated with the Federated Colored Catholics, a group formed from the earlier Committee for the Advancement of Colored Catholics. The federation was organized by Howard University biology professor Thomas Wyatt Turner in 1925. It invited white clergy and laity as associated members, an inspired move at a time when no lay Catholic organization would admit blacks. There were white priest-leaders such as John LaFarge, S.J., and William Markoe, S.J., who endured the ire of their own fellow religious in order to fight discrimination. Falls would recall over sixty years later that he couldn't understand the title "Federated Colored" that preceded "Catholics" in the title. "It should have been just 'Catholics,'" he said, stressing his theme of catholic as universal. He recalled, however, that the federation, which broke up in the early thirties, did some pioneer service. Ironically, although the federation lingered on until 1958, its effectiveness had ended by 1933 when its direction shifted from black solidarity to interracial justice, largely because of the influence of these Jesuits. According to historian Patrick W. Carey, the white presence in the interracial group eclipsed the black solidarity.

"This isn't very Christian," Falls said, "but at one of our meetings, we discussed whether or not there was such a thing as a decent white man." The Federated Colored Catholics eventually evolved into the Catholic Interracial Council of New York, which spread to many other cities, including Chicago, where Falls tried to initiate a chapter. But he never quite succeeded in turning racial justice into a popular movement among Catholics. It's safe to say that Dr. Falls respected Fathers LaFarge and Markoe, but he may have considered them too genteel. According to Cyprian Davis, author of *The History of Black Catholics*, La Farge thought that racism could be combatted by good manners and reasonableness. Falls had already been treated with good manners and reasonableness and nothing had changed. He had a file filled with letters like that from church leaders. "The Federated Colored Catholics couldn't stand up to pressure," he said. "Many just backed down." (Thomas Wyatt Turner, founder of the movement, continued to speak out on racial justice. He lived until 1977. At ninety-nine, he received an honorary degree from Catholic University of America, a school he could not enter in the early 1900s.)

"You know," Dr. Falls added by way of explanation, "people who are discriminated against are loathe to discuss it. It's very painful. So, it was very hard to get even colored Catholics to challenge the Church to abide by its own teachings."

Even LaFarge, the immensely effective Jesuit, refused to call segregation a moral offense, at least in his early writings. He pleaded for a "separate but equal" society; Falls wanted integration in everything, especially the Church.

Dr. Falls was born into a church dominated by clergy. In his archdiocese and elsewhere, little would happen until the clergy changed. In Chicago, this would not come until 1936 when seminary education under the legendary Reynold Hillenbrand changed radically. During his eight years as rector of the enormous seminary at Mundelein, Illinois (named for the cardinal after he gave the town a fire engine), he educated a core group of priests who would work tirelessly to effect change. There were earlier individual priests who were in "nigger work"—the common description of the period—but, by and large, an educated, black physician such as Dr. Falls worked alone and often fruitlessly. Segregation was the accepted culture. The colored had their own Catholic church. Typically, when his younger sister decided to enter the convent, her only choice was an African-American congregation in New York. "I don't think that any other option was even discussed," he recalled.

Ed Marciniak, whose roots in church reform and social change trace at least six decades, reviewed Avella's book for the *New Theology Review*. In a particularly painful chapter on race relations, Avella mentioned Arthur Falls, who had almost single-handedly fought for more than four decades against racial discrimination in Chicago hospitals, public places, and Catholic institutions.

I called Ed and discussed the review. When I volunteered that Falls was surely dead, Marciniak corrected me. He gave me an address in Western Springs, Illinois, where Falls had lived since 1952. (I learned that he bought property in this all-white community over forty years ago. When he tried to build on it, he learned that his land had flunked obscure soil tests. He took the case to court and won, but the Chicago suburb harassed him every inch of the way. "They examined every nail that was going into the place," his niece, Vilma Falls Childs, said. "The city claimed that it wanted the house completely fireproof in case neighbors tried to burn it down. They looked for any way to keep my uncle out. It even has a cement roof!")

I called his Western Springs number for nearly two weeks without an answer. (The bunker-like house is now for sale.) Later, my wife had lunch with Patty Crowley and Rosemary Arrott. Coincidentally, Rosemary knew Arthur Falls' sister, Regina Falls Merritt, now living in a Carmelite retirement home. I would learn later that Arthur Falls was one of eight children, six of whom are still alive. "We're all stubborn," he said with a laugh. "I had relatives that lived to be over 100."

Rosemary supplied Regina's phone number and Regina willingly supplied Dr. Falls's new address in a one-pickup-truck town in Lawton, Michigan. I reached Falls through his niece and we arranged an interview at a nursing home where Dr. Falls had been living since 1993.

Ed Marciniak called Msgr. John M. Hayes, an eighty-eight-year-old Chicago priest, who had spent much of his life in "colored work," as the jargon at the time described it. Hayes knew Dr. Falls through the Catholic Worker storefront meeting room on Taylor Street, a place that Falls had established and for which he had paid the rent.

During the nearly three-hour drive to Lawton, Michigan, the two old men gave me a course in Chicago church history. Hayes was ordained in 1931; Marciniak had entered the high-school seminary the year before. Ed spent five years at Quigley Preparatory Seminary before leaving, but he remained tied to the Church for the rest of his life. He protests that he isn't a product of the tight grip of "the Church with the capital 'C,'" but, during one visit to his office, our conversation was interrupted four times by phone calls, all from clergy. Marciniak is a lay activist who has been strongly influenced by the creative leadership of priests like Bernard Sheil, Louis Putz, and Reynold Hillenbrand. But he was just as strongly influenced by Dorothy Day, John McDermott, Pat and Patty Crowley, and his brother-in-law Russell Barta—all leaders in lay ministries that did not wait upon clerical initiatives. He was a popular teacher of urban affairs at Chicago's Loyola University and an expert in city housing. As stubborn in his views as Falls in his, Marciniak is a creative, opinionated double agent for both institutional and lay church.

The two men had keen long-term memories. They could recall, for example, a maverick labor reporter who attempted to track down Cardinal George Mundelein, Chicago's omnicompetent archbishop from 1915–1939. The writer wanted a statement on a particularly bitter strike that was splitting Chicago. He traced Mundelein to New York where the prelate was ensconced in a hotel, preparatory to sailing to Rome. Bishop Bernard Sheil, an activist for many causes but one who always excused lack of social progress with "We've got to be practical," blocked the reporter's way. (Sheil would later say the same thing to Dr.

Arthur Falls.) Voices were raised in the hotel and the reporter ended the discussion by socking Sheil in the jaw. He didn't get his interview.

Driving back to Chicago, the Irish Catholic reporter's conscience got the better of him. He stopped in Detroit, sought out a priest and confessed to socking a bishop—a reserved sin in those days. "The priest gave him three Our Fathers and three Hail Marys," Msgr. Hayes remembered with a dry laugh.

Most of the stories, however, had to do with the racial climate in Chicago and in the nation when Arthur Falls was growing up. Segregation was an integral part of the culture. If one were white, one simply accepted it without much thought. Cardinal Stritch, a native of Tennessee, was often heard to say that "the conversion of colored people was his highest priority." But if someone pressed the issue with him, it would likely become clear that he didn't envision that African-Americans would live, study, or pray in integrated harmony. His predecessor, Cardinal Mundelein, had segregated the parishes even more after the 1919 race riots that saw thirty-nine deaths and a house bombing every twenty days through 1921. Mundelein believed in churches for Negro Catholics—segregated churches.

Only rarely would Cardinal Stritch bring himself to chastise a pastor who used his pulpit to keep blacks out of his parish. Typically, the Garfield Improvement Association was little more than a euphemism for an overwhelmingly Catholic group whose sole focus was to keep blacks out of reach. Clearly, no pastor, however racist, was removed for racism in an era when pastors were plentiful and could be removed for failing to wear their hats when leaving the rectory. In a period when the pastor was the social and political arbiter of all that happened in his parish community, racist priests set the pattern for their followers. There were exceptions. As early as 1901, a black student had been accepted in a Waukegan parish after she had been rejected at the local public school. But such veins of gold were rare.

THE WHITE OAK RETIREMENT HOME is just down the street from a large Welsh's Grape Juice plant, one of the many processing places in the Lawton area that grows commercial fruits in the rich fruit belt near Lake Michigan. It is quiet country, 135 miles from Chicago's South Side, where Dr. Falls practiced for over sixty years. With a physician's practiced eye, Falls had recognized that he needed assisted living and entered the nursing home near his favorite niece. He now lives in a private room in an intermediate care facility that provides three meals in common each day, abundant activities, and medical supervision.

Falls is now a small man, slightly bent with age. Although somewhat feeble, his overall body tone is good. He speaks slowly, only after thinking things over. But when old emotions are aroused, he can become very animated. The fires inside him may be banked by age but they are still there. He has a coffee-with-cream complexion and a largely bald head. He dresses neatly but casually in the comfortable oversized clothes favored by people who no longer have to be pressed. One could call him distinguished, if it didn't seem so patronizing.

Falls is the son of a post office employee and a dressmaker; his parents were Creole Catholics, people descended from or culturally related to the French settlers of the southern United States, especially Louisiana, which still has the largest number of black Catholics in the country. Falls has some family roots around Baltimore, another heavily Catholic populated area dating to post-Revolutionary War times. Born in 1901, he attended public elementary, high school, and junior college before entering Northwestern University's Medical School.

"There was no universal acceptance then," he recalled, repeating his favorite theme. "I was raised to believe that 'Catholic' meant 'universal.' But it doesn't seem to apply. It was a universal church, all right, but 'universal' didn't mean us. The Catholic Church never really welcomed me, but if you believe in something, you have to stick with it."

His parish as a young man was Our Lady of Solace, a small church and school wedged between two thriving parishes, Visitation and St. Brendan's, in Chicago's Englewood area. His first years were at St. Monica's, one of a few parishes exclusively for colored. Later, the family moved to Englewood and Our Lady of Solace. "There was very little solace there," he recalled with a hearty but asthmatic-sounding laugh, the product of an angina condition. He remembered that, while denied entrance to any Catholic elementary school, he could attend Mass. "Officially, we didn't have to sit in a separate part of the church as in some parishes," he said. "But as children we had to go to the children's Mass where the children in the parish school sat together. Since I couldn't get in the parish school, I couldn't sit with them on Sundays. Further, when we went to Confession, whites had their confessions heard first. Each parish had its own ways of telling you that you didn't belong."

"At least he could get into the church," his niece, Vilma Falls Childs, recalled with lingering bitterness. "My parents brought me to four churches before finding a priest who would baptize me. When I was enrolled in St. Margaret of Scotland, the sister principal looked my mother and me over and over. We are light-skinned, so she accepted me.

But when the pastor returned from vacation, he came to my classroom, made me stand up, and said: 'We don't want any niggers in this school and we don't want you in the church.' He threw me out." (Vilma Falls Childs would close her career as principal of a virtually all-white Catholic elementary school. There has been some progress. But the earlier wound still hurts. "You don't get over those things," Dr. Falls said.)

Dr. Falls's parish closed in 1975, long after he had moved to the suburbs. Many of the neighboring parishes closed around the same time. It's a great irony that white observers claimed that the parishes dried up because the majority of blacks were non-Catholics. Dr. Falls views it differently. He was a Catholic who couldn't get into most parishes and their schools because he was black.

When Falls was born, the African-American population in Chicago was less than 2 percent of the total—about forty thousand in a population of over two million. The rising troubles in Western Europe before and after World War I shut off much European migration and opened a path for blacks from the rural south. By 1920, when Falls entered medical school, there were 110,000 Negroes, now over 4 percent of the population. Two decades later, when Samuel Stritch became archbishop, the city was 8 percent black.

Chicago's first African-American priest was Augustus Tolton, ordained in Rome in 1886 at the age of thirty-two. He was the son of two Catholic slaves from Missouri. He was born in 1854, the same year that James Augustine Healy, America's first black priest, was ordained. But Healy and his two brothers—all priests—"passed" as whites. One became bishop of Portland, Maine, and another president of Georgetown University at a time when the D.C. school did not accept blacks. (The third brother died as a young priest.)

Tolton's father escaped to St. Louis and became attached to the Union army. His mother rowed across the Mississippi with her three children to Quincy, Illinois, then crowded with refugee slaves. Tolton's education was hobbled by his need to work in the tobacco factory, but he managed to be tutored by a German priest in Latin, Greek, and German. When no seminary in the United States would accept him, he gained entrance to the Vatican's Urban College with the understanding that he would be ordained for the African missions. Instead, he returned to what is now the diocese of Springfield, Illinois.

Father Tolton lived in fear and loneliness. At a time when clergy tended to socialize only with each other, the "nigger" priest, as he was called, was abandoned by his bishop and ignored by most of the other clergy. In fact, they resented him because, although he had only a handful of black parishioners, a good number of whites attended his Sunday Mass.

When Chicago's Archbishop Feehan agreed to accept him in 1889, he virtually escaped to the larger city, bringing his nineteen black parishioners with him.

Chicago Catholics had been worshiping in the basement of St. Mary's Church since 1880. There may have been one hundred of them. Two years after Tolton arrived, work was begun on what became St. Monica's Church, the first official black parish. According to Cyprian Davis' *History of Black Catholics*, Tolton may have had a regular congregation of 260 black Catholics out of some 500 in the city. He worked among his black parishioners, sharing their poverty, once allegedly living in a storefront.

In 1897, he returned from a retreat in Kankakee and, while walking home, suffered a stroke. One story has it that he was brought to a local Catholic hospital where he was refused treatment. By the time he got to the colored hospital where Dr. Falls would later practice, he was dead. Augustus Tolton was only forty-three.

Four years later, in a city whose first settler was Jean Baptise Point du Sable, a Catholic black man from Haiti, Arthur Falls was born. His life was not too far removed from older black Catholics who once had to ask the permission of their owners to receive Communion.

Catholics had no monopoly on racism. In fact, they may have been slightly less prejudiced than Chicago's Protestants who lived several rungs up the economic ladder and were thus safe from competing for jobs and housing with blacks. Further, there were priests who dedicated their lives to the conversion of African-Americans, if not their inclusion in the city's social fabric.

Integration was made more difficult by the large number of national parishes. Although officially changed from ethnic to territorial parishes, the language barriers lingered.

At Northwestern's Medical School, Falls was largely ignored by his classmates. He had to endure the jokes of the professors. "If you're not sure what to do," they told their students, "go find a nigger and use him as a guinea pig." (After nearly seventy years, the university made amends. In October, 1994, the alumni association honored him and asked him to be a role model to black medical students now young enough to be his great-grandchildren.)

Dr. Falls got his medical license in 1925. He established an office on the South Side, near Provident Hospital, the only hospital that would accept black physicians. It was years later before one Catholic hospital would grudgingly accept black patients, putting them in a large, unused ward, males and females together, with little privacy.

For years Falls bristled under the pressure of prejudice, especially from his church. "My practice was heavily obstetrical," he said. "I was always careful to explain the Church's position on reproductive issues. Then, I asked them to follow their consciences. I never did an abortion in my life. I don't believe in it. I was able to help a good number of women to keep their children. You know, it's much easier to have a position on a moral issue. But this was a church that wasn't universal. It couldn't abide by its own teachings. It just wasn't interested in racial issues. It had no real position."

Dr. Falls believed in the Church's teaching. His mother used to tell him that he should remain a Catholic because he believed in its teachings, regardless of its failure to live up to them. It's a supreme irony that, if the Church had put as much effort into racial equality as it has into the abortion issue, it could have held and increased its black population. Instead, Dr. Falls recalls with sadness, he was asked repeatedly why he remained in a church that closed baptismal, educational, and vocational doors in his face.

Sometime after 1934 Peter Maurin, co-founder of the Catholic Worker Movement, contacted him and invited himself to Falls's home. The aging doctor knew of the movement from a representative of the *Worker* who came to Chicago from New York earlier. Perhaps he read the *Catholic Worker*, a famous one-cent paper, written largely by Day and Maurin. The paper translated Gospel values into everyday living. "Peter Maurin stayed a week in my house. He spoke of a church I never knew before. He told me of a church that might be. It was the church I believed in and had waited for," Falls recalled.

Perhaps Day's leisurely articles, filled with her insightful asides, or Maurin's direct "Easy Essays" inspired Falls's own writings. Whatever the case, he attended meetings in the basement of Old St. Patrick's Church in downtown Chicago, and began sending letters to the *Worker*. His contributions became an regular column, titled "Letter from Chicago."

Dr. Falls wanted a center in which people could gather to discuss issues of social justice. At his own expense, he funded the storefront meeting room in two subsequent locations. He had no quarrel with the better-known Houses of Hospitality that were being opened by Catholic Worker volunteers, but he preferred meeting and teaching facilities that would not only provide the loaves of bread to the needy, but would work to change a society into one that would permit minorities to bake their own bread.

The storefront was unheated, "at least physically," Falls said with more wheezy laughter. "Of course, we were accused of being Communists. We sure had some rousing meetings. We helped people; we even established a credit union."

The early editions of the *Catholic Worker* displayed a masthead showing two workers clasping hands. Both were white. Soon after they appeared, Falls pointed out the anomaly to Day and suggested that one worker be black. She immediately made the change that has endured to this day. Falls understood symbols. He is proud of that logo.

"There isn't a dime's worth of difference between Mundelein and Stritch," Falls said with remarkable frankness when we returned to the institutional church issue. "When you appealed to them, the answer was always the same. They saw themselves burdened with administrative issues that took all their time. They were always going to get to the race issue, but the time was never ripe."

"When I wrote letters or visited the chancery office, I always stated my business right away. Then I ended the letter or I left the chancery. I wasn't looking for anything except the issue. I never tried to push myself on others. But when you are colored, you are always accused of being uppity. I learned a lesson: If you write a letter and get no answer, then the lack of response is an answer. I got lots of non-answers."

In 1941, soon after Stritch was installed, Falls wrote the former bishop of Toledo and Milwaukee in a typically Falls fashion. "On more than one occasion," he wrote, "efforts have been made in Chicago to develop an active Catholic interracial group which would be able to make a distinct contribution to the program of interracial cooperation. . . . I therefore should like to request that Your Highness consider the possibilities of a Chicago Catholic Interracial Council, developed under your auspices. . . ."

Stritch rarely responded directly to letters involving sensitive issues. He was compulsively prudent, at least in the eyes of his admirers. Ordained in 1910, he was a bishop just eleven years later and an archbishop for ten years before coming to Chicago. He would be named a cardinal in 1946 and would rule Chicago with a permissive hand until, in a move still shrouded in secrecy, he was elevated to the Roman Curia. He died in 1958, just two months after his appointment to the Curia.

Stritch was used to being a bishop in a triumphalist church where he seldom encountered direct opposition. He commuted in style between his two Chicago mansions and his third in exclusive—and segregated—Hobe Sound, Florida. He was always accompanied by an entourage, often including a personal physician, who received a papal knighthood for merely monitoring the prelate's grumbling bowels. In his clerically sealed world, he had only to raise his ringed hand to shut off conversation. There were ambitious flunkies to do his dirty work. Against this background, any letter from a lay person would seem uppity. But one from a black man only stirred the larval prejudices deep in his southern gut. It was as if he couldn't help himself. (Once, when boarding a train, he ordered a subordinate who was carrying his luggage to "give the nigger a good tip." He never quite caught on.)

Stritch responded to Falls in a noncommittal way. Privately, according to Avella, he saw a Catholic interracial group as one that might stir up racial troubles. Almost at the same time, he had rejected a petition from the cloistered Dominican sisters who wanted to open a cloistered convent for colored girls. Again, he said, "the time was not opportune."

Between 1946 and 1953, there were six race riots in Chicago. Stritch regretted them but said nothing publicly. After one known as the Peoria Street riot, Falls wrote to him:

"It would not be correct to state that only Catholics have participated in these recurring evidences of group hatred, but certainly Catholics have been most active in them and frequently have been in positions of leadership. The last riot was clearly a reflection of the anti-Negro and anti-Jewish attitudes which for years have characterized the clerical and lay leadership at Visitation Parish. . . ."

The evidence was obvious. News reports showed teenagers wearing Catholic school sweaters taking part. Stritch answered with another "just give it time" letter.

Generally, Stritch assigned someone to answer the doctor's letters. They were masterpieces of obfuscation, promising nothing. "When I used to see Stritch at meetings," Falls recalls, "he would never look at me. He always turned away. The time wasn't ripe." And he laughed again.

Visitation Parish was not far from Our Lady of Solace. Its pastor prided himself on the fact that there were no "colored" in his parish. The annual all-white May procession up Garfield Boulevard was his pride and joy. "He is a magnificent pastor," his fellow priests used to say. "He has only one weakness." The tolerance of the "weakness" is what bothered Dr. Falls. Other moral lapses would have been met with instant dismissal. Instead, pastors who openly fought integration were given only a mild slap on the hand while those who promoted it were bar-coded as troublemakers. The pastor at Visitation, for example, retired and was replaced by another just as racist. The situation festered until the arrival of Cardinal Meyer.

To this day, church watchers still regard Cardinal Stritch as kindly and caring. He was gentle, almost shy. While he had trouble making decisions, he allowed good things to happen, including limited integration. Thus, it was a measure of how deep-seated the anger was when Dr. Falls leaned forward in his easy chair, waved his arthritic hands, now too gnarled to permit him to write, and said: "This is very unchristian of me, but Stritch was a bastard."

For the remainder of his time in office, Stritch assigned a subordinate to answer Falls's pointed letters. Meanwhile, little happened. Stritch did write to Southern bishops, urging them to accept black candidates to their seminaries, but Chicago did not accept its first until 1942. (He was Fr. Rollins Lambert, ordained in 1949.) American bishops as a national body did not speak out on the constitutional rights of African-Americans until the early 1940s and did not make racial discrimination the exclusive subject of a national pastoral until 1958. There was some integration in the elementary schools, virtually none in the high schools or colleges—even in some of the elite, small Catholic colleges. The hospitals remained closed to both black physicians and patients. Again, Falls's colleagues would ask him repeatedly, "Why do you bother? Why remain a Catholic?" "I'm stubborn," he would repeat. "This is supposed to be a universal church."

When Albert Meyer came from Milwaukee in 1958 to succeed Samuel Stritch, he determined to study the problems of Chicago firsthand. He spent much of 1959 visiting every area of the city, from the Gold Coast to the slums, talking to people on the street about the effects of discrimination. He sought the advice of veteran priests such as John J. Egan, head of the Office of Urban Affairs; Daniel Cantwell, chaplain to the Catholic Interracial Council, which had finally been founded in 1946; and Joseph Richards and Martin Farrell, two highly successful pastors of black parishes. Almost immediately, Meyer began to exert pressure on pastors who were dragging their feet on admitting blacks to their parish. He did the same for elementary and high schools and encouraged his priests to participate in local and national civil rights demonstrations. "The heart of the race question is moral and religious," he wrote. "No one who bears the name of Christian can deny the universal love of God for all mankind. Our Christian faith is of its nature universal; it knows not the distinction of race, color, or nationhood."

It was strong stuff, especially when measured against the much softer prose and lack of action by Stritch. Ed Marciniak and John Hayes viewed Cardinal Meyer as a strong leader both in Chicago and at Vatican

II. They were convinced that he made a heroic effort to turn the racial issue on its head. They were surprised, then, when Dr. Falls paused and then said quietly, "I think he was weak."

Perhaps only one who has endured a lifetime of prejudice can make such a statement. During the Meyer years, Falls withdrew from most church issues. He was now into his sixties. "I think my uncle had just grown tired of bashing his head against walls," his niece and godchild said. During Meyer's seven years as archbishop, Falls concentrated largely on integrating hospitals. The Catholic hospitals were private, largely out of reach, even for a bishop's influence. Falls succeeded by threatening to sue the hospitals. To the best of his recollection, he filed only four suits, but the word spread. The larger society was getting the word through the courts.

When Meyer died in 1965, Vatican II had ended; the first civil rights legislation was in place; there was significant integration in the churches and schools and Falls had gained entry to some hospitals for his colleagues and patients.

Meyer's successor, John Patrick Cody (1965–1982), reintroduced the imperial style of George Mundelein. His reign was marked by Romanism, triumphalism, and centralization. Gradually the black belt in Chicago widened. To its credit, the church made genuine efforts to maintain a Catholic presence in the inner city. Long after other mainstream churches, banks, stores, repair shops, and other stable social structures had left the inner city, the Catholic churches remained as long as they could. But they continue today to merge or close.

But by the civil rights era, Arthur Falls had aged. According to Ed Marciniak, he had worked almost single-handedly against racial discrimination in hospitals, public places, and Catholic institutions. "He was a leader in his own right," Marciniak said. "He never became a card-carrying member of the civic or church establishment."

Now, he rests happily in a rural nursing home, looked after by his niece, waiting for God. He practiced medicine until he was eighty-eight, fueled by the stubborn streak of which he remains so proud. Many members of his extended family live in the area and call on him often. He retains a sunny humor, often laughing so hard that he gets short of breath. His wife of over sixty years, Lillian Proctor Falls, died on Easter Sunday morning in 1988. She had been an effective welfare office administrator, supervising over three hundred employees. The daughter of an Atlanta bishop, she never converted to Catholicism. Their only son and grandson live in New Jersey.

From time to time, there are Catholic services in the retirement home. Eucharistic ministers from the local church bring him Communion. Falls walks hesitantly, sometimes using a walker. His niece and godchild looks after his finances. He refuses to have a phone installed in his room. The elderly often have their peaceful years interrupted by calls from investment vultures. He wants peace.

The piece of steel he had in him all those years has begun to bend somewhat. But he's still stubborn—and proud of it. Another priest friend, who remembers him from his Catholic Worker days, confirms the stubborn streak. Asked if an apology from the present archbishop, Cardinal Joseph Bernardin, would mend past hurts, he said: "No, I don't think Arthur would be impressed by that. He was a perfectionist, a lone fighter. He was just too stubborn."

"When he goes to Heaven, I think he would qualify as a martyr," Msgr. John Hayes said. "He certainly has earned it." He was clearly one without honor in his own country, profession, or church. The institutional church owes him an apology, but Dr. Arthur G. Falls had best not wait.

"This is an unchristian thought," Dr. Falls said at the end of our interview. "I hope to live to be a hundred, but when I die I want to go to Heaven and sit next to St. Peter at the Last Judgment and listen to all those explanations about why the time was never ripe."

Then he laughed until his breath grew short again.

12

The Women of CTU

"Evil in the Church arises from authoritarianism, not true authority. The word 'authority' comes from *ab audire*. It means that I move from what I hear within; it is that truth which speaks to me. When I move from the truth that is in me, I hurt no one—but I scare the whole world."

—Irene Dugan, 84

Sr. Irene Dugan is a Religious of the Cenacle, a once-cloistered congregation of sisters best known for their retreat ministry. Since entering religious life in 1938, her career has evolved dramatically. She is still attached to the Institute of Pastoral Studies at Loyola University of Chicago. Because she is now confined to a wheelchair, students come to her convent at the Fullerton Cenacle in Chicago. She is a forerunner to the women of Catholic Theological Union at Chicago (CTU). They, too, move from what they hear within; they, too, scare an awful lot of people.

"It has been a long haul," said one of them, Mary Huffman. "I hope that it's worthwhile." Huffman, of St. Louis, Missouri, matriculated at CTU in 1991. She is in her third year of a four-year program that will award her a master's degree in divinity. She will complete 36 quarter hours common to all M. Div. candidates and 72 quarter hours in one track of a two-track advanced program that is tailored to the needs of lay and religious women and men who will not be ordained. The second advanced track generally adds another year, requiring 105 quarter hours beyond the basic 36, and leading to ordination. This track is closed to Mary and the other seventy-one lay women enrolled in CTU, but she doesn't feel that she is limited. In fact, the women of CTU view the clerical candidates as the ones trapped in an ecclesiastical cul-de-sac.

"I don't have to commit myself to the Church," Huffman said. "I can commit to ministry. I have already experienced church in many other ways than Rome envisions.

"Sure, I'm frustrated with the Church," she continued. "But CTU has taught me that the Church is bigger than that and that we're called to make things better. So, we are quietly pushing forth this vision. We would be living without hope if we just took things the way they are."

"I like it here," she continued. "I like the smallness of this place. I like the multicultural aspect. I like the fact that there are women on the faculty and that they are always trying to bring more women into the school. It's a great place to be hopeful about the Church."

The women of CTU are beyond anger and politics. Like any minority—which they are, practically if not numerically—they are more sensitive. They have a deeper understanding of the dominant male Church which barely bothers to understand them. "Oh, sure, I'm angry," Huffman said. "I have so many friends who have left the Church, and I've had to explain myself so often in the past three years.

"Other women think I'm crazy. They think I'm putting myself in a position to be oppressed. But I'm not going to allow myself to be stomped on. This school has taught me that the Church can be bigger than that. What I want to do doesn't have to be done in a parish."

The presence of women at CTU has made the theologate not only a community of inquiry but a community of faith. They speak a different language and have a different vision. Typically, while Mary was aware that her native see at St. Louis was open, she evidenced no interest in who would succeed the ailing and retired archbishop, John May. "Does it matter?" one of the other students asked rhetorically. "I care who gets St. Louis, but it isn't going to affect what I'm going to do." (In January, 1994, the job went to a conservative Vatican careerist named Justin F. Rigali.)

Huffman is enrolled in a collaborative A.M./M.Div. program with the nearby School of Social Service Administration of the University of Chicago. It will permit her to complete both degrees in one year less than if she had pursued them consecutively. "I wanted to bring both disciplines together," she said. I'd like to do parish work with other M.S.W.'s [Masters in Social Work] in other parishes. I'd like to apply the principles of organizing to revitalize neighborhoods, to make the Church more viable.

"I don't know if I can reform the Church from within," she added, "but the social work degree will give me other options."

It isn't easy. At $215 per credit hour, the seventy-two hours following the foundational courses costs over $15,000, exclusive of the usual nuisance fees and books, as well as board and room. For Huffman, there is the substantial added cost of the M.S.W. degree. She survives on student loans, a Dorothy Day Scholarship, and a grant from Mary's Pence, a program spawned by Chicago's Call to Action which funds projects for women. She has also worked at CTU in research, library work, and old-fashioned maintenance. Presently, she also has a position in retail sales in downtown Chicago.

The economics of earning a degree at a theologate that educates 159 seminarians from the thirty-one participating religious communities, together with 15 from other communities, invites comparisons. It addition, there are 45 women religious, 30 diocesan priests and 44 lay men, making its total enrollment of 356 into the largest theologate in the United States. (CTU accepts ordained diocesan priests only; they don't want hovering bishops. Further, technically CTU is a theologate, not a seminary. Strictly speaking, a theologate is a school of theology in which candidates for the religious priesthood study; a seminary—the word means "seed bed"—educates candidates for the diocesan priesthood.) Religious are supported by their congregations. Lay men and women receive few subsidies. It is a rare parish or diocese that educates its future lay leaders. Those that do spend only a fraction of what they spend on seminary education for their priests. (It is extremely difficult to pinpoint precise costs for a seminary education. Factors such as fund raising, contributed salaries of some faculty, enrollment decreases, cross registration, library and faculty interchange, and expanded use of seminary property all make it difficult. One informed source said that it would be a fair estimate to say that an academic year at a seminary can cost about as much as the same year at the quality university. One estimate says that the final four years of theology now cost approximately $111,500.)

The women of CTU were concerned about the number of Catholic women who have enrolled in seminaries and divinity schools of other Christian faiths. One unconfirmed report said that half of the students at Harvard's Divinity School are women and that 50 percent of those had Catholic roots. Clearly, there are growing numbers of former Roman Catholic women who are now ministers in other faiths. One graduate of the Divinity School at the University of Chicago remains a practicing Catholic while ministering full time in a United Church of Christ parish.

CTU was founded in 1967 by three religious congregations—the Franciscans, Servites and Passionists. Officially, it opened in the fall of 1968 with 108 students and a faculty of 24. It now has sixteen hundred alumni working in sixty countries on six continents. In the past year alone, the number of female lay students has risen from fifty-eight to seventy-two.

No one is quite certain when the first theologate opened its doors to a lay person, but by 1987, 40 percent of the student bodies of the forty-nine Catholic theologates nationally were composed of students who were not preparing for ordination. Nationwide, according to Dr. Joseph O'Hara of the Center for Applied Research in the Apostolate at Georgetown University, there are now some fifty theologates in the United States. "I don't know precisely how many of them accept women," he said. "Some of these are theological unions, so it's hard to trace. But in academic 1993, there were 314 full-time and 833 part-time female students enrolled." O'Hara reported that the number of full-time women has decreased slightly in recent years while the number of part-time female students has increased.

It was the lay students, in fact, that broke down the pervasive isolation that once characterized religious formation. It's likely, too, that lay students helped the theologates by forcing them to become accredited.

Women tiptoed into CTU. First, three came only to audit courses. Then, a clutch of religious sisters enrolled for credit. Finally, in 1972, a lay woman named Alacia Lakey arrived. She wasn't formally snubbed, mostly simply neglected. She got little assistance with course planning or housing. After a year, she transferred to Yale's Divinity School. According to the founding president, Paul Bechtold, C.P., "The tensions were not unlike those that surfaced in the early days among the several faculties of the different religious orders."

Clearly, not everyone at CTU liked the idea of women students. Bechtold recalled: "Some priests were still wedded to the idea of a clerical caste and male superiority." There were concerns about celibacy, already fragile. Some students were concerned about the impact of women in the classroom. Gradually, however, the presence of religious sisters appears to have cleared a path for lay women. From the start, the sisters established the principle that the education of women would be no less inclusive than that of men. Presently, the women of CTU see the challenge from a reverse angle. "It's important for the men being trained here that they come to understand the reality of women," one female student wrote.

Mary Huffman is twenty-nine, younger than most of her female classmates at CTU. The third of seven children, she was a cradle Catholic raised in a thoroughly Catholic home in St. Louis, where her father runs a barge-towing business on the Missouri River. She graduated from St. Mary's, once viewed as the sister school to the University of Notre Dame in South Bend. Mary spent the next three years volunteering with the Holy Cross Associates, two of them in a Catholic Worker community in Phoenix, Arizona.

"For a while, I thought I was going to law school," she said. "It even crossed my mind to become a nun, but it wasn't a strong feeling.

"In Phoenix, I got the idea that I wanted to study theology. So, I wrote to my old theology prof at St. Mary's and he recommended CTU. He said it was a good place for women to be."

Huffman's classmates agree. "It's a great place to feel good about the Church," one said. "It's culturally diverse, and there are at least a dozen women on the faculty who keep us looking beyond the institution into ministry."

"I'm here because one of my recurring dreams is that I'll go to church some day for Communion and it won't be there," Jo Dresden of Aurora, Illinois, said. "It seems as though I'll never get out of here," she added, "but after working at Wal-Mart for years, I had to look at the values in my life. When I get my master's in theology, I'm going into a liturgical consulting program and, if I'm needed, into ministry in my parish."

"I feel the invitation to explore here. My boundaries are tested," said Charlene Klabacha, who commutes from Orland Hills, Illinois, a good hour away. She is a full-time student now but was part-time for nearly five years, working for her master's in pastoral studies. With three children, two of whom are still in school, she will return to be a full-time director of religious education in her parish. "People here are so willing to tell their story," she added. "I feel like a co-learner on a journey."

Even the language of these women is different. In a standard seminary, generally an ecclesiastical pyramid created by a square-jawed bishop with bricks and mortar in his veins, the language of these women would sound hokey. But their use of words such as "co-learner," "discernment," and "journey," represent an entirely new way of looking at their theological quests. It is a far cry from the militaristic language of the old seminaries whose bulletins sounded more like army training manuals.

"This isn't a seminary," Tina Moreau of Massachusetts said. "This is a school of ministry. The faculty doesn't even use the word 'seminary.' We even have lots of non-Catholics." (Chicago has become one of the largest centers of theological education in the world. It has twelve seminaries with over four thousand students and a faculty of over four hundred. At least four other theology schools are within walking distance of CTU and seven others are part of a collaborative association. The interlibrary loan program alone gives CTU access to 1.2 million volumes in theology and allied fields.)

Moreau worked in church-related programs in Bolivia and Haiti before coming to CTU. She wrote to some twenty theologates before enrolling in CTU's world mission program.

"This place will give me more credibility," Kara McBride, at twenty-four, the youngest of the students interviewed. McBride, whose mother is also a CTU alumna, expects to complete her M. Div. in 1995. She graduated from the College of St. Thomas in Minnesota and spent at year at Chicago's Amate House, a sanctuary for recovering addicts, before coming to CTU.

"I can't picture myself graduating," she said lightly. "But if I do, I'll have some background. I can go toe-to-toe."

McBride was part of CTU's program in Israel, one dominated by male seminarians. "They couldn't use inclusive language if they tried," she said with youthful exaggeration. "So I just told them that they simply couldn't understand what it's like to be on the outside. At least twelve priests stopped talking to me."

"At one Mass by the Sea of Galilee," she continued, "I was asked to arrange the chairs while a seminarian was asked to do the reading. But by the end of the summer, at least one priest was saying in strong language that he also objected to the oppression of women."

On balance the women of CTU have few complaints about oppression. "I'm respected and challenged," Tina Moreau said. "I'm looked upon as an equal." Any male-female tension seemed to be in line with comparative ages. The younger women sensed more repression and were more outspoken about it, largely because young people are simply more outspoken. The older women were more maternal in their judgments or else they simply by-passed the male-female issue on their way to ministry. All agreed that the theologate was making trend-setting efforts to overcome societal and institutional sexism.

The importance of sound academic preparation was not lost on these women. "There is a whole issue of competency behind this women's thing," one said. "There are other programs geared to lay people that simply don't have the breadth and depth."

Judy Logue, a convert mother of three grown children, now directs the Rite of Christian Initiation of Adults (RCIA) at St. Francis Xavier Parish in Wilmette, Illinois, and leads retreats and workshops for women. "I've got CTU in my hip pocket," she said. "My education there is very important toward my status with clergy. Women have to know that you just can't be good-hearted and expect equal treatment."

CTU's modest campus is located on the outer edge of the University of Chicago. Its school building has been formed from the old Aragon Hotel, a 180-room single-occupancy hotel that was once home to people of modest means, some of whom may have worked at a nearby military facility that had closed. By the time CTU acquired it, the hotel was down on its luck and its residents. (One room had six phones, an insight into the clientele.) Yet, the founding religious orders were not anxious to drive poor people away, the way their massive university neighbor had done to protect its turf against an influx of African-Americans. As things turned out, the area stabilized and the CTU neighborhood has become integrated and reasonably safe by big-city standards, an important consideration for a school that would attract commuting women.

Barbara Anderson attends CTU part-time. She works for the Department of Health and Human Services and is a youth minister at St. Helena's Parish. "I want to work in a youth program. I don't care if it's archdiocesan or not," the lively and feisty Anderson said. "I'm just tired of seeing girls pregnant and boys dead."

Anderson is a black woman, attending CTU on an Augustus Tolton Memorial Scholarship, funded in memory of Chicago's first African-American priest. She serves as an unpaid youth minister—commonplace for women in parishes that still find ways to pay male bowling coaches.

"We put on plays," Anderson said proudly. "We write our own. We don't get them from a book. We deal with sex and drugs. We perform at the Baptist church and before the Girl Scout troop. Our youth group is ecumenical. We work on the strains between parent and child and we look at the parents' viewpoint.

"You know, the archbishop should be doing more for us. It's very difficult for an African-American to accept a European-American to minister to us."

Anderson attends CTU part-time. She hopes to graduate in 1996. "I'd like to be taking more courses," she said, "but I need more money."

"We're pushing for change. We can't have a Polish pope telling us what to do. I was in Denver when the pope came. They had at least five sessions for the Latino youths, just one for us. We've got to change that."

Anderson's anger was typical of the anger of the other women. It was focused on issues rather than the institution. Like Mary at Cana who informs her son that they had no wine, she addresses the problem while men would likely look for a political plot behind the empty wine casks.

The women of CTU have little interest in the chain of command that absorbs so many hierarchial energies. Yet it is abundantly clear that they do not intend to use their earned graduate degrees to head the altar and rosary societies. While earnest but severely hobbled bishops issue platitudes about the role of women in the Church, the women themselves are gradually taking over. They are now in the majority on most parish staffs and, more important, are assuming more significant roles. Women now direct most of the education, sacramental preparation, counseling, liturgy and social programs, and visits to the sick and elderly. In more enlightened parishes, they routinely give homilies (called "reflections" to avoid chancery office inquiries) and preside at paraliturgies such as holy hours, rosaries, and stations of the cross. Gradually, especially as religious sisters grow older, lay women are assuming leadership in parishes without resident pastors. Meanwhile, ordained clergy continue to hold the purse strings and to control the cemeteries and seminaries. But only those directly involved in their parishes have any real influence.

There is some movement for ordination, but there is little energy for this among the women of CTU. Dr. Dean Hoge, a professor of sociology at Catholic University of America, has done studies that suggest that, if the pope relaxed the prohibition that bars women from the altar, there would be no massive rush towards ordination—perhaps only thirty-six hundred or so by the millennium. "It isn't the Eucharistic part," one student said. "I'm attracted to that. It's the clericalism, the celibacy, and the political system that I couldn't stand."

"They would have to break down the whole idea of hierarchy before I would be ordained," another said. "They would have to redo the whole job description. I'm much freer without ordination."

(The women's testiness sounds vastly exaggerated here, largely because the author was trapped in his own institutionally framed questions. It's important to understand that their responses were triggered by the questions. There remains a good chance that if the author's wife, who was present for the group interview, had selected the questions, the interview would have focused more on ministry after the graduate degrees.)

"When I started my theological education at Mundelein [a Catholic college for women now affiliated with Loyola/Chicago], I had to ask myself 'Where has all this knowledge been?' I had never even connected homilies with the Bible!"

That's what Marionette Phelps, another Tolton scholar, said. A single woman, she is now in her third career. "Mundelein was great," she added, "but it didn't meet my needs. When I saw the bulletin board at CTU, I knew this was it!"

For CTU women the search seems to be one of discovery. "It's all there," Phelps said. "The Church has laid it out. We just have to grab it."

Phelps, a white-haired, pre-Vatican II Catholic, gets emotional when she is seen in church as just another visitor. Like other CTU students, her education is a discovery process into a theology that was closed to her, as if it were a secret seminary initiation process.

The female professors, still largely banned from diocesan seminaries, lead the way. CTU's faculty is nearly one-third female. "They are mentors," one student said. "They break down the paradigms. They're not afraid to take on the harder things to teach."

Sue Terranova is a widowed mother of four. After five years as a part-time student, she is now full-time, hoping to become a hospital chaplain. "CTU has a reputation," she said. "We're raising awareness among people about women in the Church. We're building something. I'm not in competition with the men here. I get help from them."

"There's a lot of pulling and tugging between the men and women," Charlene Klabacha said, "but there is a great respect for each other."

"Ordination is not the issue here," Rev. Donald Senior, C.P., professor of New Testament studies and president of CTU, said. "Ministry is." The women of CTU agreed.

"We look progressive," he continued. "But we are really quite centered in the Church. We're not out of step. Our faculty, for example, would have little trouble with *Veritatis Splendor* [John Paul II's recent encyclical]. We even briefed Cardinal Bernardin on the encyclical at his request.

"We are creating a process of formation for the laity. The theology of the future will be to be inclusive across the spectrum. We are also proving that someone who is ordained later or who enters ministry later can get along."

None of the women of CTU was finding it easy. This is not a learn-by-numbers curriculum; the economics and time constraints make the program much harder for laity then religious. Typically, Denise Douglas is teaching fourth grade in her parish and commuting over one hundred miles round trip to CTU one night each week, completing a master's in pastoral studies. "I've become an expert in overnight mail, getting my assignments in under the wire. The profs are very understanding. It's tough but it's life-giving and very affirming."

"They should give credits here for lunch," Judy Logue said. "I've learned more at the lunch table, trying to talk issues through. Diane

Bergant [a religious sister of St. Agnes and professor of Old Testament studies, who joined the faculty in 1979] has wired my mind. Diane says that no one is going to run her out of her Church. I agree."

Logue was the homilist at the recent ordination of a fellow student. She preached while twenty priests listened. "We had ordained him," she reasoned. "We called him to priesthood. He asked me to preach. Why shouldn't I?" No one objected.

"Oh, why are we even discussing this?" Logue added. "Sure, we need the hierarchial church in order to pass on the tradition. The Church never gets rid of anything. But the Church must be a place where one can re-image the tradition and that's what CTU is all about."

English cardinal and scholar, John Henry Newman, wrote in his *Development of Christian Doctrine* that Christian education often enters upon strange territory and that dangers and hopes appear in new relationships, and old principles appear in new form. "It changes with them in order to remain the same," he wrote.

The women of CTU are teaching the Church that, in Newman's words, "To live is to change, and to be perfect is to change often."

13

Tom McMahon:
A Priesthood That Is Fast
Becoming a Memory

———◆◆◆———

In June, 1994, twenty-five men gathered in the Sierra Mountains outside South Lake Tahoe, Nevada, for a *gaudeamus* ("Let us rejoice").
They were celebrating their fortieth anniversary of ordination. Just as
they had done on the day of their ordination, they had answered a call
with an *adsum* ("I'm here").

Most came from the San Francisco Bay area, but there were priests
from Boston, New York, Los Angeles, Salt Lake City, Fresno, and Las
Vegas. Two classmates couldn't make it; one was ill and the other was ministering in Guam. Seven more had died before reaching their fortieth
anniversary, but their classmates called out their names during the Eucharistic liturgy and the group answered "*presente*" on their behalf. "*Presente*"
is a Spanish word for 'present'," Tom McMahon remembered. "It means
much more than simply being present. It's something that comes from the
gut."

In a society that has only recently rediscovered male bonding, Roman
Catholic clergy have practiced it with enthusiasm since the twelfth-cen-
tury when celibacy became mandatory. It became even stronger when
seminary training lengthened and priests came out of their monasteries to
form a diocesan priesthood, rectories were founded and the life span of
people increased. Centuries ago, priests were ordained at twenty-five,
lived a decade or so and died. Today, most clergy make it to their Golden
Jubilees, a factor that requires another look at the celibacy discipline and a
number of other issues. Meanwhile, clerical bonds remain exceptionally
tight.

This fortieth reunion brought back memories of the old Baltimore
Catechism and its pronouncements about the "indelible" marks or

"special character" engraved on the soul by ordination. (The new Catechism still uses the word "indelible" and adds "special character" or "seal." It holds that Holy Orders is "a vocation to divine worship and service to the Church" and states that ordination, together with Baptism and Confirmation, can never be repeated. See #1121 of the 2,865 statements in the massive new work.) If there is a special character, it may be that its strongest component is friendship.

The "Men of Menlo Park," from the class of '54, as they called themselves somewhat derisively, were now an ecclesiastical scrambled egg. Ten were still pastors, but nine others were married and fathers of teenagers and young adults. There were retired probation officers, nonpracticing Catholics, recovering addicts, retired military chaplains, former missionaries, and various others whose life experiences had never been anticipated when they prostrated themselves on the sanctuary floor on ordination day.

Priests love to party. They have more anniversaries than the medieval church, which once had at least 180 feast days that had to be celebrated with holidays, processions, and pilgrimages. Since their lives are primarily voluntary, there is a tendency to count the years and varieties of service. Generally each spring, diocesan papers are filled with pictures of priests who are marking one jubilee or another. The gilded plateaus are booster shots to their egos, replacements for spouses and children who would have marked such passages with hugs, gifts, and celebrations.

Priesthood is a portable Canterbury pilgrimage, complete with storytelling, drinking, raunchy jokes, and sincere prayers. Perhaps the procession of anniversaries *is* a celibacy substitute. Perhaps it is just the bonds of friendship.

Tom McMahon, one of the earliest members in the class of '54, is writing a book. He had barely entered his teens when he started a twelve-year program leading to that indelible mark. His class figures highly in the book. He will recall this anniversary celebration to which at least five came with their wives while others came with stoles and albs. "All came open to truth," he said, "and in humble condition, grateful to a God of love for the opportunity to gather." Tom preaches even when he writes. His style is highly emotional. His sentences often remind one of Irish lace. They are curlicued.

"There was a great outpouring of emotion," Tom continued. "The prayers summed up the class's fear for the Church. One of the guys, a retired high-ranking military chaplain, a real powerful guy, led the prayers. 'Please God,' he said, 'speak to the pope and the bishops. Tell them that the Church is in trouble and that they need to loosen up concerning priests.'

"Vatican II had split the Church but not the class of '54," Tom continued. "Each one of us could speak of his personal calling from his God.

We ended the liturgy with a thunderous *Salve Regina* and with the sad conviction that our time and type of priesthood is just a memory."

The organizers of the 1954 class reunion of St. Patrick's Seminary of Menlo Park, California, had done a thorough job. Each member had been asked to reflect on the past forty years. Even the dead spoke in essays written by classmates. The testimonies were fascinating. In spite of a training geared to turning out duplicate copies, each of these men had played out their forty years in vastly different ways. All had made accommodations in order to fit their priesthood through the camel's eye of ecclesiastical expectations. The essays had been gathered in a loose-leaf book distributed to each classmate. A few were guarded, but most were honest reflections of lives that began with heavenly ideals which had been battered by the realities of the human condition.

It was hard to get precise figures on the class. The appendix listed fifty-four names of graduates of St. Joseph's College at Mountain View, California, the undergraduate portion of the twelve-year training program. Sixteen were still priests; forty-two had departed either before or after ordination. On June 11, 1954, twenty-one were ordained at St. Mary's Cathedral in San Francisco. There were others who had been ordained in Rome or were from other dioceses such as Los Angeles, Salt Lake City, Hawaii, Guam, and Sacramento. Thirteen of thirty-nine had survived since freshmen year of high school; twenty-two joined the group during high school and college; four came from the military, and twenty-five others had come and left.

The numbers revealed a rather inefficient system. Medical or law schools with defection rates as high as seminaries would lose accreditation. But seminaries are as Catholic as the Vatican Museum, which hangs much donated art and lets it stand the test of time.

Tom McMahon's reflections did not appear in the class book. Although one of the best-liked members of the class, his outspoken thoughts proved too strong for his fellow priests. Tom had named names. He wrote nothing that others didn't know. Everything in his reflections was public knowledge, stories that had been common currency for years. But priests are intuitively prudent. They are like police officers who will cover for a buddy who has swallowed his gun and blown his head off or a fellow country club member who falls off his bar stool every night. Tom's notes had reflected on some who were alcoholic, neurotic, homosexual, overly ambitious—even one pederast priest—strong stuff for a jubilee book. "It was all well-known to everyone," Tom said simply. "I'm sorry if it offended anyone." But priests are reluctant to blow the whistle on authority figures and even more reluctant to say anything about the dead. It's a noble tradition but one geared to the continuance of an unhealthy system.

Tom mailed his unedited reflections to his classmates, some of whom had been his friends for fifty-two years. There was more anger in his testimony than in those of others. On balance, the class had a lot of anger, especially about their seminary experience and the hierarchy. It seems to be part and parcel of large institutions and professional schools. They remembered the silly rules: one needed to obtain a bathroom key from the rector in order to ease nature during the night; one had to give a list of one's companions if walking off campus. They recalled that sports were often rated ahead of intelligence and grades—even character. They could still taste the creamed chip beef and the stewed apricots. But they could also remember the guys who laughed easily and who made you laugh.

Fr. James P. Gaffey, an alumnus now in the diocese of Santa Rosa, wrote a history of St. Patrick's Seminary in Menlo Park that appeared in 1992. It was remarkably objective. He describes the seminary culture as one that nourished friendships well beyond ordination. There was a bias in favor of students from San Francisco and those with Irish surnames, but gradually that began to change. Few liberties were granted by the Sulpician faculty, so friendships tended to grow among the students themselves. Radios were banned; students rarely got off campus, except to give blood or vote. McMahon recalls that he hardly knew that the country was absorbed in an ugly war in Korea.

In 1954, the year of ordination, the class was allowed to watch only "The Catholic Hour," Bishop Fulton J. Sheen, and philosopher Mortimer Adler on TV. Bike riding was permitted until 1949 when a student was killed on a public road. With classic overreaction, Archbishop John J. Mitty (1935–1961) prohibited all further bike riding. The superior, Fr. Thomas C. Mulligan, allowed attendance at one football game at nearby Stanford, but Mitty objected because he could not allow them to attend without their clerical collars and he was worried about the reaction if they attended with collars. Movies were confined to religious themes such as *The Song of Bernadette* or *Monsieur Vincent*, together with Mickey Mouse movies that must have lowered I.Q.'s and artistic tastes by dozens of points. Fr. Mulligan, an echo chamber for the severe archbishop, ruled without compromise, often bordering on being unreasonable and infuriating. He was just as rigid on himself, often contorting his face simply to avoid a healthy sneeze. (Poor Mulligan was just doing his duty. It earned him the lifelong hostility of his seminarians and the indifferent gratitude of a changing archdiocese. A broken man, he resigned in 1967 and died in 1970. Mitty wrote him a two-sentence acknowledgement of his thirteen years of service and, when he died, neither a representative of the archbishop nor a member of the seminary community attended his funeral. According to Gaffey, it was "an omission bitterly resented by his family." Yet such institutional insensitivity is part of the syndrome that causes priests to have such bittersweet memories.)

McMahon's love-hate relationship with the Church has a history that pre-dates his ordination. A series of bitter experiences have left Tom with enough anger to blow up the Vatican.

A rare native Californian whose parents were born in the West before the 1906 quake, he had an uncle who was ordained for San Francisco in 1922. "After forty years of service during which he built two churches," McMahon recalled, "my uncle, dying now of Parkinson's disease, was refused retirement by Archbishop Mitty. In fact, he was summoned to the chancery and let stand in front of Mitty's desk for a full five minutes, swaying from his illness.

"Finally, Mitty looked up and said 'McCarthy, I have had it with your drinking.' My uncle's name was Tom Bresnahan.

"My uncle drew himself up; looked at the archbishop and said 'You goddamn fool. Forty years ordained and you don't even know my name!' He walked out and five days later, after my intervention, he was allowed to retire. He died two years later, still bitter.

"My uncle never visited me during my twelve years in the seminary. I wonder if he was trying to tell me something?"

McMahon was raised in San Francisco's Mission Dolores Parish where his widowed mother was secretary to the pastor, Thomas A. Connolly, who would later become the archbishop of Seattle. She had been baptized in old St. Joseph's Church in 1898. The family grew up with priests processing in and out of the house. "We cut them no slack," Tom recalled. "We demanded genuineness of them."

From second grade on, he served at the liturgical pageants, carrying the bishop's gloves at the Christmas masses. But his highly romanticized faith was sorely tested when Connolly expressed disgust with him when he struck out with the bases loaded, making the final out and losing an important parish school game. 'You son of a bitch,' I said to myself. 'Have you any idea how I feel?' I viewed most priests as father figures, especially since my father had died in 1931."

McMahon's mother stayed close to her brother, Father Tom Bresnahan, during his years at St. Vincent de Paul Parish. The pastor, Fr.

Martin Ryan, knew of her struggle to raise four children as a widow. When he died in 1941, he willed his estate to her. But when the executor, Tom's priest-uncle, attempted to probate the estate, the archdiocese declared that Fr. Ryan had left no will. The money went to the archdiocese. That wound is still festering.

It didn't keep Tom McMahon out of the seminary, however. He recalls that he entered St. Joseph's College, which included a prep school seminary, in 1942. "For three years, I was obedient, pursuing a spirituality that would prepare me for service to people. I got good grades and was heavily involved in athletics. I cut trees every day. I did it so efficiently that they made me the head sacristan. God, if they only knew what I was thinking all those years. They never would have ordained me!"

One evening in 1946, he went to the common john about 10:30 P.M. and tuned in on a drunken conversation coming in the window from a faculty member's room. It was two faculty members talking about others. They were criticizing their colleagues. He listened for two hours. "I lost my church virginity that night," he recalls with mixed laughter and cynicism.

"I lost interest in studies," he continued. "I became skeptical of the corruption of clerical power. It was something that never left me.

"My next six years at St. Patrick's, the major seminary, were a pattern of hiding my true feelings, trusting few priests, and making sure that I did not run afoul of the loony-tune people who ran the place. I tried to be functional in a dysfunctional environment. Clericalism and humanitarianism were at odds. But I still played to win."

McMahon's pastor in his home parish, Bishop Guilfoyle, an auxiliary and chancery official, told him that he had been given the best assignment in the archdiocese, but the pastor proved to be a hopeless alcoholic. "God, I used to have to take the chalice out of his hands during Mass," Tom recalls with both genuine sadness and outrage because his condition was closeted. After five years, he took an assignment to South San Francisco. The crafty, miserly pastor, who used to break hosts in half to save money, cheated his way to a $1.5 million personal fortune. After the pastor's death, when questions were raised about his money grabbing, McMahon was cautioned about the need for silence about his huge estate. The pastor, it seemed, had clout in Rome. The cover-up policy infuriated McMahon.

His next pastor was a hardened former military chaplain who spoke endlessly about how Oriental women smelled. He hated Mexicans. One day, when Tom arrived at the church door with some two dozen Mexican kids, the pastor ordered him to "get those goddamn Mexican kids out of my church!"

"When I told that pastor to get out of the way or I would beat the shit out of him, I was called on the carpet for insubordination. I told the bishop [Joseph T. McGucken (1962–1977), Mitty's successor] that I was going to the *San Francisco Examiner* to turn him in as a race-prejudiced bishop. McGucken nearly swallowed his cigarette. He sent me to another pastor where I spent six months saying Mass for a convent of nuns who weren't talking to each other.

"After some time in that parish, I preached a sermon on the dignity and the rights of women. The six hundred people at that Mass gave me a standing ovation, but I was cashiered.

"By this time, I had been working some twenty years. Yet it took my next assignment with Tom Murray at Holy Spirit for me to find my first good pastor.

"In the meantime, I had gotten into hot water with the chaplains at the San Francisco Presidio. I was an army reservist and had spoken out against the Vietnam War as early as '69. It just seemed that my clerical world was falling apart."

McMahon is not a hostile man. He's as friendly a man as one could hope to meet in a stereotypical Irish pub. Yet, as anyone who has frequented such pubs can testify, veins of anger run just under the surface of many conversations. He does have a refined sense of justice and an array of ideals that were violated too early in his life. He reminds one of a young police officer who finds senior officers on the take or a novice surgeon who discovers that his mentor had botched an operation. "I don't mean to sound as if I comparing myself to him," he said, "but I'm like Erasmus in some ways. He didn't want to take on Luther, but he was terribly irritated by what Luther said. I suppose my anger has to do with pricking consciences."

"At an appreciation dinner in 1972," he said, "the cooks got drunk before they could feed the crowd. I was attacked by some tipsy parishioners on the issue of birth control. I told them all what I had said from the pulpit: that I had never even seen a contraceptive and that I would never make a decision on the sex lives of people.

"After that remark, I spent the remainder of that dinner evening watching television with my friend, Elaine, whom I had known for years. I returned at midnight, missed by no one. I knew then that clerical living was on its way out for me."

In 1975, McGucken had McMahon open a new parish. McGucken thought the parish would fail. But it thrived.

Elaine and Tom were bonded by now. Many of the parishioners knew and supported the relationship. Elaine recalls that she did not fall in love with a priest. "I fell in love with a man. He happened to be a priest."

Tom McMahon had met Elaine when she was an eighth-grade student, enrolled in a teenage club in his San Francisco parish. They kept running into each other over the years, gradually becoming friends. Elaine is as shy as Tom is outgoing. When a TV station came to interview them some years ago, Elaine found the experience as painful as Tom found it enjoyable. They are opposites, yet she supports his vision. Tom could turn a supermarket opening into a joyous event. "He's just trying to make life meaningful for people," Elaine said. "He's absorbed in the priesthood because it's part of his past and he believes that you can't talk about the present or the future if you don't talk about the past."

When Elaine conceived, Tom went to the archbishop with his resignation. Instead, according to Tom, the bishop bargained with him in an effort to get him to give up their child. In the peculiar politics of clerical ethics, a mistress is tolerated but not a mother. McMahon went back to his parish and waited for a replacement. None came. He continued to be a pastor, husband, and parent. "I should have felt guilty," he said, "but I didn't. It didn't affect my ministry and the bishop never asked."

Three years later at sunrise on Easter morning, their second child was born. Word of this event got out—the McMahons made no attempt to hide anything. A few families left the parish but, for the most part, Father McMahon performed his pastoral duties without any complications. Seven months later, after negotiations with Bishop Frank Quinn, the auxiliary bishop (later bishop of Sacramento), McMahon left church-structured ministry. "It was tough," he recalled. "Priests who fall in love with women are treated much more harshly that those who have affairs or those too drunk to say Mass in the morning." Fourteen years and four pastors later, Archbishop John Quinn still occasionally refers to the parish as "Tom McMahon's place."

Within a year after he left active ministry, a group of some fifteen families called him to be their pastor in a unique Christian community which came to be called the Community of Jesus Our Brother, modeled on the original name of the parish he had founded. The group began informally in 1980 when one of the study groups within his former parish asked Tom to continue the adult religious education they had been receiving. Now, some fourteen years later, the Christian community continues to meet three times monthly, usually on a Sunday. They share a simple liturgy, including bread and the cup. Tom doesn't vest or preside. Members adhere to a liberal theology, much of it based on Vatican

II. They support two Pearl Buck children and food kitchens for the homeless and the needy in the San Jose area, together with an annual education program that deals with issues that are still too sensitive for the institutional church to probe fully (1994's topic: "The Role of Women in the Church"). McMahon eschews the role of pastor. He prefers the designation "responsible one" which contains only a suggestion of authority.

The community remains static. McMahon observes that the close-knit bonds of the group make it awkward for newcomers to feel comfortable. There is also an age factor; most members are in their sixties. There are no small children. Members gather in each others' homes, attend plays together, and organize picnics.

"We're a kind of beacon light to the local parishes," Tom says. "We own no property and we are powerless, save for the love and justice we have for one another." The community has no links to the institutional church. Tom's links are strained to the breaking point, often because of a pervasive institutional pettiness practiced by chanceries toward resigned clergy. (Typically, when the sisters who cooked at the seminary for some ninety years retired from service, the seminary sponsored a farewell service and party. Tom's name was struck from the list of invited guests. He is no longer considered an alumnus. He went anyway.) The Community of Jesus Our Brother willingly funds his correspondence with his classmates and others on church matters. If Tom is distanced from the Church, it can't be very far.

The McMahons' children have not been baptized and have received no formal religious education. Now teenagers, they are well aware of their father's background and are curious about religion. "Steve is now seventeen," Tom said. "He's conservative and identifies himself as a Roman Catholic, but says that he has neither the time nor the desire to learn about it. Last year, Tommy questioned me about the Resurrection."

While still in active ministry, Tom got certified as a therapist and drug counselor. Today, he makes his living as a private therapist and professor on the staff of the University of Phoenix, which has satellite campuses in the Bay area. He teaches courses in critical thinking, world religions, and chemical dependency. With Elaine, he also manages two income properties.

McMahon is happy. He praises God for his life. But the anger remains. "I hope that what I've said is truthful," he concluded. "The years in the priesthood were a nightmare in some ways. The realities were so ugly. But they were also wonderful."

There are contradictions. He holds the pope and nearly all the bishops as virtual anti-Christs. He calls for clerical reform but encourages the demise of the clergy. His dearest friends remain his fellow priests, especially his classmates. He has been active in the Corps of Resigned Priests United for Service (CORPUS), a group that actively promotes the use of married priests, optional celibacy, and women priests. But he differs strongly with them, especially when they exhibit trace marks of clericalism. "I shall die genuine to my understanding of faith, but in my will I have forbidden that I be buried from a Roman Church," he said. "I will not be controlled by Roman godlessness in life—and surely not in death."

The indelible mark on Tom McMahon's soul won't rub off, however. He continues to write letters on church-related matters to national publications such as the *National Catholic Reporter* and to the local press in the greater Bay area. He almost always sends copies to the archbishop and the chancery office. He has kind words about Archbishop John Quinn. He regards him as chaste, pious, and alone, but he recognizes that San Francisco clergy have an independent streak and that Quinn will forever be an outsider. (Quinn was ordained for San Diego and spent time in Oklahoma City before coming to San Francisco in 1977.) He views Quinn as extremely quiet and prudent. The bishop's emotions are so hobbled, however, that when he attended the late Archbishop Oscar Romero's funeral in 1980, he was shattered when he found himself being surrounded by peasants who were using their bodies to protect him from gunfire. Quinn was overwhelmed by their willingness to die to protect him. The clerical culture has few examples of such faith.

The archbishop, now under pressure for closing eleven churches and for questions of sexual impropriety among his clergy, continues to answer Tom's letters in polite, measured sentences. But Quinn remains noncommittal. Further, there always seems to be a clerical flunky willing to scratch Tom's name off another list.

"I try not to let the anger get to me," Tom said. "I was on a ski lift with Warren Halleran, now a prof at the seminary, not long ago. He was a class ahead of me; we've skied together for thirty-nine years. He told me not to waste my time. He said that the walls are crumbling and that I should exert my efforts at building a new church.

"I got a handwritten letter from a California bishop the other day. He asked me not to be too hard on those who stayed." Tom wasn't certain how to interpret the letter. It was both a plea and a rebuke. Tom reasoned that he wasn't trying to be too hard, but he did want to see a system that wasn't working change for the better.

"People are still defenseless in a system that doesn't have to be the way it is. Hell, we're still selling Mass cards and making rules. We have enough mystery to deal with after death. We don't need all this."

McMahon was emotionally exhausted when he drove home from Lake Tahoe and his class reunion. "The best of Christian tradition had been passed on at that reunion," he said. "I knew that I had been born into a era of fine persons. I am proud to be one of those Men of Menlo. I can only pray that those to whom we have entrusted the future of the Church will be as noble of character and genuine of heart."

14

Liwwat Boke:
"Dear Bishop"

Liwwat Boke had lost her patience with her pastor, Fr. Henry Herzog. She lived in what is now the archdiocese of Cincinnati. In the mid–1800s, it was largely farm country tilled by industrious immigrant Germans. She was a resident of an area called St. John, near Minster, Ohio. Chances are she was better educated than most of her neighbors. She could write in High German, spoken largely by the better educated. She worked as the local midwife and, by her own account, she had a happy marriage. ("He was my beloved. He loved me. I loved him. As two, we were in all things one—in work, viewpoint, suffering. At the table, at prayer, with the children, with everything. Our relationship, experiences and sexuality delighted us both in the same way. That was to us another gift from God.") She was a pioneer in the region. She had been born in Germany in 1807. It's likely she married quite young because she speaks of her husband who "concerned himself for me in 1820 or so until his death." She died in 1882. She was thirty-seven when she wrote to her bishop, a forty-four-year-old Irishman who had been bishop of the area for eleven years. He would spend fifty of his eighty-three years as bishop and archbishop of Cincinnati. He was John Baptist Purcell, the second bishop of the area, and one of the pioneers in the advancement of parochial school education.

There is a good chance Bishop Purcell had heard other complaints about Fr. Herzog, who had a history of antagonizing people. But this letter may have forced Purcell's hand.

Clearly, Liwwat Boke had been pushed to the edge. On August 25, 1844, she wrote the following letter to Bishop Purcell:

"Dear Bishop:
"We wives of this entire region here are obedient to our Bishop.

160

"We are not obedient to our pastor, name of Henry Herzog, in his incorrect and erroneous dominating regulation of our privileges and privacy in our married lifestyle.

"The cleric, Henry Herzog:

- Teaches the womenfolk here, "You are in mortal sin if more than twice a year you provide sex with your husband.
- "You must confess everything, every time you do penance."
- Says that we dare not talk over with our own husband or wife sex-related words, things, acts, feelings, or deeds.
- Says that kissing and petting bring on intercourse and sexual desire; that is a sin.
- Says that all married couples must live more in a self-controlled and continent lifestyle with one another.

"Dear Bishop, we women are not yet entirely crazy, but are now so greatly guilt-ridden, worried, and hopelessly confused with this apostle and adherent of Jansenism. He is a silly fool! His singular inquisitiveness, deep into another's most intimate sexual attraction is miserably shameful!

"Is the Catholic Church again back in those hypocritical or phony times, the people encouraged to the virginal state over any other one? Roman Catholics particularly regard sex as dirty and married sex just a little less dirty. The Bishop knows better! It is a wrong approach for getting near to salvation!

"One reads and sees that also in earlier Christian times, the unhealthy view that the 'virginal state' is a better and higher way to heaven. Such a sickly attitude plus the complaining, lamenting, and reviling by spiritual sisters, brothers, and clerics against natural sex in marriage is at least bizarre, eccentric, and at worst unhealthy. The severity of the first learned fathers of the Church held sinful every little thing that was related to sex, and showed their abhorrence of all pleasure that might gratify worldly desires and lessen the spiritual.

"Herzog the cleric would forever like all people to live in the state of virginity or 'purity.' He would want us to be considered as harmless, innocent vegetables. Perhaps this human paradise here in the sexless forest can, generation after generation of people, make a new paradise of innocent and imperishable things come alive.

"The use of marriage is permitted by Herzog because, to the 'fallen descendants,' sex is only a noxious and bitter need of humanity that persists, and restraint, however imperfect, against natural licentiousness of pleasure and desire [isn't possible for everyone]. He sees pleasure and desire as a disgrace. Marriage is tolerated but is pictured as a defect. His outlook, as with many sisters and priests, always carried cultic overtones.

"The praise of the virginal state is overemphasized. That state is a sacrifice freely assumed. Marital intercourse between consenting men and women partners is a healthy, enriching pleasure. We have enough trouble in St. John. It is not necessary that we try virginal ways, not between married people.

"Watch out! Watch out lest your loss of sensual pleasure be replaced by spiritual pleasure . . . pride.

"Dear pope, sisters, clergy—listen to me! You are not a finger-breadth better than I. I am a woman, a human. I am sensual. I am a woman, Lord Bishop Purcell, a married woman, a midwife, with a little more acquaintance with people outside of the confessional. I was a bit educated as a young girl in the cathedral school in Osnabruck. I see and listen to pain, to conjugal behavior, to the personal conduct of life's course, to the honorable conduct between people—man and woman, wife and husband. We must not draw off and take away altogether from the value of sex which brings and carries new life into this world.

"Altogether, here in this area, more than one hundred women now and then tell to one another, to me, to anyone who has ears for hearing, their expectations, disappointments, indescribable humiliations, their hesitations, lack of cooperation and participation, their fear of sin, of hell, and, many times, of the misunderstanding of most of our clerics. That is why the majority of the women folk have asked me to write to you with these thoughts. You are the last judge before God and the Catholic Church.

"Natural sex must have a common equality for both the husband and the wife. Both must have the same freedom to express their sexual wishes, dreams, delights or actions. What the unmarried celibate must understand is that the holy sacrament of marriage gives the married couple the complete freedom to express, experience, examine, explore and enjoy their inner sexual individuality, their physical selves, without explaining or accounting to anyone. It is their own personal concern. It is one part of their common life together. Sex is powerfully important to people. Married people must have the freedom to express, as husband and wife, their love for one another—in, by, and through sex.

"In sex one can feel. In the surge of sexual desires and pleasures, one comes alive with strong feelings. One does not often find strong emotions in this forest. Therefore, sex is precious and welcome.

"In sex one feels absorbing pleasure. Sexual pleasure easily absorbs your entire consciousness into itself. But pleasure also brings fear. Yet in the security of love you choose to let yourself go with pleasure—sexual pleasure—to give yourself up to it, to identify with it. With the overflowing pleasure, the personality that you yourself are knows the other in a unique way. You are together in an overflowing emotion from both yourselves.

"I regret the awkwardness with the use of expressions like 'are together' but words such as 'communion' and 'sexual intimacy' are so much laden with romantic, intangible overtones that such expressions fail to evoke the simple, plain, earthy experience you and I are discussing here and now.

"Of any occasion filled with happiness, such enjoyment as sex is the high point. Today, here in the forest, in our hectic, short, active life, men and women often are alone a long time, and often they are tired. They sleep. They are exhausted from work. Sex is sometimes the only way possible to hold love together.

"So how important moralists will judge all this depends on how important they judge natural human feelings. If moralists rate the worth of human feelings far below responsible chastity and intellectual insight, they might consider that being together in sex is not important at all. They will consider it even less important if they also rate enjoyment as one of the lowest feelings.

"But you clerics may become completely dismayed if husbands and wives also let it be admitted that they both together have sex—for fun! The moralists can learn something. Having fun is one of the best and most profound ways, one of the most personal ways for human beings to be together. About all this, humans don't even ponder. It is as natural as eating, kissing, breathing, and urinating.

"Sex is always in the right season. Sex is the sign of an overpowering drive in both husband and wife. Sexual passion is beyond question an urgency, difficult and even impossible to resist in an individual's life. Husband and wife come to this stage in their relationship when the desire to touch one another springs up wildly throughout their consciousness. It doesn't matter what they're doing. They must get their clothes off!

"Let us not be embarrassed or ashamed to stress these commonplace, often gallant, often comic, often funny, often tragic facts about sex. Sex with the one we love is not just an appealing option, like reading a book with someone, or singing or praying with another. It is a raw need inside our body. It is like hunger after a fast day, or like the need to sleep after thirty hours of hard work. When the need is fulfilled, the contentment can and does permeate our whole being—similar to a good meal after hunger.

"This power of a natural need dwells in all our lives. This was proved by the austere Jesuits years ago when they continued to smoke although the pope had forbidden them to do so. The importance to their personal lives of satisfying their need to have tobacco outweighed the force of a papal edict or authority.

"Listen, Bishop. Listen well, Lord Bishop. Tell your clergy what you know is natural and God-given—one of the most worthwhile things in our married lives together. We must include this most lovely expression and experience, the at times overpowering need for sex. Even though there may be other ways, sexual passions stubbornly draw their desires towards the singular way of being together.

"I cannot understand why theologians do not try to understand this themselves! One can eat sugar, drink wine, or whatever—as the Jesuits with their tobacco smoking. But this is a compulsion that does not go away. It calls intensely, personally, toward togetherness in rare awareness and joy.

"Lord Bishop Purcell and all theologians, I have tried on behalf of all the many Catholic women here to explain their views, their awareness against that foolish 'mortal sin' which only exists in Herzog the priest's twisted mind! You clerics must understand, not let it be ignored in your calculating, your rating of this prize, this value, this precious gift from God himself!

"Humans can live without sex, the same as without hearing. They miss a human experience involving sound, noise, confusion, singing, voices, music, etc. Yes, they live without hearing but we wish that they could hear because they live better with hearing. Hearing and sex are powers that we cannot help wanting. They are important. They bring us to life in human ways.

"With thanks and respectfully, your co-worker,

Liwwat Boke, 1844"

N.B.: Late in the fall of 1844, Bishop Purcell sent a Father Navarron to the area to quiet the troubled waters. These notes were found in translation in a church rectory. They were together with another letter by Liwwat Boke. They appeared to consist of six to ten pages of a book, but the pages were loose. The book—or diary—appears to have been given by Boke's descendents to the parish priest who did the translation.

15

Brendan Fay:
"It's not such a human
way to be living."

————◆•◆————

I waited for the foam to settle on New York's St. Patrick's Day parade.
Then I called Brendan Fay, an immigrant Irish Catholic, who is gay.
He is one of the leaders of the Irish Lesbian and Gay Organization
(ILGO) that put the church of New York to a test of its faith.

The church flunked.

Beneath its grand smiles, green ribbons, watered silk, and Blessed
Mother banners, the faith of New York's institutional church proved
thinner than boarding-house soup. Based on their reaction to a handful
of gay Catholics trying to march in the St. Patrick's Day parade, New
York's official faith appeared to be composed mostly of fear, prejudice,
and hypocrisy.

"It's not such a human way to be living," Brendan Fay said. "I'm
fresh out of jail and I'm late returning your call because I've just come
from giving a talk at a conference on gays and lesbians in Irish history.

"You know, Ireland and Irishness aren't presented very well. For
years, I thought that the only gay Irishman was Oscar Wilde. Then I
began to find all kinds of others. There was John Atherton, for example,
one of the first bishops in Ireland. He was appointed by Henry VIII who
made church law into civil law and then had Atherton executed by the
very laws against homosexuality that he had set up. In 1822, there was
Percy Jocelyn, the lord bishop of Clogher, who was the head of the
Society for the Suppression of Vice. He was sent off to jail himself for
being a homosexual."

"Well, of course, they were both Protestants," Brendan continued.
But he was making a point that his life experiences had confirmed: homosexuality is as common among churchmen as it is among society at large.

165

Indeed, there may be a higher percentage of gays among clergy than the population at large. Further, while it may be true that St. Patrick drove the snakes out of Ireland, he did nothing to reduce its gay population.

Brendan Fay carried on like that until 1:30 A.M. It must have been a three-hour call. He told me of the beautiful poetry that came from monasteries where monks often went off in pairs and lived together, and of both the words and art in the early Irish texts that showed clearly that the Irish were well aware of sex in all its forms.

He spoke of Roger Casement, an Irish nationalist and a hero of the 1916 revolution, who suffered in jail for his homosexuality. Casement, another Protestant, worked for the British consular service. In 1904, he exposed the atrocious exploitation of the rubber gatherers in the Congo. He later exposed similar conditions in South America. In 1911, he was knighted for his services. After the outbreak of World War I, he went first to the United States and then to Germany to secure aid for an Irish uprising against the very people who had knighted him. The Germans promised help, but Casement considered it inadequate. So in April, 1916, he returned to Ireland, hoping to secure a postponement of the Easter Rebellion. After landing from a German submarine, he was arrested, tried, convicted, and hanged for treason. To further blacken his name, some British agents had circulated his diaries, which showed him to be a homosexual. Casement had priests coming to him, pleading with him to just say he was crazy, not gay. They promised to get him out. But Casement answered that he could not deny "a love that God had made, not I."

Fay recalled the young Jesuit, Gerard Manley Hopkins, a poet and priest, who spent some time in Dublin. Hopkins' life was marked by continuous inner conflict, which arose, not from religious skepticism, but from an inability to give himself completely to his God. He produced only a small body of work but it profoundly influenced twentieth-century poetry. His poems reflect an intense dissatisfaction with himself as a poet and priest, perhaps because of the ambiguity and shame attached to his sexual orientation.

Fay is a lover of Irish history and literature, a member of the Celtic League, a dancer at Irish ceilidhes, a former Irish Christian Brother and seminarian, and a religion teacher in New York's Catholic schools. He would much rather talk about a rich Irish culture than about a parade that, as often as not, gives a shanty Irish impression of a nation where words are sacred and the culture is rich.

I had called Brendan to talk to him about the St. Patrick's Day parade, in which he had proudly marched for years after he came to this country in 1984. A few years ago he and over two hundred other immigrant Irish and Irish-Americans announced that they were homosexuals and lesbians and wanted to celebrate both their orientation and their Irishness by having their own contingent in the parade. Then the New York police horses reared, the bishops used their croziers like shillelaghs, and the bagpipes nearly split their kidney-shaped sides.

The parade always stepped off with a contingent of New York's finest on their horses or marching behind in their double-breasted greatcoats. The police were followed by the Irish pipers and their wailing, haunting pipes. No one asked how many of them were gay.

At the reviewing stand, the mayor, other politicians, and the top men of the Ancient Order of Hibernians (AOH) elbowed each other for a chance to show off their green sashes at the front of the platform. Under their top hats and ample bellies, there might have been some gay Irish Catholics.

On the steps of St. Patrick's Cathedral, the cardinal and his clerical entourage, all of them grinning under their birettas with the colored balls that signified their rank, stood and blessed the marchers as they passed the brass doors. No one dared ask how many of the clergy were gay.

Brendan Fay came across the pond from Drogheda, a city of seventeen thousand in County Louth, north of Dublin, facing the Irish Sea. Back home, he had spent four years with the Congregation of Christian Brothers and three in the seminary, and was involved in a medley of justice causes. He visited Taize, an ecumenical community in France, and the Vatican, "where I became disenchanted."

His search for peace of mind took him to an Irish Cistercian monastery where he went on his knees to a saintly priest who listened uncritically to his revelation that he was a homosexual. "Get off your knees, lad," the monk said. "Sure, I'm the same as you are."

"Stay away from rigid people," the old gay monk told him. "And remember, Brendan, that you are made in the image and likeness of God."

HOMOSEXUALITY IS A TERM coined in the nineteenth century to describe a sexual and emotional interest in members of one's own sex. Today, the correct phrasing is "homosexual orientation." Orientation suggests that the boundaries between heterosexual and homosexual are not as rigid as many seem to believe. Recent studies suggest that about six percent of males have some erotic interest in both sexes, whether publicly pronounced or not. In the Western culture from which most church theology is drawn, such an observation would draw strong objections, particularly from churchmen, a contingent that may have a higher percentage of gays than any other defined group.

In 1994, Yale professor and researcher John Boswell released a book titled *Same Sex Unions in Premodern Europe* in which he stated that the Church has sanctioned and idealized same sex unions for nearly two thousand years. Indeed, he contended, bonding of brotherly equals was seen as the highest form of human contact. Boswell acknowledged that same sex unions have met with moral ambivalence which, over the centuries, has given way to intolerance. He cites some seventy liturgies that bless such unions. Church scholars quickly pinioned the book, claiming that Boswell had distorted historical facts.

There are at least a dozen theories as to how homosexual orientations are formed—everything from inherited genes to domineering mothers—but the real roots remain a mystery. The American Psychiatric Association no longer considers homosexuality a disorder, unless sexual orientation becomes an object of distress for the individual.

The gay and lesbian civil rights movement began in 1969, when patrons of a gay bar in New York City rioted after police attempted to close the bar. For five days, the Stonewall Riots continued. The gays not only fought back: they started a movement. Twenty-five years later 1.2 million gays gathered in New York City to celebrate the twenty-fifth anniversary of the riots. They marched down Fifth Avenue, past St. Patrick's Cathedral which was locked, barricaded, and protected by New York City police and private security guards. The archdiocesan Catholic paper continued to deepen the divide by characterizing the participants as "drag" men, "bare-breasted" women, and "militant homosexuals." Their coverage went on to say that the archdiocese gives "loving care" to people with AIDS, thus reinforcing the stereotype that AIDS is an exclusively gay disease. "Their loving care is both admirable and Christ-like," attorney Donald Maher said, "but their complete lack of loving care provided to gay and lesbian people is neither admirable nor Christ-like." Maher, one of the founders of the Gay and Lesbian Catholic Ministry at St. Paul the Apostle Church in New York, made repeated calls to a number of church officials in the weeks prior to the gay pride parade. He was seeking some expression from the church—just a word of welcome, a service or a Mass—but his calls were not returned.

Today, about half the states have removed laws forbidding homosexual activity among consenting adults from their books, but as late as 1986 the Supreme Court upheld states' rights to have laws prohibiting homosexual conduct. Typically, in Cobb County, Georgia in 1994, the government passed an anti-gay resolution. It was a terrible irony in a county with a 20 percent illegitimacy rate and two divorces for every three weddings. Somehow, the local politicians and churchmen felt it more important to pass a resolution that would put the brakes to an estimated three hundred gays rather than address the social problems introduced by 1,545 unwed mothers and 2,739 divorces.

Prejudice against gays has to do with Western notions of the nuclear family, fear of AIDS, legal recognition of same sex couples and the teaching of churches. The United States may have the highest level of paranoia concerning homosexual orientation. A massive study of some 190 cultures revealed that nearly 130 of them considered homosexual behavior as normal.

The percentage of gays in the population is thought to be at least 10 percent, a figure that may date to the studies of Dr. Alfred Kinsey, an American biologist who died in 1956 and who had done pioneer sexual research. Kinsey's research is now regarded as deeply flawed. A biologist by training (his expertise was the gall wasp), he compromised science and took his research subjects where he could find them: in boardinghouses, college fraternities, prisons, and mental wards. For fourteen years he collared hitchhikers who passed through town and quizzed them mercilessly. It was hardly a random cross-section. A recent study, released in 1994, and conducted by the National Opinion Research Center at the University of Chicago, revealed that only 2.8 percent of American men said they were gay or bisexual and only 1.4 percent of women identified themselves as lesbian. It is the first truly scientific survey, based on face-to-face interviews with a random sample of nearly thirty-five hundred Americans, ages eighteen to fifty-nine. Organized gay groups challenged the results, partly because the earlier 10 percent figure gave them significant political clout. "We're queer and we're here," they continued to chant.

Kevin Calgeri, former president of Dignity, an independent national group of gay and lesbian Catholics, dismisses most estimates. "I used to play 'gaydar,'" he said. "Now, I find it isn't important. What's important is how we are perceived and treated."

BRENDAN FAY LEFT IRELAND and tried New York. "I wanted to get away from my own hypocrisy," he said. "I used to go to the pubs and bath houses in Dublin where I met other Irish gays, including priests, but we were all afraid to come out. We simply couldn't be Irish and gay. We couldn't break the hermetic seal."

Being Irish, Catholic, and gay seemed to be a contradiction in terms. "It was like expecting a God who could do all things to make a rock he couldn't lift," Brendan said.

In New York, Fay completed his master's degree in theology at St. John's University. He taught at LaSalle Academy and later at Mary Louis Academy, an all-girls' school in Queens. He also studied with philosophy professor Dick Westley at Chicago's Loyola University where he "learned a whole new way to be Catholic."

Fay became active in the loosely organized ILGO, another decision that brought him "out of the darkness." They had few members and few purposes other than to celebrate their Irishness, their faith, and their gayness.

In 1991, ILGO was banned again from taking part in the St. Patrick's Day parade. However, the then mayor of New York, David N. Dinkins, arranged for the group to participate under the banner of another group. (Political banners, except those attacking England, are banned from the parade, but the group's identity is permitted. ILGO's banner was considered political, although pro-life ones are not.)

Dinkins, an African-American who knew something about the nature of prejudice, was loudly booed as he marched up Fifth Avenue with the small group of gays. Brendan was among them and his picture appeared in the paper doing an Irish step dance with the mayor.

Shortly after, Fay was called to the principal's office at Mary Louis Academy and fired. At the school, Fay never advertised his gayness, but he made no secret of it either. There were administrators, faculty, parents, and students who knew of his orientation and accepted him. The students signed a petition, but the wall of fear held.

It isn't clear whether or not outside pressure was exerted. The school where Brendan taught is in Jamaica Estates, part of the diocese of Brooklyn. Brooklyn's bishop, Thomas V. Daily, is viewed by some as even more reactionary than New York's Cardinal John O'Connor.

Brendan took a job in a lamp shop. He appealed his dismissal. There was a settlement with the school. Checks were issued and cashed, but there was the usual confidentiality clause. After the settlement, he left the lamp shop. He is now doing research on the life of Roger Casement.

Mayor Dinkins boycotted the parade in 1992 and 1993. Given the enormous problems of drugs, crime, education, race, and a crumbling infrastructure, the issue of a few gays marching in a parade was hardly a big one. However, little issues are often more easily understood than larger ones, and the two-edged one of race and homosexuality played a part in Dinkins' loss to Republican Rudolph W. Giuliani in 1993. Both sides trashed the core of each other's culture with the church constantly issuing statements that favored Giuliani's positions.

In 1994, the *New York Times* wrote a strong editorial, urging Giuliani to "distance himself from this benighted display of bigotry." New York's archbishop, Cardinal O'Connor, a man known for taking consistently Republican political positions in both local and national races, took issue with the editorial, labeling it "Catholic bashing." He denied even a trace of prejudice, claiming that the Church's teaching on homosexuality "came from God."

O'Connor has a way of raising the temperature of an issue by putting himself in the center and adopting the role of martyr. "If it is a disgrace to be Irish or to be Catholic, I am proud to stand before you in disgrace," he said. The faithful at St. Patrick's gave him a standing ovation.

ILGO was organized in 1988 as a social organization to offer mutual support to Irish gays who needed a place to be honest. The group found some acceptance from the local church, especially at St. Paul the Apostle, a Paulist Church on West 59th Street in Manhattan. Prior to the 1993 parade, over two hundred people attended a very moving service there, organized by Donald Maher, a New York labor lawyer. One U.S. Congressman showed up; Mayor Dinkins sent a message, and there were messages from Ireland, as well as Irish dancing, scripture readings, and sermons. The Church sent someone to observe, but did nothing to stop the preaching or the praying.

ILGO had a more important agenda than marching in the St. Patrick's Day parade. In 1991, however, they filed an application with the AOH with no other thought than to enter a small contingent as part of their own efforts to break the seal that bound them. Initially, there was no objection, but when it came to the attention of Church authorities, their reaction found ILGO placed "on a waiting list to nowhere."

They marched anyway, without a banner and with Mayor Dinkins on their arms. "Die, fags!" the crowd shouted. "Queers!" "AIDS!" were just a few of the printable epithets hurled at them, along with the beer cans.

Fay remembers the experience as one of the most important spiritual moments in his life. "I only wanted it to be a celebration of our Irishness," he said, "but it broke the seal on our silence."

The next year, the Hibernians used their clout to have the contingent banned again. Indeed, the AOH almost canceled the parade. ILGO managed to march in front of the parade, not officially a part of it. There were arrests and charges. Fay recalled that the majority of the arresting officers were embarrassed at having to place plastic cuffs on the peaceful demonstrators. "But those plastic cuffs hurt," he remembered.

In 1993 things got worse. The Church joined in with editorials and speeches that likened the Hibernians to martyrs for the faith. Now, the AOH announced, it was a "Catholic parade." A spokesman for the Hibernians called ILGO "Irish sodomites."

There is hardly a scripture scholar who still has his own teeth that views Sodom's offense as a sexual one. The scholars cite adultery, lying, unrepentance, pride, gluttony, indifference to the poor, and inhospitality—not sodomy, as it is presently understood. Jesus mentions Sodom but no specific sin. But gay-bashers seem to like the word.

Whenever homosexuality is mentioned in the Bible, it is condemned. It is described as a crime worthy of death and a sin against nature. It must be remembered, however, that various forms of sexual intercourse were considered a necessary part of worship by contemporary pagan groups. Thus, according to University of Notre Dame theologian, Fr. Richard McBrien, the condemnations   must be seen in this context. "The worship of Yahweh was to be unconditionally exclusive," McBrien said. "No trace of pagan influence was to be countenanced." One trace was homosexual activity.

Even after the danger of ritual intercourse had passed, the prohibition against homosexual activity was retained. Not until late in the New Testament is an explicit link made between Sodom and sexuality. (See Jude 6–7.)

The Christian writers were consistent in their condemnation of homosexuality. They linked it to laws protecting children. (The stereotype that molesters are gay still exists, although, as mentioned in chapter 6 here, the majority of sexual abusers are heterosexual.) St. Thomas Aquinas linked it with sins of lust, along with masturbation and bestiality—a pretty wide grouping.

The Church's most recent statement on homosexuality was issued in 1992. Entitled "Observations Regarding Legislative Proposals Concerned with Discrimination Toward Homosexual Persons," it reminds the faithful that official Catholic teaching has consistently judged all homosexual acts as at once unnatural and gravely sinful. A 1986 letter from the same Congregation for the Doctrine of the Faith stated that a homosexual act was "an intrinsic moral evil" and that even an inclination toward homosexuality "must be seen as an intrinsic moral disorder."

There are hints in earlier documents that homosexuality is transitory or at least not incurable. Those that are deemed incurable "must certainly be treated with understanding and sustained in the hope of overcoming their personal difficulties and their inability to fit into society."

Yet, while theologians disagree, the official Church seems to be inching toward a better understanding of the issue. The Church still holds that homosexual acts are always sinful in themselves. But it now counsels kindness on the issue, stating that confessors "must avoid both harshness and permissiveness."

The new *Catechism of the Catholic Church* does not lay blame on the homosexual for the orientation or the condition. It now states explicitly that homosexuals "do not choose their condition," and insists that they "must be accepted with respect, compassion and sensitivity" and are not to be subject to "unjust discrimination."

It's a start.

Other theologians hold that homosexual acts are morally neutral, a position that argues that the morality of the sexual act depends upon the quality of the relationship. Theologians such as John J. McNeill, who was dismissed from the Jesuits for his activist position on the issue, believe that the basic norm is love and that sexual relations can be justified morally if they are true expressions of human love.

Moral theologian Charles E. Curran holds a position that says that homosexual acts are essentially imperfect. His position is a kind of moral middle ground. For him the ideal meaning of human sexual relationships is in terms of male and female, but he also holds that an irreversible, loving homosexual relationship which is striving for permanency can be morally good. (It get more complicated than that. Readers can learn more from McBrien's *Catholicism*, from which these notes are adapted, or Richard A. McCormick's *The Critical Calling.*)

Back in New York, Cardinal O'Connor stated that ILGO was trying to bring down the Catholic Church. ILGO was linked to the AIDS Coalition To Unleash Power (ACT-UP), a militant gay group with whom they have no connection. ACT-UP once invaded a Mass at St. Patrick's Cathedral; at least one member of the group took Communion and then threw it on the floor. Today, because of the desecration, it is still common to find a police officer at St. Patrick's near the priests as they distribute Communion. It's a gun-toting church.

Brendan's message machine, which greets callers in Gaelic and English, began to log obscene and threatening calls. It informed him that he was a British spy sent to New York to discredit the Irish race. Most calls, however, simply spewed filth in the name of God.

A series of clout-laden injunctions kept ILGO from the 1993 parade. They formed a group anyway and attempted to march. Singing

"We Shall Overcome," they walked into a sea of police who arrested 238 of them. "We got only one block," Brendan said. "I was with my friend Tarlach MacNiallis, the first Irish gay I met in New York. I was holding my rosary. We were charged with criminal contempt, parading without a permit, and disobeying an injunction. But there were straights and even a priest arrested with us."

At the 1994 parade, 102 protestors were arrested and charged with disorderly conduct, 56 with an additional charge of resisting arrest. Since 1991, all arrests have resulted in court actions in which the charges were dropped.

The experiences have decimated ILGO. Membership has declined to just a few dozen. Most left the Church in disgust before the spit dried on their coats. Cardinal O'Connor bragged that all their efforts "were not worth one comma in the Apostles' Creed."

The crowds watching the parade have dwindled considerably, although in 1994 the organizers boasted over 700,000 viewers. Part of the reason is that big city parades aren't what they used to be. Fear of crime and high prices for food along the streets near the parade route have kept people away. The Catholic schools, once the main contingents in the parade, have dwindled. School administrators are taking a second look at the political correctness of a holiday for one ethnic group and none for another. There's a chance that the annual event is coming to an end.

In 1994 in Boston, the organizers canceled the parade rather than admit a gay group. Lawyers, including William Kunstler, are poised to challenge the church-state question in court.

In Dublin, Galway, and Cork, gay Irish units marched without incident while their heritage of tolerance was trampled on across the sea. One group of marching gays in Ireland won the trophy for best float. "The Celtic heritage is one of bonding and friendship," Brendan said. "It appears that the Church, while blathering about compassion and forgiveness, only wishes to isolate its gay Catholics."

In 1992, Brendan had been walking in the Williamsburg section of Brooklyn when a young man came up behind him on a bike. Yelling words like "faggot" and "queer," he plunged a knife into him, cutting him badly. Fay staggered into several local shops in an effort to get help but shop owners in Brooklyn do not see, hear, or speak evil. It was forty-five minutes before an ambulance was called.

The incident made the news. Giuliani, who was later to be mayor, visited him in the hospital; Bishop Daily of Brooklyn did not. Fay was helped through the assault by a group known as the Anti-Violence Project. Political statements were issued decrying violence against gays but the Brooklyn and New York church maintained an official silence. Later, ILGO and the Anti-Violence Project picketed Brooklyn's St. James Cathedral. The bishop decried the picketing.

Meanwhile, however, the institutional church has heard the cries for justice. They appear to be inching toward both a better treatment and a better understanding of gays.

"There has been a lot of silence from the Church," Donald Maher of the Gay and Lesbian Catholic Ministry of St. Paul's says. "The local church's real concern is that it present an absolutely uniform ministry to its people. Any service to the gays would contradict this."

Yet, as St. Paul's continues its apostolate to the gays, the official church appears to be learning. When the group announced another prayer service prior to the annual parade, auxiliary bishop Patrick J. Sheridan cautioned that it should not take place. It was clear, however, that he would make no effort to stop it. Further, he assured the group that the church would cooperate in other ministries sponsored by gays and lesbians.

The prayer services continued. They included a reflection from Brendan Fay. In June of 1994, a right-wing group came to the Mass with a well-prepared attack. The Morality in Action Committee, an ultra-conservative group headed by a Paul Morrissey, had tipped off the media and had their own VCRs to record their effort to preserve the faith. They ran into the sanctuary shouting "You're all sodomites!" "Faggots!" and "Queers!" they yelled while waving their crucifixes and rosaries. "This Mass is a sacrilege! Get off the altar!"

The gays answered by trying to pray the rosary over the church's P.A. system. The right-wingers attacked the small choir, yanking their music from their hands and tearing it up.

It was decided to start the Mass anyway, but the group attacked the priest. He had to withdraw to the sacristy. Finally, the police were called and some members of the Morality and Action Committee were arrested.

"At their trial, the group claimed the right of religious expression," Maher recalled. One female protester, who had sat through the trial with a picture of the Blessed Mother pinned to her chest, got thirty days. The sentence is being appealed.

The Morality in Action members had recorded the protest. They brought it to Bishop Sheridan confident that he and Cardinal O'Connor would be proud of their sword-carrying faith. Both bishops were sickened by the scenes. They may be conservatives, but they are decent men. They still tend to speak of "our people" when referring to the Hibernians or even the conservative protesters on trial. They have yet to make the leap of faith required to think of gays as "our people." But they vigorously protested the circus antics of the extreme right. The cardinal strongly denounced the interruption of the Mass and the violence against homosexuals. He called it "absolutely reprehensible" and added: "No violence or expression of hatred, verbal or physical, against homosexual persons can be justified by anyone purporting to act on behalf of the Church."

Later, Cardinal O'Connor visited the parish to listen to the concerns of the Catholics on Manhattan's West Side. Virtually every question he parried was on homosexual issues.

Courage is a gay and lesbian group that was founded out of New York's St. Michael's rectory in 1980 by Fr. John F. Harvey, an elderly but vigorous Oblate of St. Francis de Sales, who is in residence there. Fr. Harvey argues that, while a homosexual is not responsible for his orientation, he or she is responsible for controlling actions that spring from this orientation. And since all sexual acts outside of marriage are objectively immoral, homosexuals are just like unmarried people. Therefore, they must lead chaste lives. It's a neat syllogism that lacks only a link to reality.

"Courage is for the chaste homosexual," Maher said. "It's a Twelve Step group that partly supports the notion that homosexuality can be cured." Potential members are interviewed and membership is contingent upon a virtual oath of chastity.

Courage appears to be tinged with other rather conservative viewpoints. It has gained acceptance by the official church in seventeen locations while groups like Dignity have been driven out. Courage would be welcomed for a liturgy at St. Patrick's, perhaps even to the annual parade, although neither option is likely.

In 1994, conservative Catholics met with other Christians in Colorado Springs to map strategies for reversing the political gains made by the gay rights movement. The emphasis at the meeting was on making the gay issues more broad-based. The idea was to appear almost sympathetic to gays, never bigoted or mean-spirited. For these Christians, homosexuality remains a curable disease. Former gays were described as "ex-confused."

The groups at the conference bore name tags with boasting titles: Focus on the Family, Concerned Women for America, Christian Coalition, Eagle Forum. But the underlying tone of the conference could best be expressed by another group at the conference. They called themselves Warriors Not Wimps for Jesus. One priest participant announced that the increasing numbers of gays in the seminaries is just another organized gay conspiracy to neutralize church teaching.

The fundamentalist coalition knows how to push buttons that will light up bishops and politicians or short-circuit the careers of those who might differ with them. Their "anti-confused" agenda is often wrapped in other conservative issues.

In June, 1994, over three hundred gay and lesbian Catholics gathered across the street from St. Patrick's Cathedral. In the pouring rain, they read Scriptures, sang hymns, remembered friends and lovers who had died of AIDS and, in the words of Marianne T. Duddy, president of Dignity, spoke of the day "when the cathedral would no longer symbolize discrimination and condemnation."

Some two hundred police officers, enough to quell a nice-sized riot, circled the cathedral, protecting it from the praying gays. It is painful to observe how institutions such as the Church can marshall protection when their perceived interests are involved.

Meanwhile, at St. Paul's, the homosexual faithful are looking at issues of concern to the larger society and applying them to their own lives. With preparations for the 1996 presidential elections already underway, the all-embracing family values issue has already resurfaced. The gays of St. Paul's are testing the tensility of their fellow Christians' faith once more. They will examine family values from the point of view of gay and lesbian parents.

Brendan Fay has returned to Ireland to continue his research on Roger Casement. The gay and lesbian group continues to meet at St. Paul's. "Someday, there will be no need for the gay and lesbian community to yell 'shame' as it passes the Cathedral," Donald Maher said. "Someday, there will be a welcome. Until that day, we are all left with much to pray for."

16

Linda Pieczynski:
"We are the Church . . .
What if we meant what we said?"

———————◆•◆———————

"**I**'m part of the criminal justice system. When the Supreme Court comes out with a decision that I consider stupid, I'm still part of the system. It's the same with the Church. It's the body of Christ and we are part of that body."

So spoke Linda Pieczynski while she poured coffee early one morning in her century-old Hinsdale home. She was dressed in a lawyerly suit, ready for work. Now, however, she was doing what she loved best, pitching for Call to Action, feminist causes, ecology, realistic family values, an end to domestic violence, an increase in small faith communities—even a closer relationship with an institutional church that continues to widen the moat between the cathedral church and the pilgrim church.

She can talk. She speaks in whole paragraphs, organized, structured, persuasive. Yet, she can speak with expression and her laughter is still as infectious as that of a Catholic teenager in her high-school cafeteria. (In fact, she did laugh often there, mostly about what the priest in religion class was telling them about boys.) Her nearly twenty years of education, all of it in Catholic schools, have supplied the thought process; her faith and natural enthusiasm supply the fuel that energizes her actions.

"I want to get the word out about Call to Action," she said. "Next year, we hope to get on a computer network, on the Internet system."

"We got the idea from the conservatives," she says with a laugh.

"People are beginning to ask 'What can we do?' Now, this year, we're going to do it. You know, about 60 percent of the crowd at last year's meeting were new people. They'll go home and tell their neighbors.

"I see the real work of the Church going on in small faith communities. Groups like Christ Renews his Parish, Scripture study groups, that sort of thing. I see groups dealing with alienation. I think we can get people to link up. And perhaps we can needle the Church to address real issues. When is the last time you heard a homily about domestic violence, for example? Whatever the case, if changes are going to come, they will come at the grassroots level."

So it goes. Linda Pieczynski is a prescription for an ailing church. She thinks big. "Maybe it's time for priesthood to end," she said, reflecting on John Paul II's 1994 encyclical that forbade the ordination of women. "That statement angered women in a way they had never been angered before. I think the Church may be self-imploding. But the average Catholic can't even get an appointment with a bishop to talk about it."

Linda Sucher Pieczynski was born into a German-American, Catholic family in St. Louis. "Everyone, it seemed to me, was Catholic," she recalled with humor. "We didn't know any Protestants, but, if we did, we thought of them as pagans. There was a Protestant grandmother on my father's side, but she didn't go to church. If she had any religion, we didn't talk about it. It's only recently that I learned that one of my ancestors was a plains Indian. I guess I'm one-sixteenth Native-American."

Linda attended St. John the Baptist Grammar School and Rosati-Kain High School, an elite diocesan girls' high school (now coed) that had been named for two long-dead bishops. It was conducted by diocesan priests, together with the Sisters of St. Joseph and the School Sisters of Notre Dame. "My high school experience was a very maturing one," she recalled twenty-five years after graduating. "I think that the two congregations of sisters competed with each other. The two orders sent their most progressive nuns to my school. I got a marvelous education. Some of those sisters became role models for me. Years later, I felt funny when some of them left the convent and came to me for advice. It was like role reversal."

Linda started high school just as Vatican II was ending. She remembers little of the pre-Vatican II days. "I was a cradle Catholic in a stable family," she said. "I made my First Communion one day and my Confirmation the next. In grammar school, we went to church every day. In class, we made coins of gold foil and put them in a box. They symbolized the gold that we would build up in heaven. That's the way it was.

"I remember the old catechism," she continued, "but I also remember getting up in class and arguing with the priest about *Humanae Vitae* [Paul VI's encyclical on birth control that appeared in 1968]. I told the priest that it just didn't make any sense to me that artificial birth control is immoral and that natural birth control is not. After all, the intent and the outcome are the same. I still feel the same way."

Linda Sucher's education taught her to think critically. A typical class project might be to write theologians such as Karl Rahner (1904–1984) and Reinhold Niebuhr (1892–1971). ("One of them answered. I can't remember which one. And we didn't save the letter!" Linda moaned.) The class's discussions were lively and serious. The sixteen documents of Vatican II were read carefully and discussed intently. Obviously as bright as she is articulate, Linda read difficult material and stayed with it. Far from looking back on her high-school days as parochial, she believes that her high-school education best represents what she is today. "Oh, there were setbacks," she recalled. "One of our religion teachers was a priest who later became a bishop. A nice man but he warned us that boys were uncontrollable and had to be avoided. We used to talk about it in the cafeteria and laugh. My boyfriends were controllable. My father sat on the porch."

"I was a good Catholic girl," she said with a smile. "At Mass every Sunday and to Confession regularly. I used Confession the way some people use a psychologist's couch. I had some very interesting discussions in the confessional.

"I am what I am today because of all that church and education. I haven't turned a corner somewhere. The beliefs I hold and the values I hold are mine."

Linda won a scholarship to Chicago's DePaul University, where she majored in sociology. She also had an interest in serious movies, a fascination that led to meeting her husband, Alan, a student at nearby Loyola University of Chicago. They met between their sophomore and junior years and were married in the summer of their junior-senior year.

Her graduation in 1973 coincided with the beginnings of the feminist movement, an interest that has remained high on her priorities. "My husband was shocked when I told him that I wanted to enter law school. We were living in Rogers Park and we had our first daughter, Sarah, during my second year in law school.

"After passing the bar, I got a job as assistant states attorney in DuPage County, outside Chicago. Eventually, I became a supervisor in the criminal division, overseeing traffic violations, misdemeanors, and the juvenile courts.

"But then my boss lost the election and I was thrown into private municipal work and the normal junk of private practice. Well before this, we had moved to this old house in Hinsdale. Our second daughter, Jenna, was born in 1981 and our third, Jessica, in 1986.

"Alan is a commuter; he's in personnel management at the Federal Building in Chicago where I had once worked part time. He's a Texan and a grad of a Jesuit high school down there and a Jesuit college up here."

Pieczynski has written a number of articles for legal journals and two volumes on criminal practice and procedure. She has taught at DePaul and presently teaches courses on child abuse for educators and another titled "Youth in Crisis." She is considered an expert on the emotional chemistry and legal issues involving the sexual abuse of children. Yet, when several priests, including one in her own parish, were arrested for abusing children, she offered to do workshops for parents and children in her parish and for the priests of the diocese of Joliet. She received polite but evasive answers and never heard from parish or chancery again.

Her marriage to the law has not been an entirely happy one. One gets the feeling that she wearies of moving the wet cement of the law with her eyebrows. More important, her daily exposure to delinquent children, growing numbers of gangs, and utterly indifferent parents have covered her ideals with skid marks. Viewed abstractly, the law can be very attractive. Translated into everyday realities, it gets muddied. Like one of her early heroes, Reinhold Niebuhr, who realized in his old age that ministry had many inadequacies, Linda's love for the law has thinned a bit. Just as with religion, it is filled with grace and grief.

"Oh, I suppose only 40 percent of lawyers really like what they're doing," she said. "I guess I'd now rather have more time for writing and teaching and for using the media to spread the things I believe in. I guess I'd just rather be working full-time for Call to Action."

Linda joined Call to Action (CTA) in 1990. Within four years, she was named president. The reasons for the choice were obvious: Pieczynski is attractive, articulate, informed, and energetic. She understands the importance of both image and substance. There is just enough anger in her to get things done. There is enough theological and legal training to get them done in appropriate ways.

She discovered CTA when its traveling performing artists did a show for her women's theology group. She attended her first national conference in 1991; helped to plan its sequel in 1992, and joined the board in 1993. She replaced Mary Ann Savard, who had headed the organization for a decade and had turned it into an effective, organized catalyst for change.

CTA was founded in 1976 out of the ribs of a massive Call to Action Conference held in Detroit under church auspices. The first meeting, initiated by the late Detroit archbishop, Cardinal John Dearden, was the most widespread consultation in recent American church history. The organizers had worked on it for over two years, sorting 800,000 responses, and eventually electing 1,340 voting delegates from 152 of the then 167 dioceses. One-third of the delegates were priests, recruited largely from the decision-making offices of their dioceses. Virtually every lay delegate was in some way attached to the official church. About one hundred bishops took part, including four of the five then active U.S. cardinals. There were ninety-two special interest groups either directly involved or camped around the edges, attempting to nudge the delegates in one direction or another on issues such as church, work, family, neighborhood, race, and ethnicity. It was an ecclesiastical Woodstock.

The conference got bogged down under its own weight. It was one of those classic "good string, bad yo-yo" situations. The agenda was too big; procedural issues consumed valuable time. Bishops, used to simply raising their ringed hands or meeting behind closed doors with docile fellow clergy, became threatened. In the men's room of Detroit's Cobo Hall, the bishops could be heard muttering, "They've gone too far." One highly placed bishop whispered to Msgr. John J. Egan of Chicago, who jointly chaired the conference with Alexis Herman of Atlanta, "You've ruined my career." The apostolic delegate, liberal-minded Archbishop Jean Jadot, made an appearance. Although at one point Paul VI addressed the group by satellite, the bishops knew that the Vatican had condemned the conference from the start. The gathering had something to do with power and power would not be shared.

Although 1,140 of the 1,340 delegates had been appointed by the bishops themselves, the outcomes were still too threatening. To this day, the agenda and outcomes of the biennial synods of bishops held in Rome are written before they even begin. Ballots, when taken, have each voting bishop's name on the cover—and results are tabulated by in-house tellers. If they do not come out as planned, the pope simply issues no report. In a church that keeps dragons to blow out candles, the CTA Conference might as well have been a meeting of the Iranian parliament.

It was Dearden's dream that CTA groups be started in each diocese. However, once each bishop returned to his own sandbox, he grabbed his familiar pail and shovel and buried the idea. CTA groups were started in only twenty-three dioceses and within ten years only Chicago's survived. Clergy support has all but vanished—about 5 percent of the attendees at the 1993 conference were active clergy—and any direct diocesan support has dried up. Typically, in March, 1994, of the thirty-eight national Catholic organizations, including CTA, that met in St. Louis to discuss diversity and spirituality, none were attached to the institutional church. In fact, the official church had publicly disassociated itself from a number of the groups. Today, while at least fifteen canons in the Code of Canon Law list the rights and obligations of the faithful, the canons stress that the laity "are bound to obey declarations and orders given by their pastors in their capacity as representatives of Christ." In short, the bishops wanted nothing to do with any organization that didn't have a desk at the chancery office.

Yet Chicago's CTA has thrived. Its annual meeting now has the status of a major conference, drawing delegates from virtually every state. While the number of clergy and religious decreases, the number of laity—including at least 10 percent under thirty-five—continues to rise.

When CTA risked a major portion of its budget and placed a full-page ad in the *New York Times*, a $60,000 bite from its pie chart, the ad served as a booster shot to the nation's lay Catholics. Signed by 4,505 Catholics, including a number of priests and one auxiliary bishop, it energized pockets of Catholics throughout the country. New CTA groups were formed in a dozen cities and core membership increased dramatically.

CTA's ad was intended to promote a dialogue. The written responses often sounded more like a shouting match, but there were thoughtful essays, including some from conservatives. Peter Steinfels, then senior religion writer for the *New York Times*, suggested that the ad may have sounded more like other mainstream Protestant churches. New York's conservative archbishop, Cardinal John O'Connor, was patronizing. He saw signers as "sincere" but "confused." Milwaukee's liberal archbishop, Rembert Weakland, an increasingly rare species, called the ad "a significant contribution."

CTA planned another ad, one that would be signed by 100,000 people. But the effort fell short, partly because it ran too close on the heels of the first one. But its roster jumped to over seven thousand members, and, while it still must operate out of a tacky old convent in Chicago's uptown area, it can afford bigger balloons. It can afford to support co-executive directors, Sheila and Dan Daley, as well as Carrie Maus and Elaine Schatzline-Behr, two younger staffers who help to organize CTA's many projects.

Their annual conference is a potpourri of deep-dish presentations, covering everything from small Christian communities to world peace. The energy at the meetings somehow reminds one of a group of old outrider scouts who ride out in front of the wagon train and report back. Inevitably, the more cautious people in the caravan hold back, reluctant to go to the "cutting edge" as John Courtney Murray described it. But eventually groups like CTA persuade the core group of the wisdom of its direction. Then, the core group makes the new idea its own and takes credit for it.

CTA is still seen as liberal and maverick. Yet its agenda closely resembles the values of middle-of-the-road Vatican II Catholics. It has its share of visionaries and radicals but, should any bishop risk his miter to attend a meeting, he would be applauded and heard with respect. It begs comparison with the present political climate in the United States—loosely organized Democrats differing on basic issues with tightly wound Republicans. Yet, the "Republican" bishops staunchly support CTA's thinking on peace, nuclear weapons, gun control, anti-capital punishment, and a host of economic issues. In short, the two camps share virtually the same campfire.

Linda's path to CTA may trace to her days at DePaul University. She studied courses in philosophy and theology, including one with a fascinating Jewish rabbi—a first for her. Once she was married, the feminist movement began to cross her vision. "I felt strange about it," she recalled, "until I started to link feminism and ecology together. There were things that were making me mad. I began to wonder why women had to assume their husbands' names and why I had to bring a marriage certificate to Marshall Field's in order to get a credit card."

Although raised a Catholic, her husband has drifted from the Church. "He remains something of an agnostic," she said. "Somehow he could shed his faith more comfortably than I could.

"I drifted away from the Church. I went only occasionally to Loyola's chapel near Lake Michigan where our first daughter was baptized. But when Alan came home one night with a lump on his neck and a report from the doctor that sounded like Hodgkin's disease, I did an awful lot of praying!" (The lump was diagnosed as benign, but Linda had reattached to the Church.)

The Pieczynskis sent their kids to Catholic schools. The education was better and gangs were verboten. But Linda left her parish and began attending St. John of the Cross in Western Springs (and the Chicago archdiocese) because both liturgies and homilies were better.

"The kiss-off letter from the pastor and the bishop on the sexual abuse issue made the decision an easier one," she recalled. "After all, one of those pedophiles had baptized my daughter. I was a supervising attorney at that time as I learned that the diocese had been covering up cases for at least five years.

"Things weren't going well at my job. When a woman friend asked me to attend a CRP [Christ Renews his Parish] weekend, I went with some reluctance. The weekend was conducted by women. I made marvelous friends. It was such an experience to talk with other women about spiritual things.

"The Christ Renews his Parish experience led me to Jesus Day [an archdiocese-wide evangelization conference] and my association with St. John of the Cross Parish introduced me to books I had never heard about. I'm a voracious reader, but hadn't read much about religion since college. I read Rosemary Radford Reuther's *Sexism and God Talk* and discovered that women like her were giving names to the feelings I was experiencing.

"By the time I attended my first Call to Action conference, I began to realize that all this development had taken place during my absence. Basically, I educated myself, gradually discovering a wonderful link between feminist theology and ecology.

"It was at this time that I started the Sunday walks once a month in the forest preserve with our daughters. We didn't give up Sunday Mass entirely. We just took a day off. The only rule was that we had to talk about spiritual things. It was a very special experience. I can recall going to the Grand Canyon and hearing my husband say that it was the most profound spiritual experience he could remember. Somehow, the canyon reminded me of the Rose Window at Chartres.

"You know, I see no division between the physical and the spiritual. I find them totally interrelated. I don't believe that God has to work outside that physical-spiritual paradigm.

"Anyway, after that first CTA meeting, I volunteered to help. Within a year, I was on the board, and now here I am! I think the board wanted a younger person so that we could bring CTA into the next generation."

CTA shares one problem with the Church of the capital "C". It is aging. The majority of the twenty-three hundred people at their 1993 conference were on or approaching Medicare. Some 30 percent were priests or inactive priests, religious sisters or former religious. Both the priests and religious have the potential for influencing others through the pulpit or the classroom. Now, however, with fewer vocations and an increasingly conservative clergy corps, CTA's informal network has been weakened somewhat. Further, there remains an element of fear. When Edwina Gately, founder of a shelter for prostitutes and an advocate for the poor, was pictured standing next to the presider and wearing a stole during the 1993 CTA liturgy, the picture appears to have landed on every bishop's desk. It appeared in CTA's own literature and in the *National Catholic Reporter*, an independent, liberal weekly. Following the appearance of the picture, Gately was banned from speaking in several dioceses. The banishment sent a chill through many priests and religious who rely on the institutional church for their support. The minor liturgical gesture may have unnerved more bishops than the appearance of theologian Hans Küng at one CTA conference, just five years after its founding. It has since had Charles Curran and Matthew Fox, an Aquinas and an Assisi, but a female with a stole was viewed as an Uzzi in the sanctuary.

"We still need to recruit younger people. But the young people are doing what I did for years—raising a family and building a career," Pieczynski said. "They just don't have a lot of time for spiritual development. They have deep spiritual interests but they aren't hung up on dogma. They just don't pay any attention to it. We must appeal to that hunger for spirituality as well as activities that help them to put their faith in action. That's why we're looking at Habitat for Humanity. It's a project that will appeal to them.

"And when I tell people my age about my involvement, they are just thrilled. There is a real hunger out there in spite of people's anger with the institutional church."

Linda's anger is measured. She has an attorney's respect for other points of view. She sees the present pope as a man who will go down in history for his work in bringing an end to communism, but she views him as "a man of the 1940s" on what she terms the "bedroom" issues.

"We are treated as the new Communists," she said. "Presently, the homosexual issues take first place but the feminist issues are just behind.

"I have to ask just how these women's issues are related to domestic violence and incest. Somehow, it reminds me of the civil rights movement. We did have some church people at the forefront of this movement, but the institutional church gave us only words, not actions. I'm still afraid that women are being told to go back to their abusive husbands.

"I'm a prosecutor. There was a time when prosecutors got promoted for covering up cases. Now we're promoted for opening them up. Now the Church has to do the same thing."

Pieczynski has strong feelings about issues that link her to a more traditional church. In some 80 percent of juvenile cases that are brought to her, she finds kids from single-parent homes. She shares the Church's concern for marriage preparation and for working at a marriage to keep it viable. She believes in strong marriage preparation and two-parent homes, although she does not support bankrupt marriages. She is saddened by the loss of credibility that the Church suffered because of the birth control question, but she believes that it can still be a moral force.

"I'm a lawyer," she reminds. "I read the Church's thoughts on sexual issues and I realize that it has no experiential component for what it says, at least inside marriage. It doesn't understand the depth of spirituality that can come from a sexual union. It doesn't understand the rituals of forgiveness and grieving. It's as if it is trying to teach a surgeon how to do surgery through books.

"I'm not going to listen when a group of elderly, celibate men try to tell me about my sexual life. It has no relevance. And it's a shame because we see what happens when it breaks down. We see sexual relations that go astray of good, positive values. We need the moral authority of the Church on the positive side of these issues, and we're wasting it.

"The hellfire and brimstone are gone now. We no longer go to Mass out of fear. And, meanwhile, we have learned to do so much in the sciences. We can extend life, manipulate genes to create news crops and yet we condemn *in vitro* fertilization for a couple that wants children desperately. It's nonsensical!

"I share the feeling of other Catholics about abortion. I think it's terrible. But as a lawyer dealing with cases that are pretty cut and dry in terms of what the law says and what society supports, I think it would be terribly hard to support an anti-abortion law on which there is no consensus. It's tough enough to apply the law when the issues are clear. People agree that murder is wrong, but there is no consensus on the prohibition of abortion. There are too many people who are willing to break the rule."

Linda's quarrel with the Church is tied to its tendency to apply the natural law in a selective manner. She hears it being cited to condemn birth control but not such scientific advances such as transplants, prosthetic surgery—"even the changing of the direction of the Chicago River," she says for emphasis.

"My office is filled with damaged kids," she said, "children of parents that were never suited to have children. For some, birth control—even abortion—may be a necessity."

Linda believes in CTA's buzz-word "We are the Church" and its sister sentiment "What if we meant what we said?" "Our people come to meetings and feel accepted," she said. She cited homosexuals, the Church's latest lepers, who can find support and acceptance under the all-embracing tent of CTA.

CTA formed a coalition—a favorite word for liberal groups—of some thirty-four organizations that share its vision for renewal and reform within the Church. Catholic Organizations for Renewal (COR) is more of a forum than an organization. It embraces groups such as Catholics for Free Choice, a pro-choice group; CORPUS, a group of resigned priests who are calling for a married and female priesthood; the National Coalition of American Nuns; News Ways Ministry, which deals with gay/lesbian issues; and visionary groups such as Catholics for the Spirit of Vatican III. None of the groups boast large numbers, but they are peopled by Catholics who have made conscious choices and are willing to work for them.

At times, when CTA gathers, it appears to be a motley group of too many chiefs and not enough Indians. However, its energies derive from its sheer lack of authoritative structure. There is a discernible underlying buzz at its gatherings. It is almost impossible to have a bad conversation between sessions. Even the most befuddled members have something to say. Unlike the core church, CTA doesn't waste vital energies insuring conformity. Its former president, Mary Ann Savard, offered this explanation to Dick Westley for his publication, *In the Meantime*:

"We're not visionaries. We don't really know the way that it ought to go. But we know who's saying what might happen. We know to bring these people together with those who are dissenting or dissatisfied. That's the secret of the conference. You bring a Pat Brennan [Chicago priest], who's reimagining the parish; you bring Dick Westley, who's talking about small groups; you bring Richard McBrien [University of Notre Dame theology professor], who has lots of ideas about change; you bring Elizabeth McAllister [pacifist], who is challenging the systems; you bring Bill Callahan [Catholics Speak Out], who's always stirring things up; you bring Richard Rohr [Franciscan priest], who says that the answer is contemplation. You bring all these people together. A lot gets said with a lot of people who are kind of professionals in the Church. [One-third of the attendees at the 1993 CTA Conference were church employees; 73 percent are practicing Catholics, a much higher percentage than most parish populations.] We build a bridge between these people. We don't sit there and say we think the Church is this. That's not how we operate. We're more into networking."

Linda Pieczynski shares Savard's views. She just wants to use her youth, her education, her knack for good public relations and her strong core faith to build a future.